DISCIPLES
AND
DISCIPLESHIP

DISCIPLES
AND
DISCIPLESHIP

STUDIES IN THE GOSPEL
ACCORDING TO MARK

ERNEST BEST

T. & T. CLARK LTD.
59 GEORGE STREET, EDINBURGH

Copyright © T. & T. Clark Ltd., 1986
Typeset by Pennart Typesetting (Edinburgh) Ltd., Edinburgh
Printed and Bound by Billing & Sons Ltd., Worcester

for

T. & T. CLARK LTD, EDINBURGH

First printed in the U.K. 1986

British Library Cataloguing in Publication Data

Best, Ernest
   Disciples and discipleship: studies in the Gospel
   according to Mark.
   1. Bible. N.T. Mark—Commentaries
   I. Title
   226'.306   BS2585.3

   ISBN 0-567-09369-7

CONTENTS

Preface

These essays all deal with subjects relating to the Gospel according to Mark and mainly centre on the disciples and the theme of discipleship. They were prepared while I was working on two larger studies on that Gospel: *Following Jesus: Discipleship in the Gospel of Mark* (JSNT Supplement Series 4) JSOT Press, and *Mark: The Gospel as Story* (T & T Clark). In these essays I provided some of the more detailed exegesis which it was not always possible to offer in the books. The first essay in this collection was the genesis from which grew the first of those books. Two articles have not been reproduced since they were almost entirely absorbed into *Mark: The Gospel as Story*. The briefest essay, the review of E. J. Pryke, stands apart. It has been included because it also contains a short discussion of the authenticity of Alexandrian or uncanonical Mark. The latter of course has its own connection with discipleship.

No attempt has been made to bring these articles up-to-date. Often the more recent literature in their respective areas will be referred to in one or other of the above books.

ERNEST BEST

Acknowledgements

Thanks are due to the following for permission to reproduce the essays in this volume:

'Discipleship in Mark: Mark 8.22 – 10.52', *The Scottish Journal of Theology*, vol. 23, 1970, pp. 323-337 and the Scottish Academic Press.

'The Camel and the Needle's Eye (Mark 10.25)', *Expository Times*, vol. 82, 1970-71, pp. 83-89.

'Mark's Preservation of the Tradition'. Colloquium Biblicum Lovaniense XXII. M. Sabbe *L'Evangile selon Marc: Tradition et redaction*. (Bibliotheca Ephemeridum Theologicarum Lovaniensium, 34), Leuven University Press/Editions J. Duculot, Gembloux, 1974, pp. 21-34.

'Mark III. 20, 21, 31-35', *New Testament Studies*, vol. 22, 1975-76, pp. 309-319 and Cambridge University Press.

'An Early Sayings Collection', *Novum Testamentum*, vol. 18, 1976, pp. 1-16 and E. J. Brill, Leiden.

'Mark 10:13-16: The Child as Model Recipient'. *Biblical Studies – Essays in Honour of William Barclay*, edited Johnston R. McKay and James F. Miller. Collins, London, 1976, pp. 119-134 and 209-214.

'The Role of the Disciples in Mark'. *New Testament Studies*, vol. 23, 1976-77, pp. 377-401 and Cambridge University Press.

'Mark's Use of the Twelve'. *Zeitschrift für neutestamentliche Wissenschaft*, vol. 69, 1978, pp. 11-35.

'Peter in the Gospel according to Mark'. *Catholic Biblical Quarterly*, vol. 40, 1978, pp. 547-558.

'The Miracles in Mark'. *Review and Expositor*, vol. 75, 1978, pp. 539-554.

Review: E.J. Pryke. *Redactional Style in the Marcan Gospel*. (Society for New Testament Studies, Monograph series 33). CUP, Cambridge 1978, in *Journal for the Study of the New Testament*, Issue 4, 1979, pp. 69-76.

'The Markan Redaction of the Transfiguration'. *Studia Evangelica Vol. VII* (Texte und Untersuchungen, Band 126), edited Elizabeth A. Livingstone. Akademie-Verlag, Berlin, 1982, pp. 41-53.

Abbreviations

AnBib	Analecta Biblica
BETL	Bibliotheca Epheremidum Theologicarum Lovaniensium
Bib	Biblica
BZ	Biblische Zeitschrift
CBQ	Catholic Biblical Quarterly
ETL	Epheremides Theologicae Lovanienses
EvTh	Evangelische Theologie
ExpT	Expository Times
FRLANT	Forschungen zur Religion und Literatur des Altens und Neuen Testaments
JBL	Journal of Biblical Literature
JSNT	Journal for the Study of the New Testament
NT	Novum Testamentum
NTS	New Testament Studies
RTP	Revue de Theologie et de Philosophie
StudEvang	Studia Evangelica
SBT	Studies in Biblical Theology
SJLA	Studies in Judaism in Late Antiquity
SJT	Scottish Journal of Theology
SNTS	Studiorum Novi Testamenti Societas
SANT	Studien zum Alten und Neuen Testament
TDNT	Theological Dictionary of the New Testament (ET of TWNT)
TF	Theologische Forschung
TThS	Trierer Theologische Studien
TTZ	Trier Theologische Zeitschrift
TU	Texte und Untersuchungen
TWNT	Theologisches Wörterbuch zum Neuen Testament
TZ	Theologische Zeitschrift
ZNW	Zeitschrift für neutestamentliche Wissenschaft
ZTK	Zeitschrift für Theologie und Kirche

Chapter 1

Discipleship in Mark:
Mark 8:22-10:52

Recent study of the Gospels has concentrated on the contribution which the individual evangelists have made to the material they received. Here, and in such matters as their selection and arrangement of material, we can discern the particular point of view of each writer. Admittedly this is relatively easy when we see the way in which Matthew and Luke have varied the material they took from Mark, less easy when we examine the material they have in common from Q, and most difficult when they use material from their special sources. In the case of Mark it all, as we might say, comes from his special source and so it is extremely difficult to determine what he is trying to say to us. But, like going to the moon, the greater the difficulty, the greater the challenge. We take up this challenge in respect of one theme in Mark, viz. discipleship. This means we are not attempting to answer questions as 'Was Jesus a Rabbi who instructed scholars with his own particular teaching?'; 'Did Jesus attempt to weld his followers into a community to continue after his death?' Indeed no attempt will be made to answer any of the questions about the historical relationship of Jesus to the actual disciples he had on earth; our concern lies with what Mark thinks a disciple ought to be. Mark is writing in a post-resurrection situation to Christians, and perhaps also to unbelievers, of his own period and in his own area, which is almost certainly Rome just before or just after the Fall of Jerusalem. The questions with which he is faced are of the order, 'How are followers of the Christ called to discipleship?'; 'How are they to be faithful to their Lord?' Mark is writing also for a Christian community which already exists and in which therefore

1

Christians have also to face the situation of their relationship to one another.

The theme is 'discipleship' and not 'the disciples'; that is to say, we are not going to discuss what Mark thought of the actual disciples as disciples. So we shall not discuss how by the employment of some theory of a Messianic secret he attempted to account for their failure to recognize the true nature of Jesus while he lived among them. Nor shall we consider possible rivalries which may have existed between followers of the different apostles and which may have left their mark on the tradition (Is Mark an anti-Petrine Gospel because at times Peter is shown in an unfavourable light? Do disputes about greatness among the disciples reflect sects formed around their names in Mark's own day?). Nor shall we discuss whether, because Mark paints whatever happens in Jerusalem in such an unfavourable light, this means that he considered the Jerusalem church had failed to grasp the true meaning of the Christ-event. Interesting though these topics may be our subject is 'discipleship'. From the instructions and directions Jesus gave to the disciples, and perhaps from their failure to follow these, what do we learn about what it means to be a disciple? or, more precisely, and this is important, what did it mean to Mark in his day? Caution warns us that it is not necessarily true that we can simply transfer to our own situation his interpretation of discipleship.

The obvious place to begin is the call of the disciples (1:16-20): after the statement of what the Gospel is (1:14f) Jesus suddenly and without any apparent psychological preparation or softening up calls Peter, Andrew, James and John, and they leave their work and homes and go away with him to a new life. But the obvious place to begin is not always the best place to begin, and we shall commence, and indeed devote almost all our attention, to the great central section of the Gospel, 8:22-10:52. Most commentators take this section to be 8:27-10:45 but there are good grounds, as the exegesis will show, for the slightly larger section.

It is a carefully constructed section. Everything in it relates either to the meaning of the Christ or to discipleship, though this may not be apparent at first sight. The long account (9:14-29) of the failure of the disciples to heal the epileptic boy while Jesus and three of the disciples were up on the mount of transfiguration might appear to be an exception, but the final sentence gives the clue to it interpretation: 'and he said to them, "This kind cannot be driven out by anything but prayer"' (9:29). Almost all the other miracles close with an account of the wonder or fear of men in the face of what has happened; here this is replaced by Jesus' instruction to the disciples on how to carry out an exorcism; in other words this incident is retold not because it sets out Jesus as a great wonder-worker but because it tells the early church how to exorcise, and exorcism is one of the tasks of a disciple (3:15, 6:7). Thus this incident fits appropriately into the section about discipleship. The same is probably true in the discussion of divorce (10:2-12); in a period of loose morals, and this was especially true of Rome in Mark's day, it was necessary that the incoming disciple should know the demands that were to be made on him in this respect.

The clue to the understanding of this section in respect of discipleship is made explicit almost at the end, though it is implicit from the beginning. 'But it shall not be so among you; but whoever would be great among you must be your servant, and whoever would be first among you must be slave of all. For (notice the 'for') the Son of man also came not to be served but to serve, and to give his life as a ransom for many' (10:43-45). The rule of discipleship is: Jesus. As Jesus was, so the disciple must be. This comes out every time Jesus says to a possible disciple, 'Follow me', in the call to take up the cross, and in the summons to give one's life, as he did, in order to save it.

It is now time to look more closely at the section. It begins and ends with the healing of blind men. First comes the 'botched' healing in which Jesus fails to give a blind man perfect sight at the first attempt, and only at the second fully restores his vision (8:22-26) At the close comes the healing of blind Bartimaeus, who then follows Jesus into Jerusalem (10:46-52). Both these accounts are transition sections from what precedes to what follows. To understand them we need to accept the widespread conception that the restoration of sight is a metaphor for the gift of spiritual understanding. The two-stage healing (8:22-26) then represents two stages of enlightenment. It is directly followed in Mark by the account of Peter's confession of

Jesus in the villages of Caesarea Philippi. Peter confesses Jesus is the Christ; that is half-sight. It is only half-sight because he does not understand the destiny of the Messiah – to suffer. When Jesus told him that he had to suffer and die, and that he would rise again, Peter refused to accept this and was rebuked. Full sight will only follow on full understanding of the purpose of Jesus. Yet Peter is not now blind; previously, he with the other disciples had been so described by Jesus; they had eyes and did not see (8:14). Now, however, he knows that salvation lies with Jesus; yet he is not willing to accept the way in which that salvation will come, or what discipleship must mean for himself. Then comes the period of instruction which Jesus gives about himself and the nature of discipleship. At its end another blind man calls on Jesus with almost the same title as Peter used, i.e. Son of David; he is completely healed and he at once begins to follow Jesus. Though Jesus normally sends away to their homes those whom he has healed, he permits Bartimaeus to follow him and Bartimaeus does so, throwing away his one possession (his beggar's mantle), and going after Jesus on the way into the city. Instruction is complete; now only its accomplishment in action is awaited. It is in this way that the section begins and ends; what lies within?

What lies in between consists of a journey. It begins with the first blind man at Bethsaida on the sea of Galilee, passes out of Galilee northwards to Caesarea Philippi, returns back through Galilee to Capernaum, on to Judea and the district across Jordan (i.e. the eastern bank), then to Jericho, and continual sense of motion; indeed this is true of the whole Gospel of Mark; he uses verbs of motion more frequently than any of the other evangelists. In our section this sense of motion is brought out by his use of the phrase 'on the way' (ἐν τῇ ὁδῷ); it is found at the beginning of the incident of Peter's confession (8:27); it comes at the end of the second prediction of the Passion when the question of greatness arises (9:33); when Jesus makes the third prediction they are 'on the way' going up to Jerusalem (10:32); lastly when Bartimaeus receives his sight it is said that he follows him 'on the way' (10:52).[1] If we go back to the beginning of the

---

[1]   The phrase is almost invariably omitted by Matthew and Luke.

Gospel and the only formal quotation of Scripture that Mark makes in the whole Gospel we find it again:

> Behold, I send my messenger before thy face,
>   who shall prepare thy *way;*
>
> the voice of one crying in the wilderness:
>   Prepare the *way* of the Lord,
>   make his paths straight.

Mark's Gospel is the gospel of The Way. It is a way in which Jesus, the Lord, goes and it is a way to which he calls his followers. 'Followers' is indeed the characteristic word which Jesus uses to men; 'Follow me' is the challenge to those who would be his disciples (1:17, 1:20, 2:14); it is the call issued to the rich man who rejects it (10:21); of Bartimaeus it is said that he followed Jesus on the way (10:52). The word 'follow' implies that the one who says it is in motion, and Mark depicts Jesus in motion in the accounts of the call of disciples: that to Peter and Andrew begins 'And passing along'; that to John and James, 'And going a little further', that to Levi, 'And as he passed on'; Jesus is leaving Jericho when Bartimaeus calls to him and then goes after him. Throughout the Gospel the word 'follow' is used almost exclusively of the disciples of Jesus. We however speak casually of the 'followers' of Jesus and the thought of motion never enters into our heads, because we think of it in terms of imitation. For Mark the meaning is wider as we shall see.

Before we do so we need to recognize that Mark's use of the conception is not peculiar to himself. Luke's long section (9:51–18:14) in which he abandons the Markan outline is also constructed in the form of a journey to Jerusalem. The book of Hebrews might well be described as the pilgrimage of the people of God.[2] In Acts Christians are termed the people of 'The Way'. Paul regularly described the Christian life as a walk. In John Jesus is called 'The Way'. All this has Old Testament foreshadowings: Abraham's summons by God to go out from Haran and seek a new land which God will show him; the

[2] Cf. the title of E. Käsemann's book on Hebrews, *Das wandernde Gottesvolk.*

wanderings of the people of God in the desert from Egypt to the
Promised Land; their return from Babylon when their captivity
was over, and of course it is from the description of this that
Mark quotes in 1:3. The conception reappears in Judaism under
the image of the 'Two Ways', one towards God and the other
away from him. Mark's idea is therefore based in the Judaistic
background of Christianity and is part of the primitive pattern of
Christian life.

The section in Mark which we are examining is cast in the
form of a journey to Jerusalem. What takes place on the journey?
Central to it are the three predictions by Jesus of his passion and
resurrection. Mark has linked his phrase 'on the way' with each
of them, thus picking them out as of first importance. The three
vary in detail, showing more or less influence from the actual
course of the passion; this detail we can leave aside. What they
do assert is that Jesus cannot be understood apart from his
passion and resurrection, and that these are a necessary part of
the plan of God for him. No more can discipleship be
understood apart from the passion and resurrection of Jesus. Let
us consider the first of them. It is embedded in the section
8:27-9:1 which consists of three separate paragraphs: first, the
confession of Peter that Jesus is the Christ (8:27-30); the second,
the prediction by Jesus of his passion and resurrection and
Peter's repudiation of it (8:31-33); third, the call to discipleship
and the description of its nature (8:34-9:1). When these three
paragraphs are examined closely we see that Mark has both
heavily edited the material within each and brought them
together.[3] One sign of his hand in the material lies in the
command of Jesus to the disciples not to disclose his nature to
men (8:30). An indication that he has joined the paragraphs
together lies in the nature of the call to discipleship as 'take up
your cross'; in the prediction of the passion Jesus does not define
the nature of his death as crucifixion; if Jesus said 'take up your
cross' to the disciples then it is post-Christian reflection that has
seen that this goes with the prediction of the passion in which
afterwards men saw that he took up his own cross. Further
indications that Mark has brought these paragraphs together and

[3] Cf. E. Haenchen, 'Die Komposition vom Mk 8:27-9:1', *NT* 6
(1963), 81-109.

put them in the present geographical context lies first in Jesus'
question as to what men are thinking of him, asked at a time
when he is far away from the area in which his ministry was
exercised, and secondly in the sudden presence of the crowd in
8:34, when Jesus is not in Galilee.

Peter's rejection of Jesus' prediction must have been universal
when the gospel was preached in the ancient world – only the
fact that we are so accustomed to it takes from the sheer madness
of the idea – so part of discipleship is acceptance of the strange
idea that Jesus the Lord should die, and acceptance takes time;
even at the end of the journey to Jerusalem the disciples do not
fully understand; and, if they do not fully understand the death
of Jesus, still less do they understand what this means for
themselves. At this stage their failure to understand discipleship
is not stressed, but discipleship is defined. Their failure is
implicit since discipleship is defined as suffering and they have
shown themselves unable to appreciate suffering as God's way.
But how is their discipleship defined? First, that they should
come after Jesus, deny themselves and take up their crosses
(8:34). It is appropriate that this definition should be given in the
presence of the crowd; it is necessary to say what it means to be a
disciple to those who are not disciples before, as we shall see
later, those who are are shown to have failed to understand. The
three commands, 'come, deny, take up', here in the aorist tense
indicating something which is done once and for all, are again
appropriate in an address to the crowd. They are followed by a
command in the present tense 'follow me' indicating a continuing attitude. Thus we have three initial actions succeeded by
a process, 'keep on following'. 'Come after me' is a general
command which specifically links discipleship to Jesus; discipleship is not just the readiness to suffer, howbeit in ever so
good a cause; it is a step to fall in behind Jesus, and no other, in
the way in which he is going. The call is not one to accept a
certain system of teaching, live by it, continue faithfully to
interpret it and pass it on, which was in essence the call of a rabbi
to his disciples; nor is it a call to accept a philosophical position
which will express itself in a certain type of behaviour, as in
Stoicism; nor is it the call to devote life to the alleviation of
suffering for others; nor is it the call to pass through certain rites

as in the Mysteries so as to become an initiate of the God, his
companion – the carrying of the cross is no rite! It is a call to fall
in behind Jesus and go with him. It is further a call to deny
oneself; the nature of this is not spelt out; but it is not a call to
deny things to oneself, which is the popular meaning of
self-denial and which leads to asceticism and self-mortification;
it is a call to the denial of the self itself. The opposite is for a man
to affirm himself, to put a value on himself or on his position
before God or his fellows, to claim his rights, not just as
someone who has special rights, but the very right of being a
human being. The full meaning of this can only be spelt out as
we continue through our section to 10:52. It is, however, an
initial act without which discipleship is impossible: at the
beginning, once and for all, the disciple says No!, and he says it
to himself.

Co-ordinate with this (there is no reason to think of them as
temporally successive acts) is the command to take up the cross.
Whatever way this phrase may have originated, and many
suggestions have been made – a tattoo mark, a corruption of the
saying about the yoke – within the present context which begins
with the prediction of the death of Jesus and goes on to talk of
losing life it must be taken in a much more literal manner. But
how literal? Luke by qualifying it with 'daily' has turned it
completely into a metaphor. If Mark however was written
during a period of persecution or when one was imminent it
may be that the disciple is being warned that before him on
Jesus' way stands a literal cross. Against this we must take into
consideration that the next part of the command, 'follow me', as
we have seen, envisages a process , and not a short journey to the
place of execution. Then also it is addressed to the crowd and
not to the disciples alone; the disciple may be in the situation of
persecution, the crowd is not there yet. Moreover Mark clearly
expects that some disciples will live until the time of the Parousia
(cf. 9:1, 'Truly I say unto you there are some standing here who
will not taste death before they see the Kingdom of God come
with power'). Lastly in the Neronic persecutions, if Mark has
these in mind, not all the disciples died by crucifixion but in
many different ways; so in that sense at least the 'cross' must be
metaphorical. We take it that the phrase does not then refer to a

precise situation of persecution but to its ever present possibility in the early church; at the beginning of his discipleship the new follower takes this on himself; it will not be something into which he will later stumble as by mistake but a possibility which he deliberately shoulders and carries from the beginning.

How next do we interpret v. 35, 'For whoever would save his life, will lose it; and whoever will lose his life for my sake and the gospel's will save it'? This saying will have existed in its original state without the words 'for my sake and the gospel's' of which the last half was probably added by Mark and the first half lay in the tradition as he received it. Our interpretation depends on the meaning we give to 'life' (ψυχή). If we have taken 'cross' in the preceding verse to refer to martyrdom then we shall probably take 'life' in 'whoever would save his life' as 'physical life'; in 'will lose it' it will then be equivalent to the personal pronoun, 'will lose himself', i.e. the real self; ψυχή then changes its meaning within the verse. However if we take the 'cross' in v. 34 in the semi-metaphorical manner which we have suggested then it is easier to take 'life' throughout v. 35 as equivalent to the personal pronoun, 'whoever would save himself will lose himself'. Certainly in the next two verses, 'For what does it profit a man to gain the whole world and lose his life? For what can a man give in return for his life?', the word must have the sense of the real man and not just relate to physical life; the outlook here is much wider than persecution and approximates more to the conception of the interpretation of the parable of the sower – the various temptations for which a man surrenders the Christian life – and to the case of the rich man who for his money loses his life. This understanding of 'life' is also much more appropriate to the idea of 'denial' in v. 34; the man who denies himself is the equivalent of the man who loses, or destroys, himself; the man who affirms himself is the equivalent of the man who saves, or gains, himself. The final two verses, 8:38 and 9:1, raise the question of the result of discipleship and may be ignored for the moment. We shall return to them.

We go on to the second prediction and the passage dependent on it, 9:30–50. This again consists of a number of sections loosely joined together. Again we can detect Mark's hand. Briefly, he has added to the prediction an argument among the disciples about who is greatest among them with a subsequent rebuke by Jesus; this is followed by an attempt by the disciples to limit membership among the followers of Jesus to those whom they recognise to be such; finally a list of isolated sayings relating to the perils to discipleship which can come from within a man himself ('If your hand cause you to sin, cut it off').

The crowd which was present at various stages from 8:34 onwards is now absent; we are dealing only with the disciples, and we are very often dealing with the disciples in their relation to one another, i.e. the existence of the community of the disciples is presupposed, or to put it more precisely the existence of the Christian community for which Mark is writing. While there are many signs of this it is completely obvious at 9:41 'For truly, I say to you, whoever gives you a cup of water to drink because you bear the name of Christ [lit. 'are of Christ'], will by no means lose his reward'; this envisages a post-resurrection situation when Jesus is acknowledged to be the Christ. If then the Christian community is in mind we are not concerned about the conditions of entry into it, hence the disappearance of the crowd, but with behaviour within it. In the light of the passion the first failure of members of the community is their desire to be regarded as important in the community. It is interesting that when Matthew repeats this paragraph he draws its sting by speaking of the kingdom of heaven, thus setting it in the eschatological situation rather than that of the existing community. The same transmutation comes after the third prediction in Mark when James and John seek the chief seats 'in glory' (10:37). Thus the desire for greatness here and the desire for reward by greatness in heaven are equally rebuked. Here in 9:36f the disciples have the example of the child set before them; the ancient world, unlike ours, was not child-centred and so the child could be put forward as typical of an unimportant person; such a person must be received. The true disciple shows himself 'great', a real servant (διάκονος), when he attends to the needs of the unimportant.

If individual members of the community can arrogate positions of importance to themselves and wish to be greater than others, the community can also do the same as a whole. This appears to be the point of the story of the strange exorcist

whom the disciples found treating the demon-possessed with
Jesus' name and whom they forbade (9:38-41). The lines of the
Christian community are clearly drawn for them and those who
do not conform to the pattern cannot belong and therefore must
be driven away. Matthew, the ecclesiastical evangelist, omits
this whole section; the ecclesiastical administrator, the church
union negotiator and the definer of the church's orthodoxy have
continued ever since to act as if it was not there. Even if the
wholly unimportant believer who offers to another Christian a
cup of cold water is through its rejection made to sin (in his
annoyance at this treatment) then those who have made him sin
would be better to go and tie a mill-stone round their necks and
drown themselves (9:42).

As a tail-piece to this, and Mark is probably led to repeat it
because of the way in which the tradition came to him, the
disciple is reminded again as an individual that it is better to be
strict with himself now than to lose eternal life. This in itself
may lead on to the discussion about divorce which is introduced
so that those who are thinking of joining the community (note
that the crowds appear again, 10:1) may understand the demands
that are to be made on them. These demands were especially
relevant to a culture ridden by sex; if sex is being continually
brought before their eyes then let them realise what discipleship
demands in that respect. But sex was not the only temptation of
the ancient world; like ours it also put among its primary aims
the possession of wealth. Before we come to that (10:17ff) we
are again told about entrance into the community through the
incident in which the disciples drive away those who bring
children to Jesus. Almost certainly we ought to reject here any
primary reference to baptism; the paragraph deals instead with
the way in which the gift of salvation may be appropriated –
with humility; the humility of the child who counts for nothing
in the ancient world and realises it. Lastly we come to the section
about wealth. It begins with the story of someone who refuses
the call to discipleship; the call of Peter and the other fishermen
seemed irresistible; but it is not always so; the primitive
community knew that the gospel was faithfully preached and yet
in some strange way one man would accept it and another reject
it; on the human level it may be possible to find a reason for

rejection (here that of the desire to cling to wealth), though, curiously, there is no corresponding attempt to explain acceptance; acceptance is always 'of grace'. Indeed it is strictly impossible to explain it; entrance into the community is impossible with men, but not with God; for all things are possible with God (10:27 – we note that this statement refers not just to the difficulty of the rich man's entrance but is universal, for the discussion has gradually passed beyond the discussion of riches as a hindrance to the general statement, 'how hard it is to enter the Kingdom of God', and there is every reason to believe that Mark himself has generalised it in this way). This discussion of entrance through the mercy of God is not given to the crowd but to the disciples alone, as is the succeeding short paragraph in which Jesus speaks of present joyful fellowship within the community: 'Truly, I say to you, there is no one who has left house or brothers or sisters or mother or father or children or lands, for my sake and for the gospel, who will not receive a hundredfold now in this time, houses and brothers and sisters and mothers and children and lands, with persecutions, and in the age to come eternal life' (10:29,30). Incidentally this particular section reminds us of a truth which is more important in other sections of the Gospel, viz. disciples are such within a community; Mark has a strong sense of the church as a community. 14:27b, 28, which he has inserted into the story of the prophecy of Peter's denial, affirms this: 'I will strike the shepherd, and the sheep will be scattered. But after I am raised up, I will go before you [as a shepherd does in the East] to Galilee'; that is to say that the disciples are likened to a flock, one of the known images of the people of God in Scripture. The saying about the destruction of the temple, 'I will destroy this temple that is made with hands, and in three days I will build another, not made with hands' (14:58), reflects acquaintance with the conception of the church as the body of Christ.

If we return now to our section about discipleship we come in it to the third prediction of the passion and resurrection which is followed by the second dispute about greatness among the disciples and which culminates, as we have already seen, in the programmatic sayings of Jesus about coming not to be ministered unto but to minister to others. A simple and

unimpressive word for service – one describing the activity of
the person who waits on others at a meal – is used to describe the
ministry of Jesus and consequently becomes the pattern for the
behaviour of his followers. There is nothing grand, heroic or
dramatic about this; it is ordinary, daily, obscure, unnoticed by
others. The last phrase of Jesus, 'to give his life a ransom for
many', may suggest the heroic action but it applies to him alone
and not to the disciples.

What does it then mean to follow Jesus? It means to drop in
behind him, to be ready to go to the cross as he did, to write
oneself off in terms of any kind of importance, privilege or right,
and to spend one's time only in the service of the needs of others.
Can this be summarised in the tag *imitatio Christi*? This is often
done, but Mark leaves us in no doubt that the Christian disciples
cannot imitate Christ. At every stage where it seems that the
disciple goes after Jesus and does what he does, Mark clearly
distinguishes between the disciples and Jesus. It is not just that
Jesus was the first to walk along the way of humble service to the
cross and that men must follow, for Jesus is set in a much more
unique position. This comes out in the final programmatic statement with its distinction: all minister to others, only Jesus gives
his life a ransom for many, and the many include the disciple who
is moved to follow and minister. But this element has been
echoing all through. The discussion of discipleship after the first
prediction of the Passion ends in the saying, 'For whoever is
ashamed of *me* and of *my* words in this adulterous and sinful
generation . . .' (8:38); this is followed by the Transfiguration
with its reminder that Jesus is God's beloved Son and with the
injunction to the disciples, 'Hear him' (9:7). The discussion of
discipleship after the second prediction says, 'Whoever receives
one such child in *my* name receives me; and whoever receives *me*,
receives not me but him who sent me', and it goes on to speak of
action in the name of Christ. The example of Jesus is the pattern
for the disciple and yet the disciple cannot really be like Jesus;
there is a dimension into which he is unable to enter. The disciple
of the rabbi in due time becomes a rabbi; the apprentice philosopher becomes a philosopher; but the disciple of Christ never
becomes a Christ.

This becomes even more obvious when we follow through the

'journey' into which Mark has cast discipleship, The journey begins with the call; its meaning is made clear by its association with the predictions of both the passion and the resurrection; so far we have made nothing of the last – the resurrection. If Mark had been intending the journey only to be connected to the passion he would not have referred to the resurrection. But the journey goes beyond the passion through the resurrection. The last prediction of the passion is introduced by the words, 'Jesus was walking ahead of them' (10:32); 14:28 uses exactly the same word (προάγειν) though unfortunately the R.S.V. does not render it exactly the same in English: 'After I am raised, I will go at your head to Galilee.' And at the tomb the young man says to the women: 'Go, tell his disciples and Peter that he is going at your head to Galilee.' Now this is a quite obvious reference to a relationship to Jesus after the resurrection; some interpreters have taken it to refer to the Parousia but it is more probably a reference to all the post-resurrection period.[4] It means that Jesus will be reunited after the resurrection with his disciples and that he will continue to lead them and they will continue to follow him. But follow him where? First they must follow him to the cross, and then onward into Galilee. Galilee is not just a place. We can see this more clearly if we understand that the geographical journey which Mark constructs and on which Jesus reveals to the disciples the meaning of discipleship is a journey to Jerusalem; right from the north they come down through Galilee and Judea to Jerusalem; there the first part of the journey ends; but it recommences and goes back to Galilee, to the place where Jesus had taught and healed and preached. In the gospel there is a sharp division between Galilee and Jerusalem; the former is the place of mission; the latter the place of death.[5] Once they are through death they are sent back on the mission with Jesus at the head. Mark records no resurrection appearances. It is not that the end was torn off the original copy of the Gospel and lost for ever. No! the risen Jesus is always present

[4] Cf. Best, *The Temptation and the Passion* (Society for NT Studies, Monograph 2), Cambridge, 1965, pp. 174ff.

[5] Cf. R. H. Lightfoot, *Locality and Doctrine in the Gospels* (London, 1938), p. 125; C. F. Evans, 'I will go before you into Galilee', *J.T.S.* 5 (1954), 3–18.

with his people; he is at their head as they go on the mission to which he has called them.

And now the end meets the beginning; the beginning of discipleship was the call and the commission to go and fish for men; the end is its fulfilment, and the disciples go off on this mission. But they do not go alone; they go with Jesus at the head. Whether it is to persecution or to service, to rejection or to success, 'Follow me' is the call; follow to the cross or in self-denial or in humility and follow to win the Gentiles for their leader.

The journey is then one of imitation, but only of partial imitation for the disciple cannot do all that Jesus did; it is also a journey of salvation; of blind Bartimaeus who sees and gets up and of his own accord follows Jesus into Jerusalem it is said, 'Your faith has saved you' (10:52); following Jesus he is on the way of salvation. In this sense the end is eternal salvation, eternal life, and Mark leaves us in no doubt that there is such an end to the journey: houses, brothers, sisters and so on are received now on the way and in the age to come eternal life (10:29f). This is the end for each one. And there is also a total end for all; Mark 13, the Little Apocalypse, implies this, an end when Jesus returns, when the terrors which afflict the way now disappear, and when victory is complete. But until this time there are always some who are on the way, and the nature of their behaviour while they are on the way is stressed much more than the goal that lies at the end. In this sense we may say that the journey is open-ended. It would be a dead-end if it ended at the cross; it is open-ended because the leader on the Way is alive. As he is followed into Galilee the possibilities open, but their full nature is not disclosed; because of this we can take the journey as our journey, the Lord at its head as our Lord, the call 'follow me' as our call, and the cross and self-denial as our cross and self-denial. The cross is not the End with heaven beyond. The cross is at the beginning and always on the way: but the way is at the same time the way of risen life, of the new possibility of service, and of that here.

The historical disciples did not understand all this. Unbelievers in Mark's day did not understand; even Christians in Mark's day were only beginning to understand; and the hesitations,

doubts and fears of the historical disciples are to instruct them
and bring them beyond into a truer understanding and a fuller
following. Mark writes to explain to the church the position of
those who seem wilfully blind, but even more to explain the
position of those who claim to be Christians and yet whose
discipleship is impoverished and inadequate, who follow and yet
may be scared off when persecution comes, or may be tempted
off by the desire for wealth or popularity or success. He does not
belittle what discipleship involves, and they knew what the
horror of the cross was, but he asserts that the risen Lord goes at
the head, the creator and the pioneer of the way of the Lord; and
their eyes are not to be on the end, nor even on the way itself,
but on the Leader, he who has gone to the cross but has gone on
through it back to be their Leader.

Chapter 2

The Camel and the Needle's Eye (Mk 10:25)

Mk 10:25 lies within a passage about wealth which is itself part of the central section of the gospel (8:27–10:45); this section sets out both the significance of the Christ-event and the nature of discipleship. 10:17–31 is almost exclusively concerned with the second of these.[1]

We begin then with 10:17–31 and endeavour to shred from it the accretions and modifications which have come to it between the time of the origin of the sayings and incidents which compose it and its appearance in the gospel. These additions and alterations may themselves tell us something of the way in which the saying was understood in the early Church before Mark and by Mark himself. 10:17–31 divides into three sections: (a) vv. 17–22, an incident in which Jesus encounters a rich man; (b) vv. 23–27, sayings about wealth and discipleship; (c) vv. 28–31, the reward for the renunciation of possessions and kinsfolk. Did these three sections always belong together? If not, did Mark bring them together or were they a unit prior to his receiving them?

The last section does not cohere easily with the preceding two. It has no explicit reference to wealth but deals with family relationships and possessions (house, farm); no promise of earthly reward was earlier made to the rich man, only a call to renunciation, yet this section deals with reward on earth. If (v.

[1] Apart from the commentaries the most recent discussions of the passage are: N. Walter, 'Zur Analyse von Mc. 10:17–31', *Z.N.W.* 53 (1962), 206–218; S. Légasse, 'Jésus a-t-il annoncé la Conversion Finale d'Israël?' (A propos de Marc x. 23–27), *N.T.S.* 10 (1964), 480–487.

28) Peter has left all why should he show such astonishment in vv. 24, 26? There are many signs of Markan editing: ἄρχεσθαι as an auxiliary verb;[2] 'for the sake of the gospel';[3] and possibly 'for my sake'[4]; v. 31 was an independent logion since it is found in other contexts at Lk 13:30 and Mt 20:16; the historical Peter had not at his call (1:16–18) left house and wife (1:29-31), and may even have continued to possess a boat (3:9; 4:1, 36) and a net (Mt 17:24–27), and so he could not have said 'we have left all'; if the saying of vv. 29f. had originally been addresed to Peter it would surely have contained a reference to 'ships' rather than 'fields'. Probably Mark introduces Peter at this point as the spokesman (cf. 11:21) and formed v. 28b out of v. 29. Since vv. 27-31 were not originally connected to vv. 17-26 we do not need to trace out the original form of the logion in them and we can drop them from consideration in seeking the original meaning of v. 25.

We cannot, however, drop them from consideration in seeking what Mark means by 10:17-31. The effect of their addition to the earlier material is to widen the challenge of Jesus (v. 21) beyond wealth into the area of family relationships. This radical extension of meaning by Mark is not, however, out of keeping with other sayings of Jesus (Lk 14:26; Mt 10:37), and it serves to make relevant the challenge of Jesus to everyone, since, though all are not wealthy, all do have families. It also makes clear the reward that follows from the surrender of possessions and family, both now (entrance into a new fellowship) and in the world to come (eternal life: here it formally answers the question of the rich man, v. 17); we should observe that, though in the incident the man asked Jesus a question about eternal life, Jesus does not answer him by saying, 'Go, sell what you have, and you will inherit a reward now and eternal life later', but 'Go, sell what you have and you will have treasure in heaven and come, follow me'. Mark's addition has thus to some extent blunted Jesus's challenge.

Turning now to the first section (vv. 17-22) there are no important modifications introduced into it by Mark, though we

[2] Cf. Taylor, *Mark*, 48.
[3] Cf. Taylor, Walter, W. Marxsen, *Der Evangelist Markus*[2] (Göttingen, 1959), 77-101; etc.
[4] Cf. Marxson, *ibid*

probably ought to attribute the first few words of v. 17 to him
since right through 8:27-10:52 he uses ὁδός in discipleship
contexts[5] and the other evangelists almost always omit it; this
addition does not affect the incident itself except in so far as it
allows us to see that Mark regarded the man as a potential
disciple. The last few words of v. 22 are probably also an
addition by Mark since he likes to add short explanatory
comments using γάρ (1:16; 2:15; 5:42; 6:14, 52; 7:3f.; 11:13; etc.).
There is, of course, no reason to doubt that this incident came to
him in the tradition.[6]

If then vv. 17-22 existed in more or less their present form in
the tradition did vv. 23-27 cohere with them there? We require
to examine their structure. V. 23 refers to wealth; v. 24
generalizes it without reference to wealth; v. 25 again returns to
the explicit mention of wealth; v. 26 expresses the astonishment
of the disciples (as does v. 24a) and ends with a question they
raise to which v. 27, again without any restriction to wealth,
answers. In v. 26b the use of σῴζειν is from the vocabulary of
the early Church and the question is therefore hardly original.
The logion of v. 27 could more easily be imagined as an answer
to this question in Paul than on the lips of Jesus; it is a theological
maxim probably based on certain Old Testament passages (Zech
8:6; Job 10:13; 42:2; Gen 18:14; see in each case the LXX).[7] V.
27a betrays the signs of Mark's hand: the use of βλέπειν and its
compounds and synonyms in seams (cf. 8:33; 10:23; 11:11 and
contrast Mt and Lk), and the historic present λέγει.[8] V. 26a is
probably also Markan: περισσῶς appears only twice in the New
Testament, here and Mk 15:14; πρὸς ἑαυτούς is also Markan.[9]

[5] E.g., 8:27; 9:33; 10:32,52. The section takes the form of a journey to
Jerusalem and the cross; discipleship consists in following Jesus toward
the cross (8:34).
[6] The passage is one often used to argue for an Ur-Markus since there
is quite considerable agreement in Mt and Lk in their omissions from
Mk. Haenchen, Der Weg Jesu[2] (Berlin, 1968) ad loc. and Walter have
argued strongly and correctly that these agreements can be explained in
terms of the editorial habits of the evangelists.
[7] Cf. E. Schweizer, Markus (N.T.D.) ad loc.
[8] Taylor, 46.
[9] E.g., 1:27; 9:10; 10:26; 11:31; 12:7; 14:4; 16:3. We would expect
either ἀλλήλοις or προς ἀλλήλους; cf. Taylor, ad loc.

Thus we conclude that Mark using a saying current in the early Church[10] has added vv. 26, 27 to vv. 23-25. The effect of this addition has been to change a saying about the difficulty of entering the Kingdom (with special reference to the difficulties created by wealth) into a theological statement expressing the impossibility of becoming a Christian except by the grace of God. Mark is but the first to have turned the edge of a 'hard' saying by transforming it into a theological proposition!

If then vv. 26f. did not originally belong here what of vv. 23-25? Here we encounter a well-known textual problem. Many manuscripts add to v. 24, 'for those who trust in riches'.[11] Part of this tradition also transposes vv. 24 and 25.[12] In the text as printed in most editions[13] (without either the transposition or the addition) there is an obvious difficulty in that v. 24 generalizes v. 23 by the omission of the reference to wealth while v. 25 re-imposes this limitation; the astonishment of the disciples in vv. 24, 26 is attached only to the restricted form of the saying and not to the general; the increased astonishment of v. 26 would follow more clearly after the widening of the logion in v. 24. The variants are an attempt to smooth out these difficulties, either by addition or by transposition. Therefore the two variants arose independently, and the D-tradition naturally began with the transposition and then gathered the addition according to the principle that variants accumulate. If D has the original reading then v. 24 and v. 25 must have been transposed to their present order so as to associate the logion of v. 24 with that of v. 23 which it resembled; at this stage the addition was made, which then worked itself back to D. If the addition to v. 24 was the original reading then at some stage this must have been accidently omitted (since the wording in its reference to wealth is different from that of v. 23, it cannot have happened because the scribe's eye slipped); an ancestor of D finding the text without the omission then attempted to correct it by transposing the verses and at a later stage added the omission.

[10]　Perhaps vv. 26b, 27 were a question and answer drawn from the instruction of catechumens.
[11]　A C D　Θ f¹, f¹³, pl. It was read by Clem. Alex.
[12]　D it.
[13]　Following ℵ B W.

All this is much more complicated than the assumption that the B-tradition represents the original. In support of this we note that Matthew's words at the beginning of 19:24 ('And again I say to you') suggest that he realized he was omitting something, and this could only be Mark's v. 24.[14] Moreover πεποιθότας (Mk 10:24b = 'trust in') is not a Markan word. The addition is not only an attempt to smooth the text but also an attempt (perhaps the first) to explain why riches are a hindrance to entrance into the Kingdom: those who have riches trust in them and this prevents trust in God (cf. Is 31:1). If then the B-tradition is the correct text of Mark the increased amazement of the disciples in v. 26 over v. 24 must be compounded of two elements: (i) v. 25 is sterner than v. 23 since it makes entrance into the Kingdom for a rich man a virtual impossibility; (ii) a rich man is the one whom we would expect to enjoy God's favour and not His rejection, and so v. 25 drives home the point of v. 24.

Turning now to vv. 23-25 themselves, v. 23a is Markan as indicated by the use of περιβλεψάμενος [15] and the historic present λέγει.[16] Mark introduces the disciples as an audience (Luke sees there is no need for them to be mentioned) most appropriately since 8:27-10:45 as a whole deals with discipleship.[17] The creation of v. 23a does not imply that Mark added v. 23b to vv. 17-22; v. 23a is his attempt to create the audience he wishes for the following sayings. V.24a in emphasizing the astonishment of these disciples states a Markan theme (θαμβεῖσθαι is used by Mark alone of the evangelists, cf. 1:27; 10:32).[18] There is nothing in the next clause, 'And Jesus said . . . ' which is exclusively Markan, and also nothing which is non-Markan; it serves to introduce the logion which ends the verse. From where does this logion come? It is perfectly general without the reference to possessions of v. 23b. It is most unlikely

---

[14] If v. 23b and v. 25 had belonged together in the pre-Markan tradition it is possible that Matthew may have known this (the tradition did not disappear once it was written down) and therefore had good grounds for omitting v. 24; this seems an unnecessary supposition.
[15] Six times in Mk; once in Lk; never in Mt or Jn. Cf. 10:27. See Légasse, 485, n. 1; Schweizer, *ad loc.*
[16] Taylor, 46.
[17] The disciples are redactional also at 8:27, 34 (?); 9:31; 10:10.
[18] Cf. Walter, 210.

that both are original; we must therefore give the preference to
v. 23b which is specific and concrete and therefore much more
like the kind of statement that would come from Jesus. V. 24b
has obviously then been created out of v. 23b and since Mark's
hand can be detected in at least part of v. 24a it sems fair to
conclude that he created it all, perhaps as a foil to vv. 13–16; its
general nature forms a preparation for the general statements of
vv. 26f. which we have seen were added by Mark. We are now
left with v. 25 which there is no reason to suggest Mark created;
at no point does it bear any sign of his hand. We conclude that v.
23b and v. 25 came to Mark in the tradition. Légasse analyses
these verses differently to find the original saying. This he thinks
may go back to the same (or a similar) logion as lies behind Mt.
7:13f. = Lk 13:23ff.: 'It is difficult to get into the Kingdom of
God.' In the tradition vv. 23–24a and vv. 24b–26a were parallel
developments of it. In the second of these an original ἄνθρωπος
was replaced by Mark[19] with πλούσιος to adapt it for its
present context. The astonishment of the disciples is not Markan
but lay in the tradition; in putting together these parallel
passages Mark added περισσῶς to v. 26a in order to create a
mounting tension from vv. 23–24a (riches as a hindrance to
entrance into the Kingdom) to vv. 24b–26a (the impossibility of
entrance). It is easier, however, to take the astonishment as
Markan and it is very difficult to see why Mark should change v.
25 from a general reference to a particular reference to the rich
since he has added vv. 26, 27 to follow it and the reference in
these is general. We note that if this suggestion is adopted then
we must give an entirely different meaning to the original form
of the logion of v. 25.[20]

   If then vv. 23b, 25 came to Mark in the tradition we have to

---

[19] Légasse is unclear whether he regards the change as due to Mark or
as occurring in an earlier stage of the tradition. Walter argues that Mk
added 24b–27 to 23, 24a and made the change at the same time. Our
argument remains valid in either case.
[20] Bultmann, *History of the Synoptic Tradition*, 22 takes vv. 23, 25 to
belong to vv. 17–22 in the pre-Markan tradition. Dibelius, *From
Tradition to Gospel*, 50, considers v. 25 alone to have been asociated with
vv. 17–22 prior to Mark. Klostermann, *Markus*, following a suggestion
of Wellhausen, *Markus*, deletes v. 25b in order to generalize v. 25 and
make the passage more harmonious.

ask whether either or both was already attached to the incident of vv. 17-22. A certain incompatibility exists between them in so far as v. 23b refers to a man who 'has possessions' and v. 25 to a man who 'is rich'. Since the tradition in the oral period tended to group sayings on the same subject this in itself is no reason for objecting to them as a unit prior to Mark. Moreover, since Mark likes to sandwich material within an existing piece of tradition his interruption with v. 24 would not be exceptional. This, however, does not answer whether either or both came to Mark already attached to vv. 17-22. It might be suggested that vv. 17-22 demand a comment of the nature of either v. 23b or v. 25.[21] This is not so. There are three other stories in the tradition which tell of demands made by Jesus on would-be disciples and in no case is there a comment (Mt 8:19f. = Lk 9:57f.; Mt 8:21f. = Lk 9:59f.; Lk 9:61f.); in none of them do we even learn whether they became disciples or not. If vv. 17-22 originally existed without any comment then we would assume that v. 23b was the first comment to be added[22] (incidents attract comments: e.g., Lk 16:1-13, where there are quite a number; Mk 9:14-29, where v. 29 is the sole one; Mk 10:35-45); for with its reference to possessions rather than directly to riches it is more appropriate to the demand to 'sell' in v. 21. At a later stage, probably prior to Mark, though not necesarily, v. 25 was added. It is interesting to note that there were several more sayings which might have been added: Lk 6:20 (and v. 24, if it is not a creation out of v. 20); Mt 6:24 = Lk 16:13 (this would have been especially relevant). Thus our analysis implies that the original context of v. 25 is not known to us. The effect of v. 25 following v. 23b is to increase the emphasis on wealth as a hindrance to entrance into the Kingdom so that it in effect becomes almost an

[21] We have already seen that v. 22b is a comment by Mark and need not enter into our discussion.
[22] It is possible that it is the original comment for there must have been some concrete situation referring to possessions to call it forth. The fullness and vividness of the narrative in vv. 17-22 contrasts with those of Lk 9:57-62 and may lend support to the idea that there always had been a comment of some nature. Fullness and vividness are themselves no guarantee of originality; they may derive from the imagination of some preacher during the oral stage; the question and answer of vv. 17f. militate against this in our case.

impossibility. This magnified severity then entered its present context during the oral period.

If v. 25 is not in its original context, can we at all determine what that context was? This is impossible; we can only make guesses. It might once have been part of a section similar to one of the three in Lk 9:57-62: 'A rich man said to him: I will follow you: let me first dispose of my wealth (*i.e.*, intending perhaps to give it to his relatives, which might take quite a while if he had to realize real estate). Jesus said to him: "It is easier for a camel . . . "'. Whether this is so or not, its original context must have been a situation in which a rich man figured. We can say no more.

Taken by itself what does it say? It asserts that it is virtually if not actually impossible[23] for a rich man to enter the Kingdom of God (without more context we cannot determine whether the Kingdom is conceived here as realized and present or eschatological and future, but for our purposes it is unnecessary to settle this), but it does not imply that a poor man will get in. It does not set down what the rich man is to do with his wealth (*e.g.*, give it away to the poor, hand it over to the common treasury of Jesus' disciples or that of the early Church) if he wishes to get in.

Where would such a saying have originated? Did Jesus create it or did it emerge from the primitive community?

There is no doubt that the primitive community was concerned about wealth. The early chapters of Acts show it practising some form of community of goods. Though much of the evidence undoubtedly comes in Lukan passages (2:44f.; 4:34f.) and Luke is apparently himself interested in poverty this does not permit us to write off this as his creation for the preservation of the incident about Ananias and Sapphira (5:1ff.) comes from the tradition, and it is hard to see it as an invention.[24] Moreover the rest of the New Testament shows no evidence that in either Hellenistic Jewish Christian or Gentile

[23] For similar hyperbolic statements see Mt 7:3-5; 23:24.
[24] Cf. Haenchen, *Apostelgeschichte,* who argues since rich men were few in the early Church the cases of Barnabas and Ananias were remembered as exceptional.

Christian contexts there was ever the same interest in a sharing of goods. Did the saying then arise in the Palestinian Christian community? It is possible to envisage the almost completed conversion of a rich man who suddenly throws up the idea on learning of the need to surrender his wealth to the community, and someone comments on his rejection of discipleship with this saying. But since it is improbable that the primitive community practised a compulsory communism (Ananias and his wife died because of their deceit not because they wished to retain some of their money) such a situation might never have arisen.

To deal more accurately with our problem we have to enquire whence the primitive community derived its ideas on wealth and poverty. They do not seem to have come from Pharisaic or Sadduccean Judaism: many of the Sadducees were wealthy; we have a fair idea of Pharisaic conceptions from Rabbinic Judaism.[25] In the Old Testament wealth is often viewed as God's blessing and poverty as indicating its absence. In the inter-testamental period this began to change, probably because the wealthy were collaborators with foreign rule, or at least acquiescent to it because of the good order it produced for their commercial enterprises. In the Rabbinic writings a balanced view appears. Both poverty and wealth can be a peril to true piety; without some wealth the study of the Torah is impossible and so poverty can be an evil; equally concentration on the acquisition of wealth hinders that study and R. Eleazar ben Harsom[26] gave up his wealth to study better. Our saying goes much beyond this, as also does the 'communism' of Acts. It has, however, been argued that the attitude of the primitive community derives from sectarian Judaism. Josephus reported that there was a community of goods among the Essenes[27] and that they despised wealth; he probably is referring to the same people as those whom we know to-day as the Qumran community. However, the literature these have left behind them

---

[25] Cf. I. Abrahams, *Studies in Pharisaism and the Gospels* (First Series), 113-117; and the articles by Hauck and Kasch on πλοῦτος and Hauck and Bammel on πτωχός in *T.W.N.T.*, vol. VI.

[26] Cf. Abrahams, *op. cit.*

[27] *B.J.*, 2:119ff.

is by no means so clear on this matter;[28] much of the evidence suggests that while the members controlled their own possessions they also used them for the common good; the community as a whole had possessions;[29] there is no reference to a vow of poverty on the part of its members. It is possible that the 'communism' of Acts could have come from here but not entirely probable; it is even less likely that such a community could have been the cradle of our logion, for the first-hand documents which come from the community itself must be preferred to Josephus' account.

If then the early Palestinian church did not derive its attitude to wealth from Palestinian Judaism it must either have taken it from Jesus or itself. Since, as we shall see, there are a number of sayings about wealth placed on the lips of Jesus by the evangelists which cannot be traced to Palestinian Judaism, it is wiser to conclude that Jesus himself is the author of this new attitude rather than that an individual or group in the primitive Church evolved it and then fathered it back on him; its practical disappearance from the remainder of the New Testament confirms this.

These sayings are:

(a) Lk 6:20. We take this to be more primitive than Mt 5:3. Within its own context it must refer to literal poverty because of 6:24. But 6:24 is probably a secondary formation out of 6:20 and cannot therefore tell us about the original meaning of 6:20 other than that its literal sense is pre-Lukan since 6:20ff. is a pre-Lukan block of teaching. 'Poor' on the lips of Jesus might have had the double sense 'poor' and 'pious', which would not have been alien to a Palestinian context. But the meaning 'poor' cannot be excluded and the saying reduced to 'Blessed are you pious.'

(b) Mt 6:24 = Lk 16:13. The original situation of this saying has been lost as its appearance in different contexts in Mt and Lk indicates. It does not say explicitly that a rich man cannot enter

---

[28]   Cf. M. Black, *The Scrolls and Christian Origins* (London, 1961), 32-39. Josephus himself (*B.J.* 2:124) implies that the community as such had possessions and even provides some evidence that individuals had them (*B.J.* 2:137).

[29]   Cf. 1 QS 6:19f.; 7:6; 9:7; CD 14:13f.

the Kingdom but only that one who serves riches cannot; in this it does not differ from Jewish piety.

(c) Mt 6:19-21 = Lk 12:33f. (cf. Lk 12:21). Mt is not as extreme as Lk in so far as his logion only forbids the acquisition of wealth and does not demand its abandonment; it may also more correctly represent the original logion in view of its stricter parallelism.[30] Again this form is at home in a Jewish setting.

(d) Mk 6:8 = Lk 9:3 = Mt 10:9; cf. Lk 10:4. The mission charge has undergone extensive adaptation but the demand that no money should be carried appears in every form. It is not the kind of demand that a rabbi would have set before his disciples, nor is there anything parallel to it in Qumran since it asks for individual as well as communal poverty. Within the gospels it may well be intended only as a rule for the Church's missionaries, but there is nothing to suggest that originally it was so limited and we can assume, that, if Jesus spoke it, He laid it as duty on all his disciples.[31]

(e) Lk14:33. This does not cohere well with its present context and was therefore probably at one stage an isolated saying. It takes up Lk 5:11 which goes a little beyond Mk 1:16-20 in its demand for renunciation of all possessions. It goes further than what we find in Judaism.

(f) Lk 9:57f. = Mt 8:19f.. This suggests that Jesus lived in absolute poverty. As a Son of Man saying it may be suspect to many scholars but it does not look like the kind of saying which would have been invented,[32] though 'Son of Man' may have been introduced into it later. Again it goes beyond Judaism.

(g) Mk 10:23. This we have seen existed at one time in isolation from 10:25. It is not as severe.

(h) Mk 10:17-22. Again we have seen that this was once independent of 10:25. But it is too rash to argue that we can generalize from it; it may only represent the demand made on

[30] Cf. M. Black, Aramaic Approach (3rd Edn, 1967), 178.
[31] What of Judas' bag? The evidence is late (Jn 13:29). Even if the disciples had a common bag this would have been only for day-to-day expenses (Give us this day our 'daily' (?) bread; cf. Mt 6:34); it could not be construed as the disciples having possessions.
[32] Cf. R. H. Fuller, The Foundations of New Testament Christology (London, 1965), 124f.

one rich man. Note also that Jesus does not instruct the rich man
to contribute his money to the common pool but to give it away
first and then beome a disciple; contrast Acts 4–5.

(i) Mk 12:41–44. Though Jesus does not say that everyone
should literally imitate the poor widow yet his commendation of
her is wholly in keeping with the preceding sayings.

These logia come from at least three strands of the tradition,
viz., Mk, Q, L. Individually some of them may not go beyond
what is found in Judaism but their cumulative effect in such a
small body of material as the gospels is considerably greater;
there are also some of them which do go beyond Judaism. Even
if private possessions were forbidden at Qumran, there was
considerable communal property as is shown by archaeology,
apart from the literature of the community. There are no real
references to communal property among the disciples of Jesus.
This new attitude to wealth and poverty we therefore attribute
to Him. But to do this is not to argue that every single one of
these sayings goes back to Jesus. Given the new attitude and
some sayings and given the early Church's sense of the risen
Lord speaking to it through prophets, we can see that new
sayings extending those which already existed might arise easily.
Equally this implies some of the sayings must have been
original, for an attitude must be expressed in sayings. This then
still leaves open the queston whether Mk 10:25 is a logion of
Jesus or not. In favour of its creation by Jesus is the vividness of
the image.[33] Yet we have to acknowledge that there was
apparently a similar proverbial metaphor curent in Judaism with
an elephant instead of a camel[34] and which was used to describe
something extraordinary. The two sayings are not necesarily
dependent.[35] So far as ours goes it is apparently explained by the
fact that a camel was the largest animal normally seen in
Palestine (Rabbis who had travelled might have seen elephants;

[33]   We do not accept the suggestion that 'camel' is a mistranslation of a
word meaning 'cable'. The supposition that there was a 'Needle's Eye'
gate at Jerusalem is quite improbable.
[34]   b. Berak, 55b; b. Baba Metzia, 38b.
[35]   Jesus, of course, could have taken up the Rabbinic saying and
adapted it to his purpose.

Jesus probably had not, still less His audience) and the eye of a needle was the smallest opening. The use in 10:25 of the phrase 'enter into the Kingdom of God' is similar to other sayings of Jesus (Mk 9:47; 10:14f.; Mt 7:21; Lk 16:16). While therefore we cannot be certain that Jesus actually uttered this saying, the evidence favours this view; if it came from the early Church it came only as the result of Jesus' teaching and in that sense is His.

If the original context of the saying has been lost we can neither be certain of its meaning nor why a rich man would find it almost, if not completely, impossible to enter the Kingdom. Is the saying to be taken as absolute, i.e., no rich man can enter the Kingdom, or as relative, i.e., only with great difficulty may a rich man enter the Kingdom? Once v. 25 came to be associated with v. 23b in the oral period the latter became the interpretation. This tells us nothing about its original meaning since the context is lost. Some of the explanations which have been offered are based on the relative understanding and some on the absolute. The first known in history is the textual variant in v. 24; this on the one hand softens the saying with its implication that it is not riches as such but trusting in them which hinders entrance into the Kingdom, and on the other hand sets trusting in riches as an alternative to trusting in God. Perhaps the rich man is encouraged by his wealth to regard life as more permanent than it is (cf. Lk 12:15-21) so that his material security breeds spiritual security. It may be that since he can arrange life as he wishes it with his wealth he finds it difficult to believe that with a true stewardship of his money, donating it to God's work, he cannot arrange his eternal life by building up for himself treasure in heaven (Paul saw that this was impossible – 1 Cor 13:3). Within a legalistic community which demands tithing the rich man when he has given his tithe and then encounters great need may be tempted to say that he has already done all that is necessary. Wealth keeps a man busy caring for it and so he may just have no time for others. It can also be a root of sin (1 Tim 6:10) – the impoverished is never a glutton. Although Scripture refers many times to the wrongful acquisition of wealth this hardly seems to be in mind in the present saying which is concerned with its possession. It is true that it is equally difficult for the poor man to abandon his few possessions as the rich his many, but this is not to be a consolation to the rich nor when v. 25 is detached from 10:17–22 is it very relevant to its interpretation.

If there have been many explanations of the saying there have been as many if not more attempts to avoid its meaning. Mark himself, we have seen, in part evades it by generalizing it (vv. 24, 26f.) and in part widens it by including kinsfolk (vv. 29f.). Clement of Alexandria discusses the passage at length and while not rejecting its literal application very quickly allegorizes it so that Jesus is made to demand the destruction of the passions of the soul.[36] He also appears to be the first to argue that since charity is impossible without money a modicum of this is necessary. This argument is often made in another way: if money is used with wise stewardship it cannot come between a man and God.

Of course all this must seem merely academic to the great majority of the readers of this journal who probably have only that modest competency that permits them to buy food and clothes and not much else. But wealth is a relative term and what is a modest competency in Western Europe would be vast wealth in most of Africa, Asia and S. America. Even the poor here are generally much wealthier than the great mass of people elsewhere and the middle class are certainly very much wealthier than all but a few. This is a saying addressed not to the wealthy by 'western' standards but to all by world standards. The ethic of Jesus was individualistic; ours cannot be; how stands it then with a wealthy nation?

[36]   *Quis dives salvetur?*

Chapter 3

Mark's Preservation of the Tradition

Formgeschichte in isolating pre–Markan material had little or no interest in the Markan residue and set it aside; Redaktionsgeschichte has fastened on to this residue and made it the starting-point for our knowledge of Mark's literary and theological work. Now that we understand the latter more adequately it is perhaps time to look back at the material which came to Mark in the tradition and ask what he did to this material as he used it in his Gospel. We shall not be concerned with the seams with which he unites incidents or with the order in which he places them or with the summaries which he writes but with what happened internally to the various pericopae as he incorporated them into the larger whole he was creating. We know that when Matthew and Luke took over the material from Mark they regularly adapted it to their needs; Matthew in particular consistently abbreviated it. Can we in any way trace what Mark did to the tradition which he had received? How far did he conserve it unchanged, apart from providing it with a linking introduction to the rest of his Gospel? How far did he adapt or mould it? What control did he exercise over it? Obviously it is much more difficult to answer this question in the case of Mark than it is for Matthew and Luke, but we must make some attempt. We can only do this by examining individual passages and as we do so the nature of the problem will itself become clearer.

Before we take up the material itself it is necessary to speculate briefly about the way in which words are used in the handing on of oral material. Any *raconteur* can probably observe what happens in his own retelling of stories. Within any material

31

which is in the course of transmission there are constants and variables. The material cannot be handed on without using the constants, e.g. it is impossible to tell the Parable of the Sower without referring to seed and, if there is only one word for this, this is a constant. These constants are of less importance than the variables when we seek to determine what has happened to material in transmission. Variables are of many kinds. There are simple variables like synonyms, e.g. μετά and σύν. Here a person will normally use his own favourite word though he may have heard the other when he was given the material. With these simple variables it is only to be expected that many Markan characteristic words would reappear within pericopae. This may not be so in the case of more complex variables, e.g. πνεῦμα ἀκάθαρτον and δαιμόνιον. Of particular interest for our purposes is the use of titles. When in Britain a man becomes ennobled and takes a title different from his original name (e.g. the British Prime Minister Disraeli became Lord Beaconsfield) some people may continue to refer to him by his earlier name and when they retell an anecdote in which he was referred to by his title they will change to the name. This suggests that when within a pericope of Mark we find a variable which has not been brought into line with Mark's normal usage we may be witnessing the preservation of pre-Markan tradition. With this in mind we shall examine some individual Markan passages.

A. Inconsistent use of Titles of Jesus

a) 1:24 Both Matthew and Luke vary the Christological titles of Mark,[1] and a priori this would seem a place where change would take place easily. In 1:24 the demon addresses Jesus as ὁ ἅγιος τοῦ θεοῦ. Commentators have difficulty in explaining

---

[1] E.g. both Matthew and Luke introduce the title κύριος where it does not appear in Mark (Matthew 8:25; 17:4, 15; 20:31-3; Luke 5:12; 18:41; 22:61); Matthew alters Peter's confession (16:16). For fuller detail see E. Best, *The Temptation and the Passion: The Markan Soteriology* (S.N.T.S. Monograph Series, 2) Cambridge, 1965, pp. 160f. I would now disagree with my tentative suggestion there that it is probable that Mark would have altered the titles in the material as it came to him.

the relevance and meaning of this title.[2] Mark's normal title of confession is ὁ υἱὸς τοῦ θεοῦ.[3] In the summary of 3:11f. where Mark is composing freely and can choose the title he wishes, he puts this latter title on the lips of the demons. If there is no clear and satisfactory explanation for the title of 1.24 within its Markan context (and it may have had a clear meaning in an earlier stage of the tradition) then it is simplest to conclude that Mark found it in his source and did not alter it to the title which would have been more appropriate to his theology. In other words it is a variable which he has preserved. Interestingly Mark never puts the title 'Son of God' on the lips of Jesus;[4] although it is the title of his preference it is always a confessional title; the title Jesus uses of himself in Mark is 'Son of Man';[5] this itself is probably another instance of the preservation of tradition.

b) In 10:47, 48 blind Bartimaeus addresses Jesus as υἱὲ Δαυιδ and in 10:51 he calls him ῥαββουνί. Commentators again vary in their explanations of the significance of the first of these two titles in their Markan context.[6] 'Son of God' would

[2] E.g. O. Procksch, *T.W.N.T* I, p. 102 refers it to the Holy Spirit; T. Ling, *The Significance of Satan* (London, 1961), p. 14 takes it as in contrast to ἀκάθαρτος; V. Taylor (*Mark*, ad loc.) traces its use to the O.T. and suggests it has Messianic significance (it expresses 'the sense of the presence of a supernatural person'); Lohmeyer gives it a more cultic connotation; F. Hahn, *The Titles of Jesus in Christology* (London, 1969) takes it to refer to 'an eschatological prophet' (pp. 231ff.); E. Schweizer (*Marcus* ad loc.) connects it with Nazareth or Nazarene through Judges 13:7; 16:17 (LXX).

[3] 1:11; 3:11f.; 5:7; 9:7; 15:39. Jesus is confessed in this way by God in 1:11; 9:7; by the demons in 3:11f.; 5:7; and by the Gentile centurion in 15:39.

[4] Although the absolute 'son' appears in 12:6 and 13:32.

[5] Cf. J. Barr, 'Christ in Gospel and Creed', *S.J.T.* 8 (1955) 225-237 (at p. 229).

[6] It would be more true to say that the commentators say very little about the meaning of the title for Mark at this point; they devote their attention to its significance for the primitive church. Their failure to relate it to Mark's view of Jesus, other than to say that Mark accepts the Davidic sonship of Jesus, is an indication of its unimportance for him. In 7:28 the Syro-Phoenician woman appeals to Jesus as κύριε; in the storm at sea the disciples use διδάσκαλε; but normally Jesus takes the initiative in healing and there is no address. It is also possible that the use of the title in a "public" scene conflicts with Mark's conception of the Messianic Secret (cf. T. A. Burkill, *Mysterious Revelation,* Ithaca, New York, 1963, pp. 188f.).

have been the natural title for Mark to use. The story is found at one of the major turning points in the gospel, at the conclusion of the central section 8:27–10:45 in which the way of the cross and the training of the disciples are expounded. It balances the story of the blind man (8:22–26) who receives his sight in two stages; Bartimaeus truly sees and at once follows Jesus. We would therefore expect him to confess Jesus as 'Son of God', the true title used by God (1:11; 9:7) of Jesus, or, possibly, 'Son of Man' which has been consistently used of the suffering of Jesus in this central section, though always by Jesus and not on the lips of others. If it is argued that the Davidic title is appropriate because of the immediately succeeding entry into Jerusalem this must be allowed, yet in view of the position of the pericope in the total structure of the gospel it is difficult to see, if another title had been originally present and a change had been made by Mark, how that change would have been made to 'Son of David' rather than 'Son of God'. If changes were being made why was ῥαββουνί permitted to remain? The Davidic title with its strong Jewish and even war-like overtones would hardly have been suitable in a Gentile Roman Church, particularly in or after a time of persecution. Moreover, the title 'Christ' (8:29) which is closely related has already been seen to be a misleading title for in 8.31 it had to be re-interpreted and 'Son of Man' is used in the re-interpretation;[7] in 12:25–37 the theology underlying its use is shown to be less important than the κύριος theology. Mark therefore preserves the title 'Son of David' from his material.[8] The Semitic form of ῥαββουνί almost certainly implies it belongs to the tradition; it can hardly have seemed to Mark's

---

[7] Cf. the similar alterations in 14:62 from 14:61 and in 13:26 from 13:21. On the inadequacy of 'Christ' as a title for Mark see R. H. Lightfoot, *The Gospel Message of St. Mark,* Oxford, 1950, pp. 35f. Even if Mark uses the 'Son of Man' suffering-sayings because he wishes to introduce the concept of suffering the point remains that on both occasions he has retained the title which existed in the tradition.

[8] Probably the retention of the title 'King of the Jews' throughout the Passion narrative (15:2, 9, 12, 18, 26) is related to this; here Mark is certainly preserving tradition, but it would have been very difficult for him to change it since it was so essential a part of the story (cf. the title on the cross), a constant rather than a variable; thus its conservation is less significant.

readers and hearers the most appropriate term with which to address Jesus when seeking the miraculous restoration of sight. ὁ διδάσκαλος is used by the father of the epileptic boy in approaching Jesus (9:17) and often in Mark it appears to carry a sense of authority as did the teaching of Jesus (1:22, 27). Mark has however not changed the traditional term ῥαββουνί to this, though it is a frequent term in the Gospel and often used editorially.[9]

c) Probably the distinction between Jesus and the Son of Man which is found in 8:38 belongs to this category of the preservation of Christological titles. Since Mark himself identifies Jesus and the Son of Man it would have been much simpler and would have produced a much crisper and better balanced logion if he had changed 'Son of Man' to the first person pronoun. The appearance of the title 'Son of Man' in 2:10, 28 falls too early according to the generally accepted view that Mark only uses this title after Peter's confession, and probably arises from Mark's desire to use at this point an existing collection of controversy stories.[10]

---

[9] ῥαββι is used three times by Mark; at 9:5 in the middle of the Transfiguration story where another title would seem more appropriate to the action of the story, unless the 'ignorance' of Peter is being emphasised; at 11:21 again by Peter when he discovers Jesus has performed a miracle; at 14:45 it is Judas' salutation at the betrayal and we would hardly expect Mark to have placed a stronger title on the lips of Judas. The equivalent Greek title, διδάσκαλος, is used within stories by disciples at 4:38; 14:14; by non-disciples at 5:35; 9:17; 10:20; 12:32; it is used in the initial address of stories, where it is most probably Markan, by disciples at 9:38; 13:1; and by non-disciples at 10:17 (10:17 is undoubtedly difficult, as Matthew's rewriting of it shows, and may represent the tradition as Mark received it; if the address is Markan it is probably derived from v. 20); 12:14 (here the title is appropriate in view of the context); 12:19. All this suggests that though Mark received the title from the tradition he also inserted it at other places; there is nothing to suggest that he altered other titles to this title. In Mark Jesus occupies a position of authority as teacher and is often referred to as teaching though in comparison with the other gospels little of his teaching is given. Cf. E. Trocmé, *La Formation de l'Évangile selon Marc*, Paris, 1963, pp. 113f.; E. Schweizer, 'Anmerkungen zur Theologie des Markus', *Neotestamentica*, (Stuttgart, 1963), pp. 93ff.
[10] Cf. H. W. Kuhn, *Ältere Sammlungen im Markusevangelium*, (Göttingen, 1971), pp. 53–99.

B. Inconsistent or Superfluous Information

a) 10:28. It is generally agreed that 10:17-31 is a Markan compilation.[11] In v. 28 Peter says 'We have abandoned everything' and Jesus replies that those who have left house, family and farm will receive a hundredfold compensation. But Peter was a fisherman and if Mark had really wished to accommodate the logion to its present position in the Gospel he ought to have added among the list of items which men might forsake some allusion to fishing-boats or fishing nets. He has thus not adapted the logion to its present context though an easy addition would have enabled him to do so.

But there is a second matter in relation to this passage. Had Peter in fact left house and family as this implies and as 1:16-18 probably does also? In 1:29 we find that Peter still maintins a home to which he goes back and 3:9; 4:1, 36 show that the disciples as a whole still have a boat at their disposal. Both the absolute nature of 10:28 and its exclusion of any reference to fishing probably derive from the passage of an original logion through the tradition which reshaped it in terms of the community to which at any time it was addressed; Mark has probably used it in the form in which it circulated in his community, without modifying it to suit the context of his Gospel.

b) There is more which merits our attention in 1:16-20. We have an unusual word for fishing, ἀμφιβάλλειν, which Mark explains with one of his typical parentheses (introduced by γάρ[12]) ἦσαν γὰρ ἁλιεῖς. ἀμφιβάλλειν is a word with many meanings[13] and to an audience not accustomed to the different methods of fishing would not normally suggest that Peter and Andrew were fishermen. Hence Mark's explanatory parenthesis;

[11] Cf. N. Walter, Zur Analyse von Mc. 10:17-31, Z.N.W. 53 (1962), 206-218; S. Légasse, 'Jésus a-t-il annoncé la Conversion finale d'Israël? A propos de Marc x.23-27', N.T.S. 10 (1964), 480-487; E. Best, 'Uncomfortable Words VII: The Camel and the Needle's Eye (Mark 10:25)', Exp. Times LXXXII (1970/1) 83-89, (infra pp. 17-30), and fuller references therein; cf. also H. W. Kuhn, op. cit., pp. 146ff.

[12] Cf. 2:15; 6:14; 7:3f.; 11:13; cf. C. H. Turner, J.T.S., 26 (1925) 145-56.

[13] See Liddell and Scott, A Greek-English Lexicon (ed. H. S. Jones and R. McKenzie), Oxford, 1951, s.v.

but it would have been easier to substitute for ἀμφιβάλλειν a more generally accepted word for fishing, e.g. ἁλιεύειν.[14] Mark, in other words, has not changrd the existing word in the tradition but explained it. We do have another word relating to fishing, δίκτυα, in v. 19 but since it cannot be misunderstood it requires no explanation. There is one other possible instance of Mark's respect for the tradition in this passage: his reference to James and John leaving their father with the μισθωταί. Commentators again offer many interpretations. The μισθωταί may be mentioned to show the love of James and John for their father in that they did not leave him alone (Schlatter, Grundmann), or to show how much James and John were giving up in leaving a family wealthy enough to employ others (Wohlenberg, Loisy), 'or does it add to the pathos – he (their father) is now left entirely at the mercy of "hirelings"? . . . can it be that the contrast is here between the apostles, who answer Jesus' call, and the "hirelings", who are held back by mercenary considerations?' (Nineham). The difficulty of commentators in finding an acceptable explanation of the significance of the word for Mark may suggest that it had none; Mark used it because it was already present in the tradition.

c) 10:35 contains the superfluous detail that James and John are the sons of Zebedee; this has already been given in 1:19 and 3:17. What has happened here is that Mark has taken up a new incident, which when it was an isolated pericope requred this information so that the scene might be adequately set, and he has failed to omit the detail when he incorporated it into the larger whole of the Gospel where it is unnecessary.

d) 11:16, καὶ οὐκ ἤφιεν ἵνα τις διενέγκῃ σκεῦος διὰ τοῦ . This clause disappears in Matthew and Luke. It fits into a Jewish situation and therefore is proabably pre–Markan.[15] It does not fit into the emphasis Mark himself lays on the cleansing of the Temple, i.e. judgment on Judaism and the admission of the Gentiles.[16] It is another case of the preservation of unnecessary detail.

[14] Cf. Lucian, Piscator, pp. 47ff.
[15] 'The prohibition implies a respect for the holiness of the Temple, and is thoroughly Jewish in spirit' (V. Taylor, ad loc.).
[16] Cf. E. Best, The Temptation and the Passion, pp. 83f.

C. Unmodified Tradition

a) 8:31; 9:31; 10:33f.[17] The kernel of these three predictions appears to be a piece of unmodified traditon. There is the use of ἀποκτείνειν rather than of σταυροῦν; we should expect the latter: (1) because Mark uses it throughout the Passion narrative (15:13, 14, 15 etc.); (2) because σταυροῦν would give a more correct prophecy of what was to happen; (3) because 8:34 with its reference to 'taking up the cross and following Jesus' in Mark's mind certainly links the fate of the disciple to the fate of Jesus. More important than this is the retention by Mark of μετὰ τρεῖς ἡμέρας; it may be that according to Semitic time-reckoning where a portion of a day is counted as a whole day this would be in no way different from τῇ τρίτῃ ἡμέρᾳ; but normally in Greek our phrase would not have the same precision as the other or necessarily imply resurrection on Sunday morning after a death on Friday afternoon. Matthew and Luke have both altered Mark's phrase to τῇ τρίτῃ ἡμέρᾳ (Matthew 16:21; 17:23; 20:19; Luke 9:22; 18:33). This latter is found more widely in the N.T.[18] and became the standard Christian phrase; we find it indeed appearing in written form in 1 Corinthians 15:4 earlier than Mark's phrase; and 1 Corinthians 15:4 is itself older than Paul's letter. Thus Mark retains an old formula although it

---

[17] Mark may not have received all three of these passages from the tradition but may have created two more of them out of the one which did come to him; if so his respect for the tradition is more obvious. I cannot accept the argument of N. Perrin, 'The Christology of Mark: A Study in Methodology', *Journal of Religion*, 51 (1971) 173-87, that he created all three.

[18] Cf. Lk. 13:32; 24:7, 21, 46; Acts 10:40; 1 Cor. 15:4; the 'three days' tradition appears also to be found in the logia of Mt. 12:40; 27:63. On the origin and meaning of the two traditions see G. von Rad and G. Delling, *T.W.N.T.* II, pp. 951-3; F. Nötscher, 'Zur Auferstehung nach drei Tagen', *Bib.* 35 (1954) 313-9; J. B. Bauer, 'Drei Tage,' *Bib.* 39 (1958) 354-8; J. Dupont, 'Ressuscité Le Troisième Jour', *Bib.* 40 (1959) 742-61; G. M. Landes, 'The "Three days and Three Nights" Motif in Jonah 2.1,' *J.B.L.* 86 (1957) 446-50; N. Walker, 'After Three Days,' *N.T.* 4 (1960) 261-2; H. K. McArthur, 'On the Third Day,' *N.T.S.* 18 (1971/2) 81-86.

would not be as immediately apparent in meaning as the formula which eventually became standard.[19]

b) 9:35. 9:33–37 bears clear evidence of Mark's redaction. Probably most if not all of vv. 33, 34 come from his hand;[20] 9:30–32 gives the second prediction of the passion; vv. 33–34 are a connecting link; vv. 35–37 are probably largely traditional material. In v. 31 the passion prediction is made to the disciples; v. 33 implies that it is the disciples who go with Jesus to Capernaum and enter a house and who are asked about the subject of their conversation on the way; v. 35 then says that Jesus sat down and summoned the Twelve. Unless we assume that Mark is here deliberatly distinguishing between other disciples and the Twelve and in the present context this is most improbable, we must conclude that in bringing in at this point a brief pericope from the tradition Mark has carried over with it its introduction for the disciples are already present.[21] Reploh however suggests that all the references to the Twelve in Mark

[19] There is some evidence in Josephus for the equivalence of 'after three days' and 'on the third day' (e.g., *Ant.* 7;280f.) but the LXX of Hos. 6.2 shows that they would normally be distinguished. J. Schreiber, *Theologie des Vertrauens*, pp. 103ff. contests the view that μετὰ τρεῖς ἡμέρας is pre-Markan.

[20] In v. 33 ἐν τῇ οἰκίᾳ and ἐν τῇ ὁδῷ are obviously Markan; references to Capernaum appear in Mark only in material introducing pericopae (Luke omits it here and Matthew transfers it earlier to 17:24); ἦλθον is probably also part of the machinery Mark uses to show Jesus' journey to Jerusalem as a journey to the cross; the question of v. 33 disappears in both Mt. and Lk.; v. 34 can hardly stand by itself without v. 33 and if a reference to the dispute about 'greatness' which it contains was in the tradition then Mark has rewritten it extensively; more probably Mark created this verse. Cf. K. G. Reploh, *Markus – Lehrer der Gemeinde*, pp. 140ff.; D. E. Nineham, *ad loc.*; S. Légasse, *Jésus et L'Enfant*, pp. 23ff.

[21] Cf. V. Taylor, D. E. Nineham, E. Schweizer; W. L, Knox, *The Sources of the Synoptic Gospels*, I, Cambridge, 1953, pp. 21ff.; S. Légasse, *op. cit.*, p. 24.

E. Haenchen, *Der Weg Jesu, ad loc.* suggests that Mark added vv. 36f. We note the use of the rare word ἐναγκαλίζεσθαι which only occurs again in 10:16. But if Mark composed vv. 36f. then v. 37 is not the proper conclusion to the implied question of v. 34; 10:15 would be much better. If vv. 36f. did not belong in this sequence prior to Mark then the use of the catch-word ὄνομα is upset in the passage.

are editorial.[22] If this is so in the present instance it would have been much easier for Mark to introduce the reference to the Twelve at either v. 31a, where he refers to the disciples, or at v. 33 where there is a neutral third person plural (both v. 31a and v. 33 come from Mark). In v. 35a φωνέω is a non-Markan word (he uses προσκαλέω) and he prefers καὶ ἔλεγεν αὐτοῖς to καὶ λέγει;[23] "sitting" (καθίσας) to teach is not otherwise emphasised by Mark; only in 4:1 and 13:3 does a reference to sitting go with authoritative teaching and in each case κάθημαι and not καθίζω is used; but regularly Mark depicts Jesus as teaching without any allusion to his being seated.[24] We assume so often that he rewrote the introductions to the pericopae which he used that it may be surprising to find him retain one where it could easily have been modified.

D. Unnecessary or Irrelevant Logia

There are a number of logia sequences whose connection at their commencement is clear and relevant but within which the final logia are both difficult in themselves and difficult to relate to their Markan context.

  a) 9:35-50.[25] It is easy to trace the verbal connections which hold this sequence together: ὄνομα (vv. 37, 38, 39, 41); παιδίων-μικρῶν vv. 37, 42); σκανδαλίζειν (vv. 42-47); πῦρ (vv. 43, 48, 49); ἅλας (vv. 49, 50). These verbal connections suggest oral transmission and therefore almost certainly imply

---

[22] Op. cit., p. 141.

[23] Cf. H. W. Kuhn, op. cit., pp. 130f.

[24] The καί is probably, as so often, his introductory link.

[25] E. W. Bundy, Jesus and the First Three Gospels, Cambridge, Mass., 1955, suggests that vv. 38-40 are a Markan insertion into an existing section, since they are dialogue in the middle of a section of logia and v. 37 joins easily to v. 41. But it is hard to see why Mark should insert these verses here and they contain the catch-word ὄνομα. Even if they are a Markan insertion this does not affect the conclusion we draw about the later portions of vv. 35-50.

pre-Markan tradition.[26] Vv. 49, 50 have proved almost impossible to interpret with any degree of certainty both in themselves and in relation to their Markan context; the final clause καὶ εἰρηνεύετε ἐν ἀλλήλοις may possibly refer back to the

[26] The most recent challange to this comes from H. W. Kuhn, op. cit., pp. 32ff., following on R. Schnackenburg, 'Markus 9:33-50', in Synoptische Studien (Festschrift für A. Wikenhauser), München, 1953, pp. 184-206 (unfortunately this was not available to me). He argues: a) Mark joins sayings and incidents by catchwords; b) Mark joins sayings together using γάρ even when there is no logical connection; c) the tradition in Mt. 10:40-42 shows that v. 37 and v. 41 were already linked and therefore Mark inserted vv. 38-40. He allows that the three 'church-rules' of vv. 37, 41f. may have been a unit prior to Mark; Mark joined these to vv. 43-8 for they have no real connection other than through 'catch-words'; v. 49 may have already been joined to vv. 43-8 prior to Mark but v. 50b is a comment of Mark relating the whole back to vv. 33f. Against this we may argue: a) That Mark uses 'catch-words' on occasions does not prove that he necessarily was the first to use them here; they were widely used and could have been in the pre-existing tradition. As Kuhn himself shows (p. 129) the root σπείρειν was the link in the original collection of the three parables (4:3-9, 26-29, 31-32). b) Mark uses γάρ no more often than do the other evangelists and admittedly does join together sayings with it. We find it here at vv. 34, 39, 40, 41, 49. But Mark also uses γάρ regularly in narrative to hold together material which was already united in the pre-Markan tradition, e.g. 6:18, 20. 8:34 and 8:35 were already a unit in the tradition as Matthew 10:38f. shows (cf. John 12:23-26); either they already had a γάρ which Mark preserved, which shows γάρ is not necessarily a sign of his hand, or he added γάρ which shows he used it with logia which were already united. In chap. 4 γάρ is used to join together vv. 21 and 22 and vv. 24 and 25, but we would hold that these were already joined in the tradition (cf. M. Thrall, Greek Particles in the New Testament, Leiden, 1962, pp. 41ff.). c) There appear to be good grounds for seeing at least in vv. 38, 39, 42, 45, 48 a connected Aramaic substratum indicating a pre-Markan union of these verses, cf. M. Black, An Aramaic Approach to the Gospels and Acts, 3rd edition, Oxford, 1967, pp. 169-71; cf. also pp. 218-222. d) The real difficulty lies in seeing what was the purpose of Mark's redaction, if indeed he was responsible, in bringing together these sections; it is possible to see a connection between the closing clause of v. 50 εἰρηνεύετε ἐν ἀλλήλοις and v. 33f. but not in regard to most of the rest of the material, in particular vv. 49, 50a. Kuhn supplies no redactional justification; commentators have always had great difficulty with these verses; lacking such justification we cannot accept Kuhn's view.

dispute about greatness in v. 34 and have been added by Mark[27] or it may have originally belonged and been the reason why Mark utilised the intervening irrelevant and incomprehensible logia. In either case Mark has included sayings which are unnecessary or irrelevant to the development of his discussion. It is conceivable that Mark and his community both understood what the sayings about salt and fire meant and saw their relevance, but this seems very unlikely. What is much more probable is that Mark had this sequence of logia; the initial logia and possibly the very last were very relevant and rather than divide the sequence he retained all of it.

b)   11:22-25.[28] Around 11:15-19, the cleansing of the temple, Mark has set according to his regular redactional method the story of the cursing of the fig-tree. Probably in the pre-Markan tradition the fig-tree stood as part of a pericope whose point was Jesus' δύναμις [29] with the addendum, already attached to it in the tradition, that a disciple could have the same power through prayer.[30] Mark now gives the fig-tree incident an entirely different meaning through its association with the cleansing of the temple but he does not omit the accompanying logia about prayer. In their present position they do not fit into the larger context and commentators struggle to explain them in it.[31] (We might say that wherever we see the commentators in confusion this is a sign of the preservation of tradition). It is therefore most unlikely that Mark gathered together a set of independent logia about prayer (v. 25 has even a different theme from vv. 22-24)

---

[27]   It was a piece of floating tradition, cf. 1 Th. 5:13; Hermas, *Vis.* III, 9, 10.

[28]   There are again verbal links: πίστις, -εύειν, προσεύχεσθαι.

[29]   Cf. V. Taylor, *ad loc.*

[30]   Taylor's remark that 'with 21 the narrative element in the story ends; it appears to have been introduced for the sake of the sayings which follow in 23-25' (p. 466a) would be true of the tradition but not as he thinks of Mark's usage. But even v. 25 does not relate to the theme of δύναμις; it must have been a part of the catechetical tradition on prayer

[31]   E. Lohmeyer simply says: 'die Sprüche haben hier mit der beschilderten Situation kaum etwas gemein'.

and set them in his Gospel at this point,[32] but they appear here because they were attached already to the piece of tradition about the fig-tree which he did want to use.

c) 4:21-5 falls into almost the same pattern but here the most difficult saying is not the final (v. 25) but the penultimate (v. 24). It s generally held that vv. 21-25 were not part of the complex of parables which Mark obtained from the tradition,[33] but did they exist as a unit prior to Mark or did he bring together here a number of isolated logia? Jeremias has argued strongly that v. 21 and v. 22 first came together and that v. 24 and v. 25 came together independently and that then these two units were joined to form more or less our present vv. 21-25 and only after this did Mark use the section.[34] On the other hand v. 23 is probably Markan and v. 24a may be also. καὶ ἔλεγεν αὐτοῖς might suggest that Mark is here introducing new material[35] but this same phrase is also used in v. 13 to re-join the interpretation of the Sower parable to the parable itself after a Markan insertion, although in the pre-Markan tradition parable and

---

[32] Contrast D. E. Nineham (p. 298) who considers vv. 22-5 to have been added by Mark himself; even if Nineham is correct we would hold that these already existed as a unit prior to Mark and that therefore v. 25 really has little to do with vv. 22-4. The sayings certainly were found in other catechetical contexts; cf. Mt. 17:20 and Lk. 17:6 with Mk. 11:23, and Mt. 6:14 with Mk. 11:25; cf. also Gosp Thom. 48, 106. The Lukan form of v. 23 (Lk. 17:6) shows that a connection between a tree and faith already existed apart from Mark 11 and this connection probably therefore predates Mark (so E. Schweizer).

[33] So V. Taylor, E. Schweizer, E. Haenchen, E. Linnemann, *Parables of Jesus*, (London 1966), p. 180; J. Jeremias, *The Parables of Jesus*, (London, 1963), p. 14 n. 11 and p. 91; W. Marxsen, 'Redaktionsgeschichtliche Erklärung der sogenannten Parabeltheorie des Markus' *Z.N.W.* 52 (1955) 255-271 (at p. 262); R. H. Lightfoot, *History and Interpretation in the Gospels*, (London, 1935), pp. 35f.; H. W. Kuhn, *op. cit.*, pp. 130ff.

[34] J. Jeremias, *op. cit.*, pp. 90-2. There may again be catch-words: μόδιος, μέτρον, -έω (so J. Jeremias, R. Bultmann, *Synoptic Tradition*, pp. 325ff.; E. Schweizer, D. E. Nineham).

[35] This view has been sustained most recently by H. W. Kuhn, *op. cit.*, pp. 130f. who apparently allows that vv. 21f. and vv. 24b, 25 were pre-Markan formations. K. G. Reploh, *op. cit.*, seems to go further and suggest that Mark found all four logia distinct from one another and brought them together.

interpretation were already joined. Mark may then have inserted vv. 23, 24a into the original unit of vv. 21, 22, 24b, 25 and rejoined the group with the aid of the phrase. Vv. 21, 22 are easily seen to be relevant to the Markan context either as another parable[36] or as related to the parable context (the light which is given in the parables is not for hiding),[37] or, more generally, as suggesting that Jesus or the Kingdom of God or the Word is not to be hidden.[38] V. 25a may fit in with this in the sense that whoever has received revelation or light will receive more; but v. 25b, 'he who has no revelation will lose it', is much more difficult to fit in. Probably v. 25 comes from a popular proverb – the rich grow richer while the poor become poorer – of which the first half is apparently appropriate to the richness which is light but the second is not since those who have no light, who are outside the church (cf. v. 11 οἱ ἔξω), cannot be deprived of what they do not have. But the difficulties with v. 24 are even greater than with v. 25b. The comment of Taylor is typical. 'The significance of the saying in Mark is obscure'.[39] In its Q form (Matthew 7:2 = Luke 6:38) it is more appropriate to its context.[40] Thus again we appear to have a sequence of sayings of which the first were important for Mark but the others inappropriate yet were retained in order not to destroy the existing unity. It is, however, just possible that Mark himself added vv. 24, 25 which already existed as a unit to vv. 21, 22 which also was already a unit. He will then have joined them

[36] Cf. J. Jeremias, *op. cit.*, pp. 91f.

[37] E.g. E. Schweizer.

[38] E.g. V. Taylor, D. E. Nineham, M. J. Lagrange, E. Hoskyns and F. N. Davey, *The Riddle of the New Testament*, London, 1931, pp. 129f. For Swete the light is the Word and the lampstand the hearers who would defeat the purpose of the Word if they put it under the 'measure' or the 'bed'.

[39] Cf. A. E. J. Rawlinson, D. E. Nineham, etc. It is this very obscurity which argues against the view that Mark collected the saying and added it to v. 25. K. G. Reploh, *op. cit.*, pp. 68f., notes the difficulty but does nothing to counter it. If Mark brought all these sayings together then a satisfactory redactional process must be offered as a supporting argument. This has never been done.

[40] In Mark v. 25a links relatively easily to the last clause of v. 24 and this may explain why in some other previous context v. 25 was joined as an explanatory comment to v. 24.

because he wished to use v. 25a. The difficulty about v. 24 still remains; he must have brought it in, though it is hardly relevant, because he wished to use the later saying.

Perhaps some of the pre-Markan collections may have been used in the same way by Mark: he desired one or more incidents and so used the whole. H. W. Kuhn[41] argues that 10:1-45 embodies a pre-Markan complex of which Mark certainly wanted 10:35-45; he used 10:17-23, 25 correcting it so as to universalise it from a discussion of the disciple's attitude to 'wealth' to discipleship in general; he then retained 10:1-12 which has really little relevance to his argument at this point, and which is difficult to reconcile with the total context. Perhaps the same is true of 2:1-3:6.[42] Earlier critics pointed out that the references to the death of Jesus (2:20; 3:6), to the Pharisees and Herodians (3:6), and to the Son of Man (2:10, 28) fall too early in the 'history' of the life of Jesus, but these earlier critics do not seem to have speculated on what this had to say about Mark's methods. It would take a longer analysis than is now possible to discuss which parts of this collection are relevant here to his redactional purposes and which are only present because he has retained an existing collection.

E. Unnecessary Retention of Names

In a number of places Mark has preserved names without apparent reason, though from time to time commentators have attempted to derive meaning, sometimes most esoteric meaning, from them. Levi's name is retained in 2:13f. though Levi is not mentioned among the Twelve in 3:16ff. (Matthew corrects this); the names of the brothers of Jesus in 6:3, though these can have been of little interest to a Roman audience; the name Jairus (5:22), again of little interest to a Roman audience; Bartimaeus (10:46), whose name is translated but not in the way in which Mark normally explains Aramaic words (ὅ ἐστιν),[43] implying

---

[41] Op. cit., pp. 146-190.
[42] H. W. Kuhn, op. cit., pp. 53-99, does not allow that 3:1-6 was part of the original collection.
[43] Mark has thus not even brought this into line with his normal convention.

that both name and explanation go back before Mark. It is often stated by commentators[44] that the names of Alexander and Rufus whose father Simon of Cyrene carried the cross of Jesus (15:21) are given because Rufus was later well-known in Rome and a cross-reference is made to Romans 16:13; but Romans 16 may not have been written to Rome and Mark may be doing nothing other than preserving names which have come to him in the tradition (this is not to say that at some point in the transmission of the tradition the names may not have been important).

In this paper we have dealt only with particular passages and not with the contradictions which many scholars find between the "suffering" Christology of Mark and the θεῖος ἀνήρ Christology of his material,[45], which if true would re-inforce our conclusions.

Conclusions

1)   The evidence adduced is not exhaustive; no systematic attempt was made to look for examples, but those which turned up in the course of other work on Mark were noted. Anyone who works at Mark will be able to produce other examples. Naturally also any particular example will be disputed. It is therefore the cumulative effect which is important. There may indeed be evidence to be produced on the other side. This paper is only an attempt to draw attention to something which appears to have been neglected.

2)   Faced with a piece of tradition Mark altered it internally as little as possible. If, as Formgeschichte has shown, notes of time, space and audience were missing then he felt himself free to set those pericopae which now lacked context in new contexts, but even where it would have suited his purpose to do so he has not altered their content nor has he abbreviated them by omitting logia which were irrelevant or even meaningless in the context he has given them. It is perhaps fair to say this in this respect he was more careful than Matthew or Luke.

[44] So V. Taylor, D. E. Nineham, etc.
[45] E.g. L. E. Keck, 'Mark 3.7-12 and Mark's Christology,' *J.B.L.* 84 (1965) 341-58; U. Luz, 'Das Geheimnismotiv und die Markinische Christologie', *Z.N.W.* 65 (1965) 9-30; T. J. Weeden, 'The heresy that necessitated Mark's Gospel,' *Z.N.W.* 59 (1968) 145-158.

3) Redaction critics argue that Mark was a genuine author and not a scissors-and-paste editor. This requires more careful definition. In the way in which he has placed the tradition in his total context supplying audience, place, time and sequence and in the summaries he has written he has been quite obviously creative. But in the way in which he has preserved the material which existed before him he has been conservative. Perhaps we should think not of an author but of an artist creating a collage.

4) Mark appears to have had a positive respect for the material which he used; this is not to say that he was attempting to write 'history', or that he possessed the journalist's ideal – facts are sacred, comment is free – or that he was positively attempting to preserve for the future what lay before him. We are only saying how it appears he actually did his work. It would suggest that he did not create incidents to illustrate general trends; as if we were to suppose that Mark believed Jesus was an exorcist but since all stories of exorcism had disappeared he therefore created some to portray Jesus as exorcist. That is not the way he worked. His positive attitude to the tradition is also seen in his retention of material, as in the logia-sequences, which plays no useful part in his gospel. Does this mean that somewhere or other he has managed to work in all the traditions which he knew? Does it imply that he did not know Q?

5) If Mark has preserved material which does not fully correspond to the view which he himself holds then are we at liberty to speak of a theology of the Gospel of Mark? Must we not rather speak of Mark's theology? If a valid distinction can be drawn between these two then it may be that we should not look for a coherent and consistent theology in the Gospel but be prepared to find unevenness since he laid his theology over an existing theology, or theologies, in the tradition he received.[46]

[46] One reviewer of my book *The Temptation and the Passion* waxed caustic because I had pointed out an inconsistency of this nature, viz., that the reference to Satan in the interpretation of the Sower parable conflicted with the view that I had argued Mark held about Satan. The reviewer was prepared to dismiss the whole argument of the book on this alone. Quite apart from the wrong idea of proof which such a dismissal implies it shows that the reviewer had not really understood the problem of determining Mark's theology.

6)   We must be careful not to press our argument too far. It would be illegitmate to conclude that all those who handed on oral tradition had the same attitude to it as Mark. Our results therefore do not permit us in any way to conclude that in the oral period the material was conserved accurately, and naturally therefore it does not enable us to make a judgment on the 'historicity' of the material Mark preserved. But equally it does not allow us to argue from 'picturesque' details in Mark to an eye-witness, e.g. Peter, who gave Mark the facts. We can say nothing about Mark's source or sources but only refer to what Mark did with what he received from them.

Additional Note

After the original publication of this article Prof. Dr. Kuhn pointed out to me that I had misinterpreted him in my n.26 where I alleged that he had argued that 'Mark joins sayings together . . .'. In fact it was R. Schnackenburg who had made this argument and Kuhn had himself disputed the facts as set out by Schnackenburg.

Chapter 4

Mark III. 20, 21, 31-35

In this paper we shall be concerned with Mark's use and understanding of these two passages and not with questions of their historicity and possible place in the life of Jesus. The vast majority of commentators see the passages as linked by Mark: the family of Jesus believe that he is out of his mind and come to seize him and presumably quieten him.[1] The scribes from Jerusalem are of more or less the same opinion, asserting that he is demon-possessed; they argue with him and are refuted. Jesus is informed of his family's arrival; he denies the importance of physical relationship and avers that the true relationship to himself is created by obedience to the will of God. Thus we have here one of Mark's frequent 'sandwiches' in which two items are related: one is placed in the middle of the other so that they shed light on each other.

Recently Wansbrough[2] and Schroeder[3] have independently put forward a view originally advanced by G. Hartmann[4] in 1913 which dissociates vv. 20 f. from vv. 31-5. They argue that: (a) vv. 31-5 do not take up the theme of v. 21, for the family of Jesus in vv. 31-5 is not actively hostile to him as in v. 21; (b) ἐξέστη does not normally refer to madness and in Mark

[1] A few commentators believe that the family learn that others are saying that Jesus is out of his mind and therefore come to restrain him (see below).

[2] H. Wansbrough, 'Mark iii. 21 – Was Jesus out of his mind?', N.T.S. xviii (1971/2), 233-5.

[3] H.-H. Schroeder, Eltern und Kinder in der Verkündigung Jesu (T.F. 53) (Hamburg-Bergstedt, 1972), pp. 110ff.

[4] 'Mk 3, 20 f', B.Z. xi (1913), 249-79 (I owe this reference to Schroeder).

elsewhere always carries the connotation 'wonder, amazement';
(c) οἱ παρ' αὐτοῦ has usually a wider meaning than 'family,
kinsmen'; and they conclude that, since the verse can be
understood in a different way, it ought to be understood in that
different way. They therefore take οἱ παρ' αὐτοῦ to refer to
the disciples[5] who are with Jesus in the house and who go out
(ἐξῆλθον) to the crowd (αὐτόν) to curb its enthusiasm for they
(the disciples) were saying that the crowd was amazed.

With these two very different interpretations in mind we
must examine Mark's redaction to distinguish what he has
written from what lay in the tradition. In v. 20 καὶ ἔρχεται εἰς
οἶκον[6] is probably to be attributed to him since he regularly
introduces the 'house' as a place where instruction is given, and
Jesus instructs in 3:31-5;[7] καὶ ἔρχεται is used redactionally to
introduce pericopae at 1:40; 5:22; 6:1; 14:17;[8] πάλιν is a Markan
favourite.[9] ὥστε μὴ δύνασθε κτλ resembles in content 6:31b
and if not composed by Mark probably represents his use of an
idea that lay in the tradition, for the need to eat has no particular
relevance to our passage[10] and we note the plural αὐτούς after

---

[5] 'Adherents' would be a natural meaning of the phrase; cf. Taylor, ad loc.
[6] In some texts and translations this is taken as part of v. 19.
[7] On the use of 'house' in Mark see J. Schreiber, Theologie des
Vertrauens (Hamburg, 1967), pp. 162 ff. No attempt should be made to
identify the present house with that of Peter in Capernaum.
[8] See also 10:46; 11:15, 27; these are redactional clauses of very similar
structure to v. 20a and used to join pericopae. Thus if the plural verb is
read in v. 20a with ℵ Af f[13] there is an equally strong case for taking it
as redactional. Note also the use of the historic present, another sign of
Mark's hand (cf. Hawkins, Horae Synopticae (Oxford, 1909), pp. 143-9;
Taylor, Mark, 46 f.).
[9] Matthew, 17 times; Mark 28; Luke 3; John 43.
[10] J. D. Crossan, 'Mark and the Relatives of Jesus', N.T. xv (1973),
81-113, argues that Mark introduces this reference in order to create a
parallel with 1:31 and 2:16. He notes that when disciples are called in
Mark we have: (a) a reference to Jesus by the sea (1:16a; 2:13; 3:7-9); (b)
the statement of their election (1:16b-20; 2:14; 3:13-19); (c) Jesus and the
disciple(s) are together in a house (1:29; 2:18; 3:20a); (d) their eating
together is mentioned (1:31; 2:16; 3:20b). The parallels are fanciful. In
the case of both 1:16-31 and 3:7-20b there is intervening material which
does not fit; two instances are not sufficient to argue that a partial
parallel in a third must be complete; 3:13-19 is not a 'call' in the same
sense as 1:16b-20 and 2:14; in 3:20b the disciples are not able to eat!

the singular ἔρχεται.[11] Thus the scene-setting of v. 20 is Markan; he puts Jesus into a house and gathers the crowd so that there is no opportunity of eating for Jesus and the disciples (αὐτούς refers back to the Twelve who have just been appointed in vv. 13–19). We are not told whether the crowd is in the house with Jesus and occupying his attention or outside so that he has to go out to them and meet their demands, presumably of healing as in 1:32–4. The verse serves at any rate to emphasize the popularity of Jesus quite apart from setting the scene for what follows. We cannot accept Crossan's view that v. 20 concludes the preceding pericope rather than introduces the following.[12]

If v. 20 may then be set to the hand of the Evangelist there is little in the way of Markan vocabulary or style in v. 21a, though equally there is nothing which would prevent us drawing the conclusion that he wrote it. Crossan[13] indicates several features which lead him to believe that it is Mark's free composition: (i) The absence of a parallel in Matthew and Luke; but both will have had good reason for omitting it; see n. 11 above. (ii) ἀκούειν is used redactionally by Mark in introductory material in 2:1; 3:8; 5:27; 7:25; 10:47 and is therefore redactional here; but it is a perfectly natural word if attention is to be drawn to the thoughts or actions of others; in the passages listed by Crossan it always relates to Jesus' healing activity, and this element is not present here. (iii) Mark uses κρατεῖν elsewhere eight times in the sense of holding someone by coercion; in some of these passages Mark is certainly not composing freely but using or rewriting tradition (6:17; 14:1, 44, 46, 49, 51); his use of the

---

[11] Crossan, art. cit., argues that this divergence is a sign of Mark's hand in both clauses. It seems easier to assume that Mark is picking up tradition which he does not completely unify. Crossan's further argument that since Matthew and Luke do not possess parallels to vv. 20 and 21 Mark must have composed them would only be valid if there were no good reason why Matthew and Luke should omit them; clearly they would have wished to eliminate v. 21 because of its harsh reference to Jesus' family; v. 20 could not then stand by itself.

[12] Crossan's argument depends on the parallel he draws with material in 1:16ff. and 2:13 ff.; the parallel is unsatisfactory (see n. 10 above) and so the argument falls.

[13] Art. Cit.

word here cannot then be taken as a sign that he is inventing an incident. The simplest conclusion from the evidence is that Mark is rewriting tradition in *v. 21a; v. 21b* however could be taken to be a Markan γάρ clause.[14] Mark normally inserts these to explain something which has come to him in the tradition. Has he then received information in the tradition that the disciples or Jesus' family went to detain him and has sought to supply a reason for this (perhaps that he was not able to take care of himself and feed himself!)? Noting this problem we must leave it until later, turning our attention first to the context of *v. 21.*

οἱ παρ' αὐτοῦ is certainly more easily understood to refer to the 'adherents' of Jesus than to his 'kinsmen';[15] evidence for the latter meaning exists but is scanty.[16] They are said to 'go out' (ἐξῆλθον); since Jesus' disciples are with him in the house this is a natural word to use if they go out to the crowd, but the crowd are not necessarily ouside and in *v. 32* they are explicitly mentioned as in the house (or in the group around Jesus). Moreover Mark does use ἐξέρχεσθαι in the sense 'set out' without explicit reference to the place from which the journey begins (8:11, 27; 9:30; 14:16). In Mark κρατεῖν regularly means 'arrest' (6:17; 12:12; 14:1, 44, 46, 49, 51), 'take hold of' (1:31; 5:41; 9:27), 'hold fast to' (a tradition, 7:3, 4, 8), 'keep to oneself' (9:10), but never 'restrain, hinder'; it only has this meaning in the NT at Luke 24:16; Rev. 7:1.[17] The referent of αὐτόν is most

---

[14] Cf. 1:16. Cf. also C. H. Turner, 'Marcan Usage', *J.T.S.* XXVI (1925), 145-56; M. Thrall, *Greek Particles in the New Testament* (Leiden, 1962), pp. 41ff.; C. H. Bird, 'Some γάρ clauses in St Mark's Gospel', *J.T.S.* IV (1953), 171-87.

[15] D. Wenham, *N.T.S.* XXI (1974-5), 295-300 notes its distance from its explanation in *v. 31* but ignores Mark's well-known editorial trick of making a sandwich in which the two outer sections relate closely to one another. J. Lambrecht, *N.T.* XVI (1974), 241-58, has shown from the structure of the whole passage, 3:20-35, how important the sandwich is here. For Wenham's second argument against the traditional solution see n. 19. His third argument depends on Mark's knowledge of the Q tradition. It is not certain that Mark knew this tradition; its very form is uncertain; *v. infra.*

[16] Cf. Bauer, *s.v.*; cf. Sus. 13.

[17] Cf. Bauer, *s.v.*

difficult. Certainly the nearest explicit and obvious possibility is
ὄχλος (ἄρτον is hardly possible!); but Jesus as a referent is
implicit throughout. Could Mark intend the crowd by αὐτόν?
Elsewhere whenever he mentions the crowd and develops the
reference he always without any exception uses the plural,[18] i.e.
according to Markan usage we should therefore have αὐτούς if
he intended us to understand the crowd; since there are at least
fourteen instances of this practice it is almost firm enough to be
described as a rule (cf. 2:13; 3:9, 32; 4:1, 2; 5:24; 6:34, 45f.; 7:14;
8:2f., 6, 9; 9:15; 15:8, 15). Finally in relation to v. 21a we require
to ask to what ἀκούσαντες refers. What is it that Jesus' disciples
have heard so that they go outside or what is it that his kinsmen
have heard so that they come to detain him? There is nothing in
v. 20 to suggest that there has been an uproar among the crowd
requiring the disciples to subdue it; anything of this nature must
be read into v. 21b. If on the other hand the kinsmen of Jesus are
the subject then the vague reference in the participle is more
suitable and is easily explained by v. 21b.

We turn now to ἐξέστη in v. 21b, In the three other places
where Mark uses the verb (2:12; 5:42; 6:51) it refers to the
wonder or amazement of the crowd at Jesus, and on each of
these occasions there is no possible doubt about the reason for
the crowd's wonder. If however the crowd is the subject in v.
21b the cause of their amazement is not mentioned. We have to
go back to vv. 7-12 to find a possible reference. Even if we can
take it in this way, and it is difficult, there is still the qestion why
the wonder of the crowd should cause the disciples to go out of
the house to restrain it. Wansbrough is forced therefore to give
ἐξίστημι the meaning 'out of control with enthusiasm', a
meaning for which he gives no evidence, and certainly elsewhere
in Mark there is no evidence for it. If the reference is only to the
crowd's wonder, and Schroeder does not take any meaning
more than this out of the word, what is the purpose of vv. 20, 21
in Mark? Neither Schroeder nor Wansbrough explores this. If
Mark is reporting an actual happening then we should probably
expect a rebuke to the disciples from Jesus in the same way as he
rebuked them when they thought that the mothers with their

[18] R. P. Meye, *Jesus and the Twelve* (Grand Rapids, Mich. 1968), p.
150.

children were giving trouble to Jesus (10:13f.). If, as is more probable, Mark is writing freely or using tradition for his own purposes and not attempting to report straightforwardly an actual happening, it may be that he is recounting the wonder that Jesus has caused among the crowd as a foil to the immediately succeeding story about the scribes who say he has a devil. If so we have the almost unique instance in Mark where the disciples act on their own and fully understand what Jesus wants them to do, whereas elsewhere it is their misunderstanding of Jesus' purpose which Mark stresses.[19] There remains finally the difficulty that Markan usage would require a plural verb if the crowd is the subject.[20]

Before we proceed to the traditional solution there are two possible mediating positions which require examination. These necessitate giving ἐξέστη the meaning 'out of one's mind, out of one's senses'. This is a perfectly normal meaning of the word, and outside the NT and literature influenced by it, is the customary meaning.[21] In passing we would wish to make clear that the statistical argument which is implicit in the discussion of Schroeder and Wansbrough is false. Because a word is used a number of times by an author with a particular sense this provides no reason for concluding that it ought to have this sense in some other passage of the same author if at the same time there is another customary and well-known meaning for the word; the context, not statistics, must determine the meaning. The first mediating position gives separate subjects to ἐξῆλθον and ἔλεγον. The crowd says that Jesus is out of his mind; the disciples go out to restrain it. The plural in ἔλεγον would here fit in with Mark's normal practice of expanding crowd references with plural verbs and pronouns; it would however still leave the singular αὐτόν as an exception to the rule. This solution gives a clear forward connection to the next

[19] This appears also to counter Wenham's argument (*art. cit.*) in relation to the activity of the disciples.

[20] See also Lambrecht, *art. cit.* (at p. 244 n. 6). He points in particular to the parallel between *v.* 21*b* and *v.* 22*b*. This parallelism in Mark suggests deliberate construction on his part and not dependence on Q as Wenham (*art. cit.*) argues.

[21] Cf. Bauer, *s.v.* See further H. Räisänen, *Die Mutter Jesus im Neuen Testament* (Helsinki, 1969), p. 27 n. 2.

pericope: the crowd says Jesus is mad, so do the scribes. But in addition to the difficulty over αὐτόν as singular there is the clumsiness of the change of subject between ἐξῆλθον and ἔλεγον, the fact that prior to the Passion the crowd in Mark is normally not hostile to Jesus and in v. 32 the crowd are quietly listening to Jesus teaching them, and finally there is nothing in the preceding material to evoke a hostile reaction on the part of the crowd. The second mediating interpretaion is to take the normal understanding of vv. 20, 21 except that in v. 21b ἔλεγον is understood as an impersonal verb. Jesus' kinsmen come to restrain him because people are saying that he is out of his mind.[22] Mark's use of the impersonal plural has often been observed.[23] H. Räisenen,[24] has urged conclusively against this view and it is only necessary to summarize his discussion. (i) We should expect the clauses of v. 21 to be in the reverse order. (ii) The subject of γάρ-clauses in Mark is always to be found in the surrounding context. (iii) 14:1, 2 is similarly constructed by Mark and here the subject of ἔλεγον is clearly that of the preceding clause: 'the high priests and scribes were seeking how to arrest (κρατεῖν) him by stealth and kill him, for (γάρ almost "and") they were saying, "Not during the feast, lest there is an uproar among the people"'. (iv) Mark reports only astonishment on the part of people generally, never the belief that he is out of his mind. (v) In addition Doudna points out that the third plural active used impersonally of matters of common report and opinion is rare in Mark.[25]

None of these views satisfactory and despite the weaknesses which have been explored in the traditional view we are compelled to return to it. Positively in its favour are: (i) The easy link created between vv. 20, 21 and the succeeding pericope, vv. 22-30. (ii) It provides the background against which vv. 31-5 get their bite. (iii) As will appear before we are finished, it fits

[22] This is how the NEB renders it.
[23] See especially C. H. Turner, 'Marcan Usage', J.T.S. XXV (1924), 378-86.
[24] Op. cit. pp. 30ff.
[25] J. C. Doudna, The Greek of the Gospel of Mark (J.B.L. Monograph Series XII, Philadelphia, 1961), pp. 6f. He instances only Mark 2:18, and here the construction is produced by the preceding ἔρχονται. Cf. Crossan, art. cit.

appropriately into Mark's total purpose. (iv) It also fits in with his known editorial 'sandwich' trick. (v) This interpretation was certainly viewed in some areas of the church as the plain meaning of the words; the amendments of DW it would not have been neessary if the Greek could have been understood easily in such a way as to avoid the implication that Jesus' kinsmen regarded him as mad. It was probably the same reason which led Matthew and Luke to rewrite the introduction to the Beelzebul incident. (vi) *V.* 20 serves to set the scene with its typical Markan reference to the 'house'.

At an earlier stage we left unanswered the question whether Mark freely composed *v.* 21 or used material in the tradition to create it. The difference between the hostility of the kinsmen of Jesus in *v.* 21 and their passivity in *v.* 31 suggests that these two verses were not originally adjacent in the tradition. We saw that the clause about not being able to eat in *v.* 20*b* was probably traditional. It therefore seems likely that in *v.* 21 Mark is using traditional material but rewriting it. John 7:5 probably also preserves early material, offering evidence for the existence of a tradition of disagreement with him on the part of Jesus' family.[26] We shall see later that Mark was not out deliberately to vilify the family of Jesus. On the whole he has a conservative attitude to the tradition.[27] Elsewhere in his 'sandwiches' he uses material from the tradition; he does not invent one or other layer of the sandwich. There was no need at this point to create a sandwich unless the material lay to hand for it; he could have made his points without it. We therefore conclude that he rewrote tradition in *v.* 21.

But it may be that, as Crossan holds,[28] *vv.* 22-7 and *vv.* 31-5 were already united in the tradition and Mark did not then create a 'sandwich'. He argues that the Q form of the tradition already had the parallel passages in combination (cf. Luke 11:15-23 and 11:27f.) and so their combination would be pre-Markan. There are difficulties here: (i) The presence of non-parallel material in

[26] Cf. C. H. Dodd, *Historical Tradition in the Fourth Gospel* (Cambridge, 1963), pp. 322-5.
[27] Cf. Best, 'Mark's Preservation of the Tradition', in *L'Évangile selon Marc* (ed. M. Sabbe, Leuven, 1974), pp. 21-34 (infra pp. 31-48).
[28] *Art. cit.*

Q (Luke 11:24-6) and Mark (3:28-9; v. 30 is certainly Markan).
(ii) Crossan holds that 3:35 probably did not originally belong to
3:31-4[29] and its addition was independent of influence from Q;
without v. 35 the remainder of the pericope which now lacks the
reference to the will of God is not sufficiently similar to Luke
11:27 to suggest a parallel. Incidentally it is amazing that
Crossan believes that Mark added v. 35 to vv. 31-4, since he
thereby destroys his whole case for the parallel between Mark
and Luke. (iii) There is a strong possibility that Luke 11:27 with
its interest in women and similarity to Luke 23:27-9 may be a
Lukan construction and not belong to Q at all. (iv) If Mark, as
Crossan asserts, inserted vv. 28-30 into the existing complex of
3:22-27, 31-4, why did he not place v. 21 (v. 20 according to
Crossan belongs to 3:13-19 and is unrelated to v. 21) immediately prior to vv. 31-5 and so sharpen its impact?

If we now move on to vv. 31-5 we have a pericope which
Mark took over directly from the tradition without, so far as can
be seen, significant redactional addition or comment; Jesus' look
(περιβλεψάμενος) appears to be the only possible Markan
touch.[30] There are certain differences between v. 35 and vv. 31-4
which suggest that the former may at one stage either have been
an independent logion added to vv. 31-4 or a preacher's
comment extending and making vv. 31-4 more precise,[31] or vv.
31-4 may have been constructed to give v. 35 a setting.[32] These
differences are: (i) The introduction of 'sister' for the first time.[33]

[29] V. infra for discussion of the relationship of v. 35 to vv. 31-4.
[30] Cf. 3:5; 10:23; cf. also 8:33; 10:27. See Räisänen, op. cit. p. 33. The
pericope however seems to need a clause similar to v. 34a, and Mark
may only have replaced a similar word by his favourite term.
Crossan, art. cit., alleges differences between Mark on the one
hand and Matthew and Luke on the other; in the latter the harshness
with which Mark leaves the family of Jesus 'outside' is softened. Matthew and Luke would naturally tend to do this in harmony with their
omission of v. 21, and there is no reason therefore to conclude that
Mark has edited the material to produce the harshness. In any case
Crossan overplays the variations of the two other evangelists from
Mark.
[31] M. Dibelius, From Tradition to Gospel (London, 1934), pp. 57, 63f.
[32] R. Bultmann, History of the Synoptic Tradition (Oxford, 1963), pp.
29ff.
[33] Some MSS read it in v. 32, but it is textually improbable.

(ii) The absence of the personal pronoun with 'sister' and 'mother'; it is repeated in *vv*. 32, 34. (iii) A change in content between *v*. 34 and *v*. 35; *v*. 34 is absolute – these people present are my mother and brothers; *v*. 35 is conditional – those who do the will of God are my mother and brothers.[34] We note also that an independent variant of *v*. 35 may be traced in Luke 11:28: 'Blessed are those who hear the word of God and keep it' and possibly another in II Clem. 9:11, 'My brothers are those who do the will of my Father'. *V*. 35 could easily have existed on its own, within a set of sayings relating to discipleship and headed, 'Jesus said'. There is some reason to believe such a set of discipleship sayings existed in Mark's community.[35] There are a number of sayings on discipleship which are found in Mark in a form beginning with ὅς ἄν (ἐάν) and which have non-Markan parallels beginning with ὅ followed by a participle; e.g. Mark 8:35 and Matt. 10:39 or Mark 8:38 and Luke 12:9. These sayings are in many cases so close in thought and wording that they must represent translation variants. If then *v*. 35 existed in such a collection did Mark add it to *vv*. 31-4 or was it already added in the tradition? It is probably impossible to determine this, but in so far as the other sayings in this set are concerned it would appear that they had been already added in the pre-Markan tradition. But even if these were added in the community there would probably still be a memory of them as a separate set and therefore they would stand out as emphatic in their addition. In passing we may note that it is most improbable that Mark himself created the saying of *v*. 35, for 'the will of God' is not a concept he employs (contrast Matthew at 6:10; 7:21; 12:50; 18:14; 26:52; cf. 21:31; Luke 11:2; 22:42); if he had created it he would probably have put 'my will' just as in 8:38 he added 'my words'.

But if Mark has not edited 3:31-5 internally in such a way as to affect its meaning and if with 3:20f. he has set the scene employing traditional material in which Jesus' family is depicted as thinking he was out of his mind and as attempting to interfere

---

[34] Schroeder, *op. cit.*, defends both the unity and genuineness of the whole pericope.
[35] Cf. Best, 'An Early Sayings Collection' (infra pp. 64–79).

in his ministry, what is the effect of Mark's insertion of 3:22-30 between 3:20f. and 3:31-5? In his 'sandwich' pattern the incidents normally reflect on one another. Mark seems to have compiled 3:22-30 in that he has joined the saying on the unforgivable sin to that of the accusation of the scribes that Jesus has a devil (which we may take as equivalent to being 'out of his mind'). He has then driven home the point by writing *v*. 30 to relate the two.[36] Thus to say that Jesus has an unclean spirit or is out of his mind is to commit the unforgivable sin. Is Mark then asserting that Jesus' family has committed this sin?[37] If this is so are we to deduce from it a polemic against the family of Jesus and in particular against James, and any James-Party or Jewish-Christian Jerusalem community that might still exist at the time of Mark's writing?[38] Certainly the insertion of 3:22-30 serves to emphasize the division between Jesus and his family.

There are two other points at which this may also appear.[39] In the story of Jesus' rejection in Nazareth the proverbial saying of 6:4*a* seems to have been supplemented by Mark with καὶ ἐν τοῖς συγγενεῦσιν αὐτοῦ καὶ ἐν τῇ οἰκίᾳ αὐτοῦ which takes up 3:21, 31-5.[40] The phrase is too indefinite for us to draw Crossan's conclusion that this transforms the story into an attack on Jesus' family. The addition serves rather to bring home the point already made in 3:21, 31-5 that opposition was encoun-

---

[36] Lambrecht, *art. cit.*, reaches a somewhat similar conclusion through a different redactional analysis.

[37] Cf. E. Trocmé, *La Formation de L'Évangile selon Marc* (Paris, 1963); Räisänen, *op. cit.* pp. 31f.; A. R. C. Leaney, *A Commentary on the Gospel according to St. Luke* (London, 1958), p. 153.

[38] Trocmé, *op. cit.* pp. 104-9; cf. J. B. Tyson, 'The Blindness of the Disciples in Mark', *J.B.L.* LXXX (1961), 261-8.

[39] Trocmé does not produce any other evidence from the Gospel to substantiate that this is Mark's view. Tyson supposes that the distinctive element in the theology of the Jerusalem church was a belief in the return of a royal Messiah and that this is rejected in Mark 12:35-7. The rejection of this idea in that passage by Mark is by no means certain and though Mark does play down the role of Jesus as royal Messiah he does not exclude it. Cf. 10:46-52; 11:9f.; instead he corrects it, not because it is erroneous, but because it is inadequate and unhelpful in a Gentile environment.

[40] Cf. Crossan, *art. cit.*; E. Grässer, 'Jesus in Nazareth', *N.T.S.* XVI (1969/70), 1-23.

tered by Jesus from his family. The second passage which has
been adduced is 15:40, 47; 16:1 where Crossan supposes that
Mark added καὶ Ἰωσῆτος in 15:40 and created 15:47. But if
Mark wished to identify an originally unidentified Mary with
the mother of Jesus and then to use this as a base for an attack on
the family of Jesus he went about it most clumsily. He would
have required also to remove τοῦ μικροῦ and there was no need
to mention Mary Magdalene in *v.* 47 and omit a reference to
James, and, assuming that 16:8 is Mark's conclusion to his
Gospel, there is no reason to infer that he intended us to
conclude that Mary failed to deliver the angel's message; there
are many other solutions to the difficulty of 16:1-8.

Before we over-hastily draw too adverse a verdict on Mark's
view of Jesus' family we must observe certain other features of
the total complex and of Mark's general editorial approach. (i)
Mark ends the complex with 3:31-5; therefore his primary
interest does not lie negatively in an attack on a party within the
church but positively on the nature of true discipleship.[41] (ii)
Mark tends to retain material which belongs to the tradition
even though it does not fully suit his purposes, i.e. he does not
adapt his material completely by erasing what he does not
require even though in some ways it may run counter to what he
is saying as a whole;[42] here he retains the hostility of his family
against Jesus because it was in the material, though he does not
wish to exploit it against them. (iii) All through Scripture we
find the retention of material which throws its heroes into a bad
light (e.g. Abraham, Gen. 20:1ff.; David, II Sam. 12:1ff.); the
material is retained if it can be used 'theologically'.[43] (iv) His
overall purpose is not to identify enemies of the true gospel or
warn his readers, even in a veiled way, against heretics but to
encourage them in their Christian faith. More generally, it seems
that too much NT scholarship today begins with the question,

[41] Cf. Lambrecht, *art. cit.*, for more general issues on alleged opposition on the part of Mark to the relatives of Jesus.
[42] See n. 11.
[43] Schroeder, *op. cit.* pp. 114f., argues in defence of his point of view
that after James and others of the family of Jesus had become Christians
any suggestion that at any period they would have thought Jesus out of
his mind would have been suppressed. This again is to misunderstand
the way in which the Bible uses biographical information.

'Against whom is this written?' While this is a necessary primary question opening up a polemical writing like Galatians it is not the key to unlock every writing. The NT writers were pastors as well as polemicists. In particular Mark's purpose is to set before his community the nature of true discipleship – to do this he used the available material.

How does this total purpose work out in our present passage? Jesus is depicted as alienated from his family, who regard him as out of his mind. Such an alienation from family must have been the experience of many of Mark's community, as was the experience of 6:1-6; their families will have thought them out of their minds for becoming Christians. The family of Jesus is thus used homiletically. Historically such opposition may have been their attitude – at any rate Mark has tradition to this effect – but he is not interested in the original tradition as such nor in how it could be used to tarnish a James-party, but instead in how his readers can be encouraged in this situation by the treatment of their Lord. If their families are guilty of an unforgivable sin, so was his; but there is no need for alarm, his family came to believe in him, so may theirs. It is perhaps right to go forward here to 4:10-12. As in 3:31, we have those who are 'outside' (οἱ ἔξω 3:31; 4·11) and those who are around Jesus (περὶ αὐτόν 3:32; 4:10) [44] The unbelieving family of the believer is 'outside' and they can be excused for this because it is the result of divine determination: God has not opened their eyes or their ears. This does not mean he will not do so in the future.

In respect of his family the Christian thus stands in no worse a position than his Lord did. In actual fact his position is much better; for if former physical ties of kinship have been broken new spiritual ties have been created with Jesus. This is taken further in 10:29, 30 where it is said that those who have left house and farm and brothers, sisters, mothers and fathers receive even in this age a hundredfold houses, farms, brothers, sisters, mothers, fathers. Both 'brother' and 'sister' were in regular use

---

[44] It is difficult to accept the suggestion of J. Coutts, '"Those Outside" (Mark 4, 10-12)', *Stud. Evang.* II (= *TU* 87), 1964, pp. 155-7, that 4:10-12 was joined to 3:20-35 in Mark's source. Why Mark should ever then have inserted the parable of the sower becomes incomprehensible (cf. Räisänen, *op. cit.* p. 37 n. 3).

among the early Christians to describe fellow members of the community[45] and Mark's readers would clearly make the jump in thought from their relationship to Jesus to their relationship to one another and see themselves as members of the new family of God. This line of thought fits appropriately into the structure of the Gospel at this point. In 3:13–19 the Twelve have been chosen and one of the purposes of their choice has been so that they may be 'with Jesus' (3:14); to be 'with him' is more important than the family bond.[46]

We may note that 'father' is not used in the logion; whether it is legitimate to employ this omission to deduce genuine biographical information about Joseph is not our concern; its absence would however at once remind the Christian that the 'father' of the new family was God. The unique position of God in relation to the family is also brought out by v. 35 – the family must do the will of God. The meaning of this phrase is not interpreted here (every Christian would have some idea of its content) but Mark recurs to it in the Gethsemane story (14:36);[47] for Jesus God's will is the cross. Later in Mark the great central section, 8:27 – 10:45, links the nature of discipleship to the fate of Jesus. If the will of God for Jesus is suffering and the cross, the same is his will for the disciples.

Mark does not work out the position of Jesus in this group. He certainly does not suggest that Jesus and Christians are all one big happy family with Jesus on the same plane as the others, or on a plane slightly higher. The very fact that Jesus enunciates the logion authoritatively sets him on a different plane.[48] In the Markan context v. 35 expands v. 34 and sets out the claims of discipleship rather than describing the nature of the relationship between Jesus and his followers.[49]

[45] The metaphorical use of 'brother' was well known both in Jewish and Hellenistic culture, cf. H. von Soden, TDNT I, 144–6.

[46] Räisänen, op. cit. pp. 34f.

[47] Cf. Schweizer, Markus, ad loc.

[48] Christians though of him as the "first born" among brothers (Rom. 8:29; cf. Col. 1:18).

[49] τοὺς περὶ αὐτόν in v. 34 means 'those of you who do . . .' since γάρ (n. 14) in v. 35 implies that it is explanatory of v. 34. It does not then identify the 'crowd' of v. 32 with the disciples or suggest that there is a third group within the crowd but identical neither with it nor the Twelve (that is if the disciples are to be limited here to the Twelve), i.e. a distinct group of 'adherents' (cf. Meye, op. cit. pp. 148–53).

But is the demand which is made in *v*. 35 to be restricted to disciples?[50] Do we not have the crowd (*v*. 32) present here in the house with the disciples, and does not therefore the distinction break down between secret and public teaching – the crowd being instructed here in the house, the place of special revelation? There is one other point at which disciples and crowd come together in what would appear to be secret teaching. This is 8:34, where Jesus 'summons' (προσκαλεῖσθαι) the crowd. There as here we have direct instruction on the nature of discipleship, on the challenge which is made on those who would be disciples; there as here the crowd are in the position of potential disciples. That discipleship means the way of the cross cannot be 'secret' teaching but is meant for all, disciples and the unevangelized masses. Those who are about to become Christians must know what lies ahead for them. Mark's own community has never fully understood and followed out the true nature of discipleship and so its members have put themselves back into the *de facto* position of the unevangelized. The simplest Christian teaching is the most profound; no one ever gets beyond it. The crowd is not therefore anomalous at this point nor is it to be identified with the disciples.[51]

[50] The immediate context, 3:13-19, would identify the disciples and the Twelve, but the very absence of both οἱ δώδεκα and οἱ μαθηταί in 3:20-35 suggests that Mark can hardly have been thinking in any restricted way of the Twelve.
[51] Cf. P. S. Minear, 'Audience Criticism and Markan Ecclesiology' in *Neues Testament und Geschichte* (Oscar Cullmann zum 70. Geburtstag. Zürich and Tübingen, 1972), pp. 79-89.

Chapter 5

An Early Sayings Collection

I

When we examine the sayings of Jesus in Mark we discover that there are a number which appear both at the expected synoptic position in Matthew and/or Luke and which appear again at another non-synoptic position in either Matthew or Luke or both. Mark 8:35a provides an example:

ὃς γὰρ ἐὰν θέλῃ τὴν ψυχὴν αὐτοῦ σῶσαι, ἀπολέσει αὐτήν.

This re-appears in the expected synoptic position in Mt. 16:25a and Lk. 9:24a but in Mt. 10:39 we find

ὁ εὑρὼν τὴν ψυχὴν αὐτοῦ, ἀπολέσει αὐτήν,

and in Lk. 17:33 and Jn. 12:25 we have further variations. It is obvious that all of these go back to the same logion and represent translation variants. Apart from verbal changes Mt. 10:39 and Mk. 8:35 differ in structure. Mark has a two–clause form, the first beginning with the masculine singular relative pronoun, followed by ἐάν; (or ἄν; these appear to be orthographical variants; the MSS vary considerably in their use of them) and incorporating a subjunctival form of the verb (we term this the R-form). In place of this first clause Matthew has a participial construction (we term this the P-form); Lk. 17:33 is in the R-form and Jn. 12:25 in the P-form. Another example is provided by Mk. 10:11:

ὃς ἂν ἀπολύσῃ τὴν γυναῖκα αὐτοῦ καὶ γαμήσῃ ἄλλην, μοιχᾶται ἐπ᾽ αὐτήν.

The synoptic parallel in the expected place, Mt. 19:9, repeats this but at the other parallel in Lk. 16:18 we find

πᾶς ὁ ἀπολύων τὴν γυναῖκα αὐτοῦ καὶ γαμῶν ἑτέραν μοιχεύει,
καὶ ὁ ἀπολελυμένην ἀπὸ ἀνδρὸς γαμῶν μοιχεύει

and a similarly structured logion at Mt. 5:32. Again these go back to a single saying but display not only translation variation but also modifications produced in transmission by local church conditions. Here again the Markan saying is in the R-form and that of Lk. 16:18 in the P-form. What these two examples disclose is true of a greater number of sayings in Mark which appear both at the expected synoptic parallel and also elsewhere in Matthew and Luke. We list them below:

Column A Markan text	Column B Parallel in expected place		Column C the extra parallel		
	Mt.	Lk.	Mt.	Lk.	Jn.
(I) 3:29	12:32			12:10b	
(II) 3:35	12:50	8:21		11:28	
(III) 8:35a	16:25a	9:24a	10:39a	17:33a	12:25a
(IV) 8:35b	14:25b	9:24b	10:39b	17:33b	12:25b
(V) 8:38		9:26	10:33	12:9	
(VI) 9:37a	18:5	9:48a	10:40a	10:16a	12:44, 13:20a
(VII) 9:37b		9:48b	10:40b	10:16b	13:20b
(VIII) 9:41			10:42		
(IX) 9:42	18:6			17:1f.	
(X) 10:11	19:9		5:32	16:18	
(XI) 10:15		18:17	18:3		
(XII) 10:43	20:26		23:11	22:26a	
(XIII) 10:44	20:27			22:26b	
(XIV) 11:23	21:21		17:20	17:6	

It will be observed that all the texts in Column A have the R-form, that all in Column B have it also, except where noted below, and that all in Column C have the P-form except where noted below.

(II) Lk. 8:21 is in the P-form.
(IV) The indicative is unusual here but see (XV)-(XVIII) below and n. I.
(V) Mt. 10:33 is in the R-form but Lk. 12:9 in the P-form.
(VII) A negative form (cf. Lk. 10:16) of this logion is found at I Th. 4:8 in the P-form.

(VIII) Mt. 10:42 is in the R-form.

(IX) Lk. 17:1f. uses a completely different structure.

(XI) Mt. 18:3 uses a conditional sentence structure.

(XII) and (XIII) Lk. 22:26a and b use a structure employing the comparative.

(XIV) All the non-Markan passages use a second plural form expressed with a conditional qualification.

The consistency of form in Column A is remarkable; when we observe also the variation in form in Column C it is reasonable to conjecture that this consistency is due to a single translator and that these sayings therefore existed together in a collection which one man translated at one time.

There is also another briefer set of sayings which have almost the same form, viz., the relative pronoun followed, not by ἄν with the subjunctive, but with a simple indicative; these are 4:9 4:25a and b; 9:40. If we examine them we see that this variation accords with their content, for the relative clause does not contain anything resembling a supposition but simply states a fact, e.g. "Who has ears, let him hear", it is a fact that all men have ears. We contrast 8:35a, "Whoever wishes to save his life . . . ;" a man may not wish to do this.[1] The difference is similar to the use of εἰ + indicative and ἐάν + subjunctive in conditional clauses.[2] We set out these verses as before:

Column A	Column B		Column C		
	Mt.	Lk.	Mt.	Lk.	Jn.
(XV) 4:9	13:9	8:8	11:15		
(XVI) 4:25a	13:12a	8:18a	25:29a	19:26a	
(XVII) 4:25b	13:12b	8:18b	25:29b	19:26b	
(XVIII) 9:40		9:50	12:30	11:23	

We note:

(XV) Mt. 13:9; Lk. 8:8 are in the P-form; Mk. 4:23, an internal Markan parallel, has the εἴ τις form.

---

[1] 8:35b has the indicative with ἄν (the subjunctive appears as a variant); both the synoptic parallels have the subjunctive; for other instances see Moulton-Turner, Grammer of New Testament Greek, p. 110; Blass–Debrunner, Neutestamentliche Grammatik §380.

[2] Cf. Moulton-Turner, op. cit., pp. 109f.; Blass-Debrunner, ibid.

(XVI) and (XVII) Lk. 8:18 has the subjunctive; the rules about the use of the subjunctive and indicative in this kind of clause were not always rigidly observed in Hellenistic Greek.[3] (XVIII) Lk. 11:23 may represent another logion altogether.

These passages like (I)-(XIV) relate to discipleship and there seems to be no reason why they should not be considered with them. If so the translator was aware of the distinction which should be made in Greek between the subjunctive and indicative in such clauses. In view of the form of both types we shall refer to the probable underlying collection of sayings as R.

II

We have suggested that a translator imposed uniformity on these sayings and that they existed as a collection prior to Mark, but may it not have been Mark himself as he put his Gospel together who imposed uniformity on the style of these sayings? Against this we would argue that Mark has many more sayings which are similar in content to those we have isolated above in relating to discipleship, which do not employ the R-form, but which could easily be rephrased in that form, e.g. 6:10; 10:12 (where the influence of 10:11 has failed to produce homogeneity of form); 10:23; 10:29f. An R-form of Mk. 8:34 actually exists in Mt. 10:38 yet the proximity of 8:35 has not produced it in 8:34. An R-form of 9:36b exists in Mark itself at 10:44. We have a P-form at 13:13b. 4:9 appears to have been part of the pre-Markan form of 4:1-34 and 4:23 to have been introduced by Mark;[4] if so Mark has re-written the R-form to produce an εἴ τις form.[5] The R-form is thus not a Markan characteristic but is pre-Markan. We should also note that the only other R-form logion in Mark is 6:11; here however the logion relates to a place and not to a person though in the parallels of Mt. 14:14; Lk. 9:5 the reference is personal; in Lk. 10:10 f., usually assumed to be from Q, it refers to place.

If uniformity was not imposed by Mark is it then a matter of

---

[3] See n. 2. The textual variants in Mk. 4:25 show how easily the subjunctive could replace the indicative.
[4] See Best, "Mark's Preservation of the Tradition", In *L'Evangile selon Marc* (ed. M. Sabbe) (infra pp. 31-48).
[5] This also applies to 7:16 if it is a part of the text.

chance? Before we draw such a conclusion there are some further facts which need to be considered and which taken together point towards our earlier conclusion of a primitive collection of sayings.

1. Many, if not all, of the sayings we have examined are clearly separable from their present contexts, i.e. these contexts are not their original contexts.

(a) 3:23–30 is generally held to be a compilation; Mark is certainly responsible for the addition of v. 30[6] and possibly for that of vv. 28f [7]; these latter verses introduce a reference to the Holy Spirit which is not demanded by what precedes and is indeed unexpected; it takes v. 30 to hold vv. 28f. tightly to vv. 22-7.

(b) 3:35 has regularly been held not to belong to 3:31–34 because it contains a reference to "sister", whereas vv. 31–34 refer to "brother" and "mother" only.[8]

(c) 10:11: that there is no inherent connection between 10:1–9 and 10:10–12 is seen by the Markan words and motifs that appear in v. 10; even if they were joined in the pre-Markan tradition[9] Mark was able to break the bond easily because it was not of long standing and so introduce the idea that vv. 11f. are secret teaching.

(d) 10:15 is an obvious insertion into 10:13–16; the incident does not require it as Mt. 19:13-15 shows.

(e) It is also generally recognised that 11:22-5 is a set of sayings which are not only loosely connected to what precedes but whose internal linkage is also loose.

We have to be careful at this point not to argue in a circle, for one of the reasons given for regarding some of the other sayings as having been at one time isolated is the very fact that they occur in Matthew and Luke at points other than and as well as the expected synoptic parallel. Yet cumulatively the evidence that at an earlier stage the remainder of the sayings were isolated (i.e. not in their present contexts) is strong.

2. When we examine the contexts of the non-synoptic parallels in Mark and Luke we often find that these contexts are

[6] Cf. Taylor, *Mark,* ad loc.
[7] Cf. Nineham, *Mark,* ad loc.
[8] Cf. Dibelius, *From Tradition to Gospel* (ET London, 1934), pp. 63 f.
[9] Cf. H.-W. Kuhn, *Ältere Sammlungen im Markusevangelium* (Göttingen, 1971) pp. 165-8.

themselves different and that the sayings are part of compilations and have no real relationship to their contexts, i.e. they are again separable from their contexts.

(a) Mt. 10:39 and Lk. 15:33 (= Mk. 8:35) have very different situations in their respective gospels; each of them lies in a separate though recognised compilation, Matthew's being added to the brief account of the sending out of the Twelve in Mark and Luke's to his first apocalyptic collection (17:20-37), which is in part paralleled in Mt. 24).

(b) Mt. 5:32 and Lk. 16:18 (= Mk. 10:11) have different situations from one another and both lie in compilations of which the Sermon on the Mount is definitely Mattthean and Luke's is also Lukan.

3. When we add to this the common form of the sayings in Mark and their common theme, discipleship, there is at least an *a priori* case for arguing that they were all translated at the same time by the same translator and were therefore either a pre-existing collection of sayings or part of a pre-existing collection of sayings and other material.

III

Have we any means of finding out whether the collection was larger at the time of its translation than the sum total of its present sayings? There would appear to be three ways by which we may determine this.

1. Is there other material in Mark which has non-synoptic parallels in Matthew and Luke and is similar in content, i.e. refers to discipleship and consists of sayings? Naturally there is a considerable amount but with exceptions there is no homogeneity within it or between it and the sayings which we have been examining. The Lukan Passion narrative is not quite the same as the Markan; either Luke adapted Mark in which case no question arises or else he had access to another passion account but, apart from 22:25-27 which we have already accepted as part of R, there is no relevant material. Luke omits the Markan story of the call of Peter and Andrew (1:16-18) but includes another story in which Peter appears as a fisherman and in which there is a variant of Mk. 1:17b (at Luke 5:10b). While the two sayings probably go back to a common source it is difficult to view the two narratives as doing so; the divergence between them is very much greater than between any of the

sayings we have examined, and the sayings themselves could not
have existed detached from their present or similar contexts
because of the "fishing" metaphor, i.e. there is a necessary
narrative element. Mk. 3:4 appears in the story of the man with
the withered hand (3:1-5) and in the story of the man with
dropsy (Lk. 14:3); the two healing stories are not variants and so
will not have at one time belonged to the common source, and
once again the sayings could not have existed by themselves but
require a 'sabbath' context. For similar reasons Mk. 6:4 and 8:12
with their parallels at Lk. 4:24 and Lk. 11:29; Mt. 12:39
respectively cannot have belonged to the source since they are
embedded in non-parallel material. 6:18 (cf. Lk. 3:19f.) refers to
John the Baptiser; again the material in which on each occasion it
is embedded forbids seeing it as part of the suggested common
source. 6:53-6 (cf. Mt. 4:24; Lk. 6:18f.) is in its present form
Markan though based probably on tradition; the parallels are
equally probably based on tradition but it would be difficult to
determine any common source; the tradition is general rather
than particular and narrative in form rather than "sayings". 8:18
(cf. Mt. 13:13, 16) is basically an OT quotation joined into the
tradition at different points; it is hardly homogeneous with the
sayings material of R; the same applies to 6:34 (cf. Mt. 9:36).
3:22b comes in a passage (3:20-35) which is generally recognised
to be a Markan compilation so that the re-appearance of the
sentence at Mt. 9:34 might be thought to be significant; however
at the latter point it is textually uncertain. Mk. 10:38f. and Lk.
12:50 go back to an original saying about baptism; both carry a
soteriological reference which may give the earliest understanding; in Mark it is related to discipleship through its positioning
in the discussion of the request of the sons of Zebedee; an
original discipleship reference may have been present if Jesus is
regarded as promising to his disciples in these verses a fate
similar to his own.[10] The theme would then cohere with that of
R; but it difficult to see how the saying could ever have been in R
(or P)-form without radical change: whoever follows me must
(will) be baptised with the baptism with which I am to be
baptised. Starting with this form and with this idea it is a long
way to the narrative context in Mark about 'dignity' in the
Kingdom and since there is no other trace of narrative in R the
narrative cannot have been original. Yet because of the

[10] Cf. J. Jeremias, *New Testament Theology* (ET London, 1971) Vol. 1,
pp. 243f.

discipleship reference this saying remains a vague possibility for inclusion in R. Mk. 10:31 has non-synoptic parallels at Mt. 20:16 and Lk. 13:30 as well as the synoptic parallel at Mt. 19:30. In all four cases the saying is put in the third person plural though it quite clearly could have been in the R-form: whoever is first shall be last and whoever is last shall be first. Again it remains a possible, though unlikely, candidate for inclusion. Mk. 9:43, 47 have non-synoptic parallels in Mt. 5:30, 29; the sayings relate to discipleship but it is very difficult to see how they could have ever existed in the R-form. In their Markan context they are related to (IX) through the key word σκανδαλίζων, and in their Matthean context to (X) through the theme "divorce"; if they had once been in R when it was split up they might have been carried in different directions through their associations in R. They thus remain a possibility for inclusion. Mk. 11:25 has a non-synoptic parallel at Mt. 6:14 and could be put in a simple R-form, "Whoever forgives men their sins will be forgiven by his heavenly Father", and it is thus a possible candidate. Mk. 12:29-31, the two great commandments, has a non-synoptic parallel in Lk. 10:27; both are attached to incidents but the passage about the two commandments could have existed separately and at some stage been brought into contact with the incidents; but would the link to a γραμματεύς, who is spoken of approvingly by Jesus,[11] have been made after translation? It therefore probably did not continue long as a separate logion and would not have belonged to R. Mk. 12:38f. has a non-synoptic parallel at Lk. 11:43; this saying has a distinct anti-Jewish bias which the rest of the source lacks and is therefore unlikely to have belonged to it. There are a number of sayings in the Little Apocalypse which have a second parallel. Some of these relate to the signs of the End and therefore have nothing in common with the sayings in the source; they are Mk. 13:21 (cf. Lk. 17:23); 13:26 (here there is an internal parallel with Mk. 9:1 but this is hardly relevant); 13:31 (cf. Mt. 5:17; Lk. 16:17; it is difficult to know if these are parallels); 13:35 (cf. Mt. 25:13; Lk. 12:38, 40: this does relate also to discipleship but none of the other sayings in R has an apocalyptic tinge). Four sayings do relate directly to discipleship, viz. vv.11,13a,13b,16; all of these could be put in

[11] R. Bultmann, *History of the Synoptic Tradition* (ET Oxford, 1963) p. 54, argues that the scene was formulated by the community as a setting for the saying; if so, this must have taken place very early in the life of the Palestinian church.

the R-form; indeed 13:13b is in the P-form; it also approximates more closely in content to the sayings of the source; since it appears in the P-form it clearly did not belong to R unless Mark or earlier tradition altered it.[12] In any case in regard to all these sayings drawn from the Little Apocalypse it is inherently probable that they themselves were in some kind of collection from an early period but it would be a collection with a different orientation from that of R. Three closely connected sayings remain, 4:21; 4:22; 4:24. The first two are miniature parables; none of the rest of the material of the source is parabolic in form; moreover in Mark these two probably refer either to the Kingdom, to the Gospel or to Jesus and not to discipleship. Only in Mt. 5:15 is there a clear reference to discipleship (i.e. it is the disciple who is the light). Mk. 4:21 is taken as more original in form than its non-synoptic parallel by Taylor[13] and Bultmann,[14] and Jeremias[15] argues that the original reference which he acknowledges is not easy to determine was probably made by Jesus in relation to his mission. Mk. 4:24b has a parallel in Mt. 7:2; Lk. 6:38; this suggests that καὶ προστεθήσεται ὑμῖν did not originally belong to the saying, and its addition appears to have taken place when v. 24 and v. 25 were brought together. The original meaning of the saying is difficult to determine; the context in Mt. 7:2 brings out a meaning most easily but it may not be the original context; the original meaning is probably irrecoverable; but though the saying does relate to discipleship, it could not easily be put into the R-form. It remains a possible though unlikely candidate for inclusion in the source.

    2. Are there any other R-form sayings in Mark? There is only one: 6:11. As we have already seen[16] not only is the reference in Mark impersonal but it is also in the non-synoptic parallel in Lk. 10:10f. whereas the proper parallels have a personal reference (Mt. 10:14; Lk. 9:4f.). It may well be that the earliest form of this

---

[12]   Since the non-synoptic parallel is found at Mt. 10:22b, which is near to 10:33 ff. in which a good number of sayings from R are found, this might suggest that v. 13 should be included; yet the sayings in 10:33 ff. lie much closer to one another than does 10:22 to any of them and we therefore doubt if there is a good case for the inclusion of v. 13b.

[13]   Ad loc.

[14]   Bultmann, op. cit., p. 79, says that Mark's interrogative form is primary; an interrogative form would be exceptional in R.

[15]   J. Jeremias, The Parables of Jesus (ET London, 1963) pp. 120f .

[16]   P. 67 above.

saying when the mission was still restricted related to people but later when the mission moved out beyond Palestine it became necessary to speak of "place" and "city". If so the original may have been "whoever does not welcome you . . . " and the logion would refer to discipleship and could belong to the source.

3. Are there any sayings which are found in company with sayings in R both in Mark and in the non-synoptic parallels in Matthew or Luke? The source includes Mk. 10:43, 44 with a non-synoptic parallel at Lk. 22:26.[17] Lk. 22:27b and Mk 10:45a are parallel;[18] they do not refer to discipleship but they move directly from how it is to be exercised to the example of Jesus' service. There is thus a strong case for the inclusion of a saying about the example of Jesus in R. The actual determination of its original form is more difficult.[19] It must be noted that there is no possibility of putting 10:45a into the R-form. The introduction to these logia about true greatness is also similar in content, though not altogether in wording, in Mark (10:42b) and Luke (22:25). Mark appears to be nearer the original wording here as all through vv. 42b–44.[20] Mk 3:29 is linked to 3:28; the non-synoptic parallel in Lk. 12:10b has 12:10a joined to it and 12:10a is a parallel to 3:28, though in present form very different. Thus probably 3:28 should be added to the source, but if so it should be added in the form of Lk. 12:10a.[21] If Mk 6:11 is accepted as part of the source then 6:8–10 goes closely with it and similarly its non-synoptic parallel at Lk. 10:4, 5, 7 is not far away

---

[17] We assume that these are independent forms of the same tradition; cf. H. Schürmann, *Quellenkritische Untersuchung des lukanischen Abendmahlsberichtes, III Jesu Abschiedsrede Lk. 22.21-38* (Münster, 1957), pp. 63–98; V. Taylor, *The Passion Narrative of St. Luke* (S.N.T.S. Monograph Series 19; Cambridge, 1971), pp. 61–4; T. Schramm, *Der Markus-Stoff bei Lukas* (S.N.T.S. Monograph Series 14; Cambridge 1971), pp. 50f.

[18] Mk 10:45b, a later addition to vv. 42b–45a, is not relevant.

[19] Schürmann, *op. cit.*, pp. 80ff. argues for the Lukan form because it posesses the greater vividness and carries through the metaphor of διάκονος

[20] Cf. Schürmann, *op. cit.*, pp. 70ff.; J. Jeremias, "Das Lösegeld für Viele (Mk. 10–45)", in his *Abba: Studien zur neutestamentlichen Theologie und Zeitgeschichte* (Göttingen, 1966), pp. 216–229.

[21] Cf. H.E. Tödt, *The Son of Man in the Synoptic Tradition* (ET London, 1965) pp. 118–120, 312–318.

from the non-synoptic parallel to Mk. 6:11 at Lk. 10:10; but since the R-form is difficult to work out we shall not put this forward though it remains a possibility. Mark 8:35 (= III, IV of R) is joined to the saying about cross-bearing (v. 34) both here and at its non-synoptic parallel in Mt. 10:38, 39, but not at its non-synoptic parallel in Lk. 17:33 (the non-synoptic parallel about cross-bearing in Luke is at 14:27). The two non-synoptic parallels are negative in form and this is probably original;[22] in the negative form it is easier to regard it as addressed to disciples (or members of the Christian community); in its positive form in Mark it is rather an appeal to men to become disciples; Mark himself has strongly edited v. 34 and probably introduced the reference to the crowd; it may then have been Mark himself who altered the original negative form. If this was in the R-form he changed it into the εἴ τις[23] form which more firmly places the bearer in the position of making a response. We thus assume that in the original source there stood a saying in R-form much more like Mt. 10:38 or Lk. 14:27 than like Mk. 8:34.

We have examined whether there are other sayings in Mark which might have belonged to the source, but it is also important to ask whether there are any sayings in the group which we have isolated which for any reason are unlikely to have belonged. An R-form might appear entirely accidentally from another translator. There appear to be three possible candidates for omission: (a) 11:23, because of its length, because of the considerable difference in content from the non-synoptic parallel which refers to a mustard seed and not a mountain and because it does not make the same kind of demand on the disciple as do the other sayings; yet it is not much longer than 9:42 and its non-synoptic parallel (Lk. 17:5f.) is contiguous to Lk. 17:1f. = (IX). Its inclusion must be doubtful. (b) 10:15, because it can be argued that Mt. 18:3 is not a true non-synoptic

---

[22] This of course does not imply that the saying goes back to Jesus. On the original wording of the logion see T. W. Manson, *The Teaching of Jesus* (Cambridge, 1943), pp. 237-240.

[23] Mark changed 4:9 into this form when he used it again at 4:23 and he may also be responsible for the appearance of this form at 9:35 (cf. 10:43f.).

parallel but was derived by Matthew from Mk. 10:15;[24] there is
no Lukan non-synoptic parallel. Mk. 10:15 does fit badly into
10:13-16 and has often been regarded as an insertion into an
earlier form of the tradition; Matthew could have observed this
and then moved it. But if he did so, why did he alter it so
extensively? It could have been incorporated more easily in its
Markan form. In Mt. 18:2 Jesus is said to take a child (sing.) and
set him in the centre of the group of disciples; in 18:4 Jesus draws
attention to the humility of "this child" (sing.); but in 18:3
"children" (pl.) are offered as examples to the disciples; this
change of number is unfortunate in the flow of the argument.
Mk. 10:15 has the singular; if then Matthew derived his saying
from Mark why did he alter the number? In view of this and the
other quite considerable changes in the saying it is easier to argue
that Matthew took 18:3 from another source and added it to his
parallel to Mk. 9:33-37 in 18:1-5 and then when he came to Mk.
10:13-16 saw that he had used a parallel to 10:15 and since Mk.
10:15 fits badly into 10:13-16 dropped it at that point. (c) 10:11,
because it has the form of a church rule rather than a direct
discipleship saying. Yet it is difficult to deny that situations
could have existed in the primitive church in which this would
have appeared as a discipleship saying; certainly in the Sermon
on the Mount it appears alongside sayings which no one would
dispute are simple discipleship sayings; if it did not appear
incongruous to Matthew's church there is no reason for us to
argue that it could not have appeared in R without appearing
incongruous to the users of R. We cannot allow the way in
which we today categorise sayings necessarily to rule how the
first Christians would have seen them. Interestingly, if a case
could be made out for the inclusion in R of Mk. 9:43, 45, 47 then
10:11 lies close to them as its non-synoptic parallel lies close to
their parallel in Mt. 5:29, 30.

IV

We can now list what the source probably contained; we give
the references to the passages in Mark, though this is not to be

[24] Cf. W. G. Thompson, *Matthew's Advice to a Divided Community,
Mt. 17, 22-18, 35* (Analecta Biblica 44; Rome, 1970) pp. 76-8, 136-7; T.
W. Manson, *The Sayings of Jesus* in Major, Manson and Wright, *The
Mission and Message of Jesus* (London, 1940), p. 499. W. L. Knox, *The
Sources of the Synoptic Gospels* (Cambridge, 1957), Vol. II, p. 16, n. 1,
argues that at least some of the variations from Mark are non-Matthean.
See also Best, "Mark 10.13-16" (infra pp. 80-97).

taken as implying that the form in Mark is more original or that the order in Mark is the original order:

3:28, 29	9:37
3:35	9:40, 41, 42
4:9	10:11
4:25	10:15
6:8-11	10:42b-45a
8:34, 35	11:23(?)
8:38	

It may be that we can produce some semblance of order in this by examining the relative position of the non-synoptic parallels in Matthew and Luke. 3:28, 29 have their parallel at Lk. 12:10 and Lk. 12:9 is the parallel to Mk. 8:38. Mk. 8:38 has also a non-synoptic parallel at Mt 10:33 which is close to Mt. 10:38, 39, the non-synoptic parallel to Mk. 8:34, 35. Also Mt. 10:40 is the non-synoptic parallel to Mk. 9:37. Mk 9:41 has also its non-synoptic parallel at Mt. 10:42. Thus there would appear to be a complex consisting of Mk. 3:28, 29; 8:34, 35, 38; 9:37, 41 the evidence for whose coherence comes from more than one gospel. Since the non-synoptic parallels to Mk. 8:38 each have a balancing and positive statement associated with them it is probable that this positive statement (Mt. 10:32 = Lk. 12:8) should also be included in the source.[25] This conclusion is reinforced by the number of couplets that the source already contains, 3:28, 29; 4:25; 8:35; 9:37; 10:43, 44. Nothing else appears to cling easily to these passages. We may thus set out the source as follows, using what appears to be the simplest and most primitive form of each individual logion, and not necessarily that appearing in Mark, and giving possible alternatives in parentheses (the reference, however, is in each case given to Mark).

Whoever does not take his cross and follow after me, is not worthy of me (cannot be my disciple?); whoever wishes to save his soul, will lose it; whoever loses his soul will save it (8:34, 35). Whoever acknowledges me before men, the Son of man will acknowledge (will be acknowledged) before the angels of God; whoever denies me before men the Son of man will deny (be denied) before the angels of God (Lk. 12:8a +

[25] Mk 9:1 probably fulfils the positive and balancing role in Mark.

Mk 8:38). Whoever blasphemes the Son of man[26] will be forgiven; whoever blasphemes the Spirit will not be forgiven. Whoever receives a child, receives me; whoever receives me, receives him who sent me (9:37). Whoever gives a child a cup of cold water will not lose his reward (9:41). Whoever makes a child stumble, it would be better for him to be thrown into the sea with a mill-stone round his neck (9:42). Whoever does not receive the kingdom as a child (turn and become as a child) will not enter into it (the Kingdom of God) (10:15).[27] Whoever does not receive you (or listen to you), when you leave shake the dust of that place off your feet (6:11).[28]

Whoever does the will of God is my brother, sister, mother (3:35).

Whoever has, to him will be given; from whomever has not, it will be taken away (4:25).

Whoever is not against us, is for us (9:40).

Whoever divorces his wife and marries another commits adultery (10:11).

The rulers of the peoples lord it over them and exercise undue authority; but it is not to be like that with you; whoever wishes to be great among you, let him be servant of all; whoever wishes to be first among you, let him be slave of all; who is greater, the one who sits at table or the one who serves? is it not the one who sits? but I am in your midst as the one who serves (the Son of man came not to be served but to serve) (10:42b-45a).

Whoever has ears to hear, let him hear (4:9).[29]

It will be seen that we have omitted 4:24; 9:43, 47; 10:31; 10:38f.; 11:23 and 11:25 for which for one reason or another we do not believe there is a strong case. 4:24 and 11:25 are not in the R-form as almost all the other sayings in R are; there would therefore need to be a very strong case on grounds of coherence through content to argue for their inclusion. 11:23 has a stronger case but we still feel it does not fit in so far as its subject matter is concerned. However if it is retained in the brief form

---

[26] See 21.
[27] We have placed 10:15 here because of the continued reference to the child.
[28] This might well have gone after 9:37.
[29] This might well have been fitted in after 9:37.

'Whoever forgives men their sins will be forgiven by his Father in heaven'

it could be associated with 3:29. If 9:43, 47 are to be included they would follow after 9:42 and would need to be followed by 10:11. 10:31 may actually be a variant of 10:44; its inclusion would add nothing to the content of R. 10:38f. is of similar meaning to the reference in 8:34 to cross-bearing; it could well be more original, but it is cumbersome in an R-form and so we have not included it.

An alternative order would be to begin with 3:28f.; 8:38; 8:34, 35. This would follow the Matthean order more exactly but 8:34 is a better introduction to the sequence and in the Markan order 8:35 and 8:38 follow it. The order we have adopted does however mean the insertion of 3:28, 29 before 9:37.

When we examine the sequence as we have set it out we note that after the initial statement of 8:34 we have three couplets (8:35; Lk. 12:8a+ Mk. 8:38; 3:28, 29) setting out contrasts in relation to salvation followed by four statements featuring "child". 6:11 may then be linked through the key-word "receive" in it, in 9:37 and in 10:15 to the sequence. 4:25 which also has a set of contrasts might go with the sequence of contrasts. Apart from this there is no easy succession.

The fact that some of the sayings are found close together in Matthew and Luke and that they can be arranged in a sequence which progresses confirms our initial arguments, drawn from the form of the sayings and their non-synoptic parallels, for the existence of R, presumably in oral form.

Looking briefly at the sayings we observe that there is no explicit Christology. The title "Son of man" may occur three times but on each occasion it can be challenged. If the title is read, and its possible appearance on three separate occasions suggests it should be, then there is nothing to assist us in settling the question of Jesus' use of it, e.g. the problems which already exist in relation to Lk. 12:8 f. are still present in the form in R. Apart from this there certainly is an implicit Christology in the frequent use of the first person. Discipleship is always being placed in relation to Jesus; the relation of the disciple to Jesus is decisive for his salvation. At one point (10:45a) Jesus sets himself explicitly as an example before his disciples. There are no parables in R; there is one ethical rule (about divorce 10:11) and one community rule (about importance in the community 10:42b–45a).

What is the relationship of R to Q? If R now appears in Mark (Mark probably did not use it directly; it was already combined with other material in the tradition he received)[30] is it also incorporated in Q? It is of course difficult to define the extent of Q;[31] not all of it may appear in both Matthew and Luke; one or other of them may have used portions of it which the other did not. But it would be generally agreed that all except Mk. 4:9; 10:15; 10:42b–45a would have appeared in any form of Q. Streeter's outline of Q[32] would agree with this. We cannot thus reach any definite conclusions; presumably Q was some time in being collected and probably R, or most of it, was gathered into it at some stage, but R was not necessarily the foundation of Q, later widened into Q by the addition of other material. One other point is, perhaps, worth observing. Before he wrote *The Four Gospels* Streeter had at an earlier stage[33] argued that Mark knew Q; the strongest part of his argument rests on material drawn from R; had he recognised the existence of R he would not have been in doubt about Mark's ignorance of Q.

[30] E.g. 10:12 was added to 10:11 before Mark received it; since it is added in a non-R-form it is probable that 10:11 was already detached from R; 4:25 and 4:24 appear to have been united prior to Mark.
[31] Q did not necessarily exist as one compact source; it may have consisted of a number of collections of material, some oral, some written, which Matthew and Luke both used.
[32] B. H. Streeter, *The Four Gospels* (London, 1936), pp. 291f.
[33] "St. Mark's Knowledge and Use of Q", in *Studies in the Synoptic Problem* (Oxford, 1911), pp. 165–183.

Chapter 6

Mark 10:13-16:
The Child as Model Recipient

In this paper we propose to examine the significance of Mark 10:13-16 for Mark and the community to which he was writing. We assume that he wrote in Rome about the time of the fall of Jerusalem. We begin by enquiring after the position of the pericope in the Gospel; is this due to Mark or did it previously stand in some relation to 10:1-12 and/or 10:17-31? It is generally recognised today that 8:27-10:45 does not represent a historical journey of Jesus from Caesarea Philippi to Jericho but is a Marcan construction. It contains two major themes: Christology and discipleship. Clearly the former of these plays no explicit role in our pericope.

H. W. Kuhn[1] has recently argued that 10:1-45 goes back to an original complex of pre-Marcan material containing three pericopae relating to divorce, wealth and position, roughly verses 2-12, 17-31, 35-45, but within each pericope we must allow for some Marcan editing. He argues:[2]

(a) Cleared of their Marcan redaction, these three pericopae are similar in 'form', that is, apophthegms with dialogue – on each occasion extended to include special instruction for the disciples. The three pericopae thus belong to the same *Sitz im Leben*.

(b) Viewed from the angle of *Traditionsgeschichte* they are similar, for in each Jewish-Christian tradition can be clearly recognised and in the second and third we find the equation of

[1] H. W. Kuhn, *Ältere Sammlungen in Markusevangelium* (Göttingen, 1971), pp. 146-91.
[2] There is a useful summary on p. 187.

'following after Christ' with 'imitation of Christ', a contribution from Hellenistic Judaism.[3]

(c) They are similar in content, taking up questions of behaviour which were of importance for the life of the community.

(d) The use of the first incident (10:2-12) and in part the second (10:17-31), which do not fit clearly into Mark's purpose on the instruction of disciples, is caused by his desire to use the third (10:35-45), which is very relevant. In order to use it he had to employ the whole complex; to it he added verse 1, verses 13-16 and verses 32-4.

We need to examine these points separately:

(a) The form of 10:35-45 is not the same as that of 10:2-12 and 10:17-31; in each of the latter we find a distinct break (before verse 10 and verse 23) between public discussion and the private teaching of the disciples. Moreover, the present form of 10:17-31 is largely due to Mark; in particular he has emphasised the element of private instruction of the disciples by the addition of verses 24, 26f., 28-31;[4] while 10:11f. may have already been attached to 10:2-9 in the tradition of Mark's church, he has probably inserted verse 10, thus producing the reference to private instruction.[5] Thus in the pre-Marcan *Vorlage* these pericopae did not necessarily have the same form. We must however agree with Kuhn[6] that they were probably used in a teaching situation – but this means little since it is true of a large proportion of the material in the Gospels.

(b) Granted that Jewish-Christian tradition is to be found in these three pericopae, this again is not unique; it is found in many Marcan pericopae. All material which did not originate in the

---

[3] On the concepts 'following after' and 'imitation of', see H. D. Betz, *Nachfolge und Nachahmung Jesu Christi im Neuen Testament* (Tübingen, 1967); A. Schulz, *Nachfolgen und Nachahmen* (Munich, 1962).

[4] See Best, 'Uncomfortable Words: VII. The Camel and the Needle's Eye', in *Expository Times,* 82 (1970-71), pp. 83-9 (infra pp. 17-30).

[5] There are many Marcan characteristics in v. 10: εἰς τὴν οἰκίαν, the private instruction of the disciples, the simple union with what preceded through καί, the use of πάλιν (linking back to previous private instruction) and ἐπερωτᾶν, probably influenced on this occasion by its use in v. 2.

[6] Op. cit., pp. 188f.

Hellenistic Christian Church passed through a Jewish–Christian stage, though this stage will have left varying degrees of impression on the material. It is moreover doubtful if the equation 'following after Christ' = 'imitation of Christ' is as clearly found in 10:17-31 and 10:35-45 as Kuhn suggests; the former is really only present in 10:17-31 and the latter in 10:35-45.

(c) This again may be admitted, but it is true of many other pericopae, for example 3:1-5; 7:1-21; 9:38-40; 12:13-17. It is hardly surprising that in a section on discipleship (8:27-10:45) there should be an accumulation of passages which deal with the theme as it affects community problems; this affords no reason for concluding that these passages co-existed as a unit – where else would Mark have placed them in his Gospel?

(d) We must agree with Kuhn that 10:17-31 and, in particular, 10:2-12 relate less directly to the main theme of discipleship, linked in its emphasis to the passion of Jesus through the passion predictions, than does 10:35-45; this does not necessarily lead to the conclusion that Mark had to use the earlier two pericopae in order to be able to use 10:35-45. Where he has used existing complexes of pericopae or logia it is normally because he wanted the first part of the sequence that he has done so (cf. 8:34-8; 9:35-50).[7] Kuhn recognises the existence of pre-Marcan collections in 2:1-28 and 4:1-34;[8] in each case it is the first pericope which carries the major emphasis.

We can go further than merely responding to Kuhn's arguments. There are positive reasons to suggest that he is incorrect:

(1) Why did Mark add 10:13-16 at the precise point at which it now appears? It evinces Mark's interest in the resemblance of believers to children or in their relationship to one another; it would have been more appropriate to place it close to 9:36f., 42, where these themes recur;[9] they are absent in 10:1-12 and 10:17-31.

[7] See Best, 'Mark's Preservation of the Tradition', in *L'Evangile selon Marc,* ed. M. Sabbe (Gembloux, 1974), pp. 21-34 (infra pp. 31-48).
[8] Op. cit., pp. 53-146.
[9] Since Kuhn, op cit., pp. 32-6, does not accept 9:35-50 as a pre-Marcan collection, it would have been easy for Mark to include 10:13-16 as he compiled it. If Mark received it and only modified it, then he could still have inserted 10:13-16 or placed it directly after 9:50.

(2) If Kuhn is correct, then Mark has introduced into an existing complex a major geographical change when at 10:32, 33 he makes the first reference to Jerusalem as the end of the journey which began at 8:27. There is no evidence for `Mark making such changes in the complexes he used.

(3) 10:35-45 were not themselves a pre-Marcan unity and therefore could not have formed the basic unit which Kuhn assumes they were.[10] If however 10:41-5 alone was regarded as belonging to the pre-Marcan complex this would not contain an apophthegm and so the pattern of three similar pericopae which Kuhn suggested (see (a) above) would be destroyed.

More recently still Morton Smith has argued that 10:13-45, with the insertion after 10:34 of the section of Mark which he has discovered in a letter of Clement of Alexandria,[11] represents a baptismal section which would have been used as a lection at the baptism of catechumens. It is impossible here to discuss the wider implications of the acceptance of what Smith calls the 'longer text' of Mark or even to examine the arguments for its existence,[12] but if we proceed from the assumption that at some time it existed, we need to consider Smith's claim that 10·13-45 as a unit deals with baptism. Either this unit existed prior to Mark and without the Clementine addition, or prior to Mark and with it and he then omitted it, or it was added to canonical Mark by Mark or someone else after the canonical Gospel had been composed, or was in the canonical Mark and later omitted by Mark or someone else. Since at the moment we are only examining chapter 10 to see if there is a pre-Marcan complex in it, all we need to do is to examine the coherence of 10;13-45 in

[10] Cf. K. G. Reploh, *Markus – Lehrer der Gemeinde,* Stuttgarter Biblische Monographien, 9 (Stuttgart, 1969), pp. 163ff.; S. Légasse, 'Approche de l'Episode préévangélique des Fils de Zébédée (Marc x: 35-40 par.)' in *New Testament Studies,* 20 (1973-74), pp. 161-77.

[11] M. Smith, *Clement of Alexandria and a Secret Gospel of Mark* (Harvard University Press, Cambridge, Mass., 1973).

[12] For a thorough examination of Smith's views, see now H. Merkel, 'Auf den Spuren des Urmarkus? Ein neuer Fund und sein Beurteilung', in *Zeitschrift für Theologie und Kirche,* 71 (1974), pp. 123-45; W. Wink, 'Jesus as Magician', in *Union Seminary Quarterly Review,* 30(1974), pp. 3-14; R. E. Brown, 'The Relation of "The Secret Gospel of Mark" to the Fourth Gospel', in *Catholic Biblical Quarterly,* 36(1974), pp. 466-85.

respect of baptism. The relevant part of Smith's argument runs as follows: 10:13–45 is the place in canonical Mark where baptismal material is to be expected; 10:13–16 states the general prerequisite of baptism (become as little children); 10:17–31 states specific requirements (monotheism, obedience to the commandements, renunciation of property) which correspend to the standard prelminary instruction for baptism; 10:32–4, the credal prophecy of the passion and resurrection, provides both the assurance and the explanation of the rite's efficacy.[13]

Smith has much in his favour when he argues that the logical place for a baptismal lection in Mark would be in chapter 10. The first section of the Gospel is directed to outsiders, but from 8:27 the teaching is esoteric. At 10:32 Jesus finally departs for Jerusalem and death; the catechumen must be ready to accompany him, and so, directly after 10:34, he is baptised. Yet the exact position of the baptism must be more problematical. In 10:38f., which according to Smith[14] refers to the participation of the initiate in the sacraments, baptism is still hypothetical and not yet an accomplished fact. Baptism would then follow 10:40 much more appropriately, or could come at any point up to the end of the chapter. Quite apart from the positioning of the baptism in this section, the acceptance of the section as baptismal requires further support from the total structure of Mark. The Gospel appears to have been written for the benefit of an existing Christian community, to correct their doctrine and reform the quality of their discipleship, and was not written for the instruction of initiates. But Mark may have taken up an existing baptismal lection and included it at this point, its baptismal nature being easily recognizable to all his community; this would only be so if the baptismal nature of the pre-Marcan material can be clearly demonstrated; as we proceed we shall see that this does not seem probable.

At this point we must lay aside the possible baptismal nature of 10:13–16, for it is the meaning of this text in its context that we are attempting to discover; when we return to it we shall see that for Mark it is not primarily baptismal in meaning.

In 10:17–31 Smith draws attention to the irrelevance of verse

[13] For this summary, see Smith, op. cit., p. 187.
[14] Op. cit., pp. 186f.

18, with its affirmation that God alone is good, takes this to be a credal confession of monotheism, and argues from it that it is a deliberate development of the original story in order to place a confession of monotheism immediately prior to baptism. He demonstrates how such a confession has a place in Judaism, and how in particular Mark 10:18 came to be quickly used in this way in Christianity, but fails to give evidence for its place in early baptismal liturgies. He also argues that the Ten Commandments were used from an early stage in Christian baptism by instancing Didache 2:1-3. This section of the Didache ('The Two Ways') is one of the earliest portions; but it is only in the existing form of the Didache, which is probably second-century, that it is related to baptism (at 7:1), i.e. the association is post-Marcan; 'The Two Ways' is pre-Christian, and so is the use of the Ten Commandments independently of baptism either in 'The Two Ways' or apart from it; we cannot then draw conclusions for Mark's use of the Commandments as necessarily implying baptism. Finally Smith draws attention to the abandonment of goods demanded in this pericope; how he expects this to support his claim to a baptismal reference is unclear since he provides no evidence for the practice elsewhere in the early Church and indeed denies its existence outside the community for which Mark wrote or which produced the complex. It is, moreover, very peculiar that if an example is to be given for baptismal instruction there should be chosen that of a man who refuses to follow Jesus! Surely there were better precedents. We thus see no reason to assume that 10:17-31 would have been taken in a baptismal sense.

10:32-4 can certainly be described as credal, but there are two parallel credal statements, 8:31; 9:31; what function do these other two play? This raises the more general point: Smith nowhere considers in any depth the total purpose of Mark's Gospel. We could argue that the disciples function in it as believers; their difficulty in understanding Jesus' words and actions corresponds to the difficulty of believers in understanding their faith; from the beginning it is addressed to believers; the logical place for the initiation of a new member would be at its commencement, where Peter and the others do begin to follow Jesus. Taken this way, the pattern of Acts is followed, in

which instruction follows rather than precedes baptism.[15]
Returning now to 10:33f. itself; if a credal type statement is
desired, that of 9:31 fills the requirement much better because of
its brevity; the details of the passion given in 10:33f. seem
wholly unnecessary for confessional purposes. Thus again, in
the 10:32-4 passage we can see nothing to support the baptismal
idea.

Finally Smith argues that 10:35-45 is the sermon, the
post-baptismal instruction.[16] Its burden for him is: 'Practise
humility, make yourselves useful in the Church, and give what
you can.' As we have already pointed out,[17] verses 35-40 and
verses 41-5 were united by Mark. Only one of them can then
have belonged to the pre-Marcan complex. There is a baptismal
reference in verses 35-40, so for Smith it would probably be
better to retain it, though, as we have shown, it does not suggest
that the baptism has just taken place. Finally we note that the
main lesson of verses 41-5 is already found in 9:33-7, which on
Smith's view is pre-baptismal; it cannot therefore have any
special baptismal reference.

We conclude that, apart from 10:3f. and what we may
discover in verses 13-16, there is nothing in 10:13-45 which
necessitates us viewing it as a baptismal complex which Mark
took up and used, nor for that matter is there anything which
suggests that Mark himself saw it as baptismal in meaning.

Isaksson [18] prefers to connect our pericope with the one that
precedes it, 10:1-12, and regards the two together as a church
marriage catechism.[19] He does not argue the case in detail: he

[15] Smith, op. cit., p. 170, denies the validity of the examples in Acts,
alleging that the argument for the absence of pre-baptismal instruction
in Acts is drawn from silence – but from where else could it be drawn?
Clearly the author of Acts could not have been expected to insert a
footnote: 'For the benefit of later generations it must be noted that there
was no pre-baptismal instruction'!
[16] Op. cit., pp. 186f.
[17] See n. 10.
[18] A. Isaksson, *Marriage and Ministry in the New Temple* (Lund, 1965),
pp. 119, 121.
[19] Put more accurately, Isaksson argues that Matt. 19:1-15 forms the
catechism; its existence would prove that Mark 10:1-16 was a
pre-Marcan unit.

holds that Matthew 19:1-12 is not dependent on Mark 10:1-12, and appears to imply that since both are united to the pericope about children (Matt. 19:13-15 and Mark 10:13-16), this linkage must be both pre-Matthean and pre-Marcan. This conclusion does not necessarily follow. Supposing Matthew 19:1-12 to be independent of Mark 10:1-12, all Matthew may have done may be to have substituted his account of the divorce pericope for that in Mark. To establish his point Isaksson would need to show that Matthew 19:13-15 does not depend on Mark 10:13-16. This he has not done and it is doubtful if it could be established; Matthew does omit Mark 10:15, but he has already used a parallel at 18:3. It is, moreover, highly doubtful whether Matthew 19:1-12 is actually independent of Mark 10:1-12.[20]

The suggestion of Jeremias[21] has commanded more general support: 10:1-31 is a pre-Marcan complex (Jeremias does not of course hold that it was pre-Marcan in its present form) dealing with 'marriage, children, possessions', three subjects on which all disciples would need instruction.[22] Mark 10:1-12 is a church rule about marriage, 10:13-16 is a rule about baptism, and 10:17-23 (25) a rule about wealth. Whether 10:13-16 dealt with infant baptism both prior to and in Mark is yet to be determined, but if in the pre-Marcan material it related in some way to the reception of children,[23] then there does exist some consistency

[20] Cf. H. Baltensweiler, *Die Ehe im Neuen Testament* (Zürich, 1967), p. 59; B. H. Streeter, *The Four Gospels* (Macmillan, London, 1936), pp. 259-61; B. K. Didericksen, *Den markianske skilsmisseperikope* (Gyldendal, 1962), pp. 116ff.; D. Daube, *The New Testament and Rabbinic Judaism* (Athlone Press, London, 1956), p. 71; J. Schmid, 'Markus und der armäische Matthäus', in *Synoptische Studien*, Festschrift für A. Wikenhauser (Munich, 1953), pp. 148-83, esp. pp. 177ff.

[21] J. Jeremias, *Infant Baptism in the First Four Centuries*, ET by D. Cairns (SCM Press, London, 1960), p. 50; cf. E. Schweizer, *The Good News according to Mark* (SPCK, London, 1971), pp. 201f.; S. Légasse, *Jésus et l'Enfant* (Paris, 1969), pp. 36f., 206-18; W. Grundmann, *Das Evangelium nach Markus*, 3rd ed. (Berlin, 1968), p. 201.

[22] Baltensweiler, op. cit., p. 73, goes much further in regarding all that lies between the second and third passion predictions (9:33-10:31) as originally a pre-Marcan complex which Mark has modified and added to. Mark 9:33-50 does not appear to have any real homogeneity with 10:1-31.

[23] We shall see later that the addition of v. 15 has changed this pericope.

among the pericopae; all of them then deal with discipleship in relation to something external: marriage partner, children, possessions. When we recall the easy way in which the early Church united the sayings of Jesus into sequences without caring much for logical consistency, we ought not to be surprised to find these three pericopae together; there is an easy progression, even if it is not logical, from marriage to children to possessions. This progression is more clearly exhibited in the pre-Marcan stage of the tradition than in the Marcan. It is difficult to see why Mark should have put the three incidents together, for the changes he has made in the second[24] and third[25] decrease their coherence in comparison with their pre-Marcan forms. If he still saw some common element in them which led him to put them together, it is much more probable that someone prior to him should have done so.

We must now turn to the content of verses 13–16 and look for signs of Mark's hand. It is joined to the preceding pericope by a simple καί, a characteristic of Mark's style. The subject of the impersonal plural (another Marcan characteristic[26]) προσέφερον is not that of verses 10–12, but it was Mark who introduced the reference to the disciples in verse 10; so this provides no grounds for rejecting a pre-Marcan connection of verses 13–16 to verses 1–10. Some scholars[27] suggest that ἐκπορευομένου in verse 17 implies that Mark, who introduced the reference to the house in verse 10, envisages all of verses 13–16 as taking place in the house which Jesus then leaves at verse 17. On the other hand, a verb of motion in relation to Jesus when he is calling disciples is Marcan (1:16, 19; 2:14).[28] It is probably safer to conclude that Mark is making no attempt to depict verses 13–16 as situated in a house. There is nothing internal to the incident which would require such a locality. The children who are brought to Jesus are not then to be considered

---

[24] See below.
[25] See Best, as in n. 4.
[26] Cf. C. H. Turner, 'Marcan Usage', in *Journal of Theological Studies*, 25 (1924), pp. 378ff.
[27] e.g. Wohlenberg, *Das Evangelium des Markus* (Leipzig, 1910), p. 272.
[28] The idea of movement is confirmed by the use of ὁδός throughout the discipleship section, 8:27–10:52.

as the children of the house of verse 10. There are thus few signs of Mark's hand at the beginning and end of the pericope. The whole of it is indeed bare of superfluous detail.[29] Verse 16 depends on verse 13a and requires it as introductory; some word must have been used to describe the approach of parents or other adults with the children to Jesus and, though the impersonal form of προσέφερον may be Marcan, the verb itself[30] is not particularly so and probably belonged to the tradition. Verse 13b is also essential to the story, though the use of ἐπιτιμᾶν may be Marcan. It also contains a Marcan theme, the misunderstanding of the disciples, but since verse 14 depends on it, in this instance the theme must have been present in the tradition.[31]

If Mark's hand is only to be traced minimally in the introduction to the pericope and not at all in the conclusion, is it to be seen anywhere else in the pericope? Verse 15 almost certainly did not belong to the story in its earlier stages,[32] for:

(1) Verse 16 is a fitting conclusion to verse 14 and fully answers verse 13a, making the pericope into an apophthegm or pronouncement story whose climax is an action and not a saying of Jesus; confirmation that the pericope could exist without verse 15 and be a true unity is seen in Matthew's omission of verse 15 in his parallel (19:13-15).[33]

(2) Luke, on the other hand, omits verse 16 from his parallel (18:15-17), for it is no longer necessary once verse 15 is there.

[29] Cf. Reploh, op. cit., pp. 186ff.
[30] 15 times in Matthew, 3 in Mark, 4 in Luke.
[31] Mark did not create the theme (cf. 9:18f.; 10:35ff.) but developed it; cf. Kuhn, op. cit., p. 182.
[32] Cf. Bultmann, The History of the Synoptic Tradition (ET, Blackwell, Oxford, and Harper & Row, New York, 1963), p. 32; Légasse, Jésus et l'Enfant, p. 38, n. 20; J. Jeremias, 'Mc 10: 13-16 Parr. und die Übung der Kindertaufe in der Urkirche', in Zeitschrift für die neutestamentliche Wissenschaft, 40 (1941), pp. 243-4; J. I. H. McDonald, 'Receiving and Entering the Kingdom. A study in Mark 10:15', in Studia Evangelica, VI (=TU 112), pp. 328-32.
[33] Cf. the argument of Légasse, Jésus et l'Enfant, p. 43. Matthew certainly does not dislike doublets and would not necessarily omit v. 15. Possibly he knew the incident in his oral tradition as well as in its written form in Mark; because his oral form did not include v. 15, and because he had already used a close variant at 18:3, he dropped it in his parallel to Mark 10:13-16.

(3) We find evidence for the existence of verse 15 as a detached logion; there is a variant in Matthew 18:3[34] and probably another in John 3:5.[35] Once verse 15 had been introduced into the pericope, it itself became the climax and verse 16 redundant, as Luke's omission of it shows; probably this process was assisted by the solemn character of verse 15 in its 'amen' form. As we shall see, its presence also transformed the meaning of the pericope. If verse 15, then, is an addition at some stage of the tradition,[36] there is nothing in the way in which it has been added which indicates clearly whether it was added by Mark or before him. The motive for the addition probably lay in the catchword 'children' and perhaps also in the reference to the kingdom of God, provided verse 14c is not Marcan.

If we go so far as to eliminate verse 15 from the original story, there is a great deal to be said for also eliminating verse 14c. Without it, we have a straightforward incident in which children are brought to Jesus for him to touch them and are repelled by the disciples who are themselves rebuked by Jesus; he then embraces, touches and blesses the children.[37] This, incidentally,

---

[34] It is not original to the context of Matt. 18:1-5, as the change of number there shows; however, it is extremely unlikely that if Matthew found it in the singular in Mark 10:15, which is the number in 18:1, 2, 4, 5, he would then change it into the plural in order to transfer it; moreover, the other variations do not suggest changes on his part from the Marcan form; cf. Légasse, *Jésus et l'Enfant,* pp. 33-5; W. L. Knox, *The Sources of the Synoptic Gospels,* vol. II (Cambridge University Press, London, 1957), p. 16, n 1; A. M. Ambrozic, *The Hidden Kingdom,* Catholic Biblical Quarterly Monograph, II (Catholic Biblical Association of America, Washington, D.C., 1972), pp. 136-8. The contrary view is argued by W. G. Thompson, *Matthew's Advice to a Divided Community, Matt. 17:22-18:35,* Analecta Biblica 44 (Rome, 1970), pp. 76-8, 136f.

[35] Cf. C. H. Dodd, *Historical Tradition in the Fourth Gospel* (Cambridge University Press, London, 1963), pp. 358f. We are not concerned to trace whether the saying goes back to the historical Jesus; cf. Légasse, *Jésus et l'Enfant,* pp. 187f.

[36] The origin of vv. 13, 14ab, 16 need not detain us; they were certainly not composed as a setting for v. 15 (cf. Bultmann, op. cit., p. 32).

[37] The reception and blessing would not be exceptional in a Jewish context; cf. J. Jeremias, op. cit. (see n. 21), p. 49; H. L. Strack and P. Billerbeck, *Kommentar zum Neuen Testament aus Talmud und Midrasch* (Munich, 1922-28), vol. I, pp. 807f.

is the way in which the story has usually been understood popularly. The addition of verse 14c, still more of verse 15, turns attention away from the action of Jesus, which is itself an example to disciples on how they should behave, into a theological statement about the nature of discipleship: being like children. In verse 14c it is possible to give τῶν τοιούτων either, (1) its classical meaning, 'the Kingdom belongs to those similar to children', in which case it means something the same as verse 15 and Jesus is not saying anything which justifies his words in verse 14ab or his action in verse 16; or (2) the meaning it sometimes has in Hellenistic Greek and in the New Testament[38] as an equivalent of τῶν τούτων, 'the Kingdom belongs to these children', i.e. to these particular children or children as a class;[39] this makes Jesus say that children may be members of the Kingdom. Whether or not this was a possible meaning in the pre-Marcan stage, it surely cannot be after verse 15 has been added, since clearly it does not refer to the membership of actual children in the Kingdom; moreover, where Mark elsewhere (4:33; 7:13; 9:37; 13:19) uses τοιοῦτος, he gives it its classical meaning. When we also observe that verse 14c is a typical Marcan γάρ clause,[40] the most probably solution is that he has written it. If verse 15 had first been inserted into verses 13-14ab, 16, then verse 14c is easily explicable as a clause making the connection firmer; by the addition, Mark has emphasised verse 15 rather than the original meaning of the pericope. It is indeed possible that Mark himself added both verse 15 and verse 14c.[41]

[38] Cf. Moulton-Turner, *Grammar of New Testament Greek,* vol. III (T. & T. Clark, Edinburgh, 1963), pp. 46f.; Légasse, *Jésus et l'Enfant,* p. 39; F. W. Blass and H. Debrunner, *Greek Grammar of the New Testament,* trans. R. W. Funk (Cambridge University Press, London, 1961), § 304.

[39] Jeremias, op. cit. (see n. 21), p. 49, takes it in the sense, the 'Kingdom belongs *also* [our italics] to children'; but *also* is neither present in the text nor clearly implied by the context.

[40] Cf. C. H. Turner, 'Marcan Usage', in *Journal of Theological Studies,* 26 (1925), pp. 145-56; M. Thrall, *Greek Particles in the New Testament* (Leiden, 1962), pp. 41ff.; C. H. Bird, 'Some γάρ Clauses in St Mark's Gospel', in *Journal of Theological Studies,* 4 (1953), pp. 171-87.

[41] On Matthew's treatment of v. 15, see n. 33. Even if v.14c was not in his oral form, he would have retained it here because it still makes the point without v.15 and because, unlike v.15, he did not have a parallel to it elsewhere.

If, then, we eliminate both verse 14c and verse 15, we have a simple account: children are welcomed by Jesus. The ancient world, unlike our own world, did not idealise children;[42] they were ignored as an unimportant section of the community; this is what the disciples wish to do; but Jesus ignores no one; he has time even for children, and to show it he is ready to bless them. Given this interpretation, we can also see how the pericope came to be attached to the preceding in the oral tradition; it follows the latter just as children follow marriage and it answers the question of their relationship to the Church – a question which certainly agitated some Christian circles (1 Cor. 7:14), though it of course contains no direct reference to their baptism. Once, however, verse 14c and verse 15 have been added, the weight of the pericope lies with them and its meaning changes.

Those who hold that the pericope was used to explain or defend infant baptism in the early Church[43] will naturally see this as an extension of the use to indicate the relationship of children to the Church. For this baptismal view in relation to children Jeremias[44] adduces four grounds:

(1) The verse was interpreted early as referring to baptism in John 3:5,[45] and then from Justin (*Apologies,* 1.61.4) onwards.

(2) The use of κωλύειν indicates a baptismal formula in which at baptism an enquiry is made whether there are any hindrances to it.[46]

(3) The imposition of hands (v. 14) is part of the ritual of baptism.

---

[42] The Greco-Roman world idealised the mature adult; in Judaism the child was 'weak' and not expected to keep the law until he became bar-mitzvah; cf. A. Oepke, in *Theological Dictionary of the New Testament,* ed. G. Kittel and G. Friedrich, trans. G. W. Bromiley, IV, p. 916; V, pp. 639–48; Billerbeck, vol. I, pp. 569f., 607, 780ff.; II, p. 373; Légasse, *Jésus et l'Enfant,* pp. 276ff.; cf. pp. 168ff.

[43]. Cf. Jeremias, op. cit., pp. 48ff.; O. Cullmann, *Baptism in the New Testament,* Studies in Biblical Theology, 1 (SCM Press, London, 1950), pp. 25f., 71ff.; Wohlenberg, op. cit., p. 272.

[44] Op. cit., pp. 48–55.

[45] Cf. M. Smith, op. cit., p. 169.

[46] Cullmann, op. cit., pp. 71–80; and 'Les traces d'une vieille formule baptismale dans le Nouveau Testament', in *Revue d'Histoire et de Philosophie religieuses,* 17 (1937), pp. 424–34.

(4) Luke's substitution of βρέφη for παιδία and various other peculiarities of the Lucan text.

We need only comment briefly on these points; they are adequately evaluated and refuted by G. R. Beasley-Murray.[47]

(1) There is no direct literary relationship between John 3:5 and Mark 10:15;[48] the former could therefore have gathered its baptismal connections entirely independently of Mark; it moreover differs so much from the Marcan form that the forces which shaped each must have been very different.

(2) κωλύειν is an inherent part of the original pericope; it would have been pointless without it; we cannot therefore easily assume that it was part of a formula; indeed, positive evidence would be required to demonstrate that Mark's first readers would have seen it as part of a formula.

(3) The laying on of hands (v. 16) was again a necessary part of the original account as a sign of blessing[49] and need not convey any idea of the impartation of the Holy Spirit as in baptism; Paul never relates the laying on of hands to baptism; when Jesus was baptised he received the Spirit in another manner. It therefore needs to be proved that Mark intended a reference to the Spirit in verse 16.

(4) Luke's substitution of βρέφη (suggesting very young children) may only indicate his adoption of an alternative word which was a favourite with him.[50]

In addition to these counter-arguments, there are also positive reasons for rejecting the baptismal interpretation of the pericope:

(a) It would be like a fish out of water in Mark's context. Throughout 8:27-10:52 he is stressing the great claims of discipleship. In the immediate context he sets out these claims in

---

[47] *Baptism in the New Testament* (Macmillan, London, 1962), pp. 320ff.; see also Légasse, *Jésus et l'Enfant,* pp. 210ff.; K. Aland, *Did the Early Church Baptise Infants?* (ET, SCM Press, London, 1963), pp. 95-9.

[48] Dodd, op. cit., p. 359; cf. R. E. Brown, *The Gospel According to John,* vol. I (Doubleday, New York, 1966), pp. 141-4; R. Schnackenburg, *The Gospel According to St John,* vol. I (ET, Burns & Oates, London, and Herder & Herder, New York, 1968), pp. 366-8.

[49] D. Daube, op. cit., p. 234; see all of pp. 224-46, and cf. our n. 37.

[50] Luke uses it five times; it is not used by any of the other evangelists; cf. Légasse, *Jésus et l'Enfant,* p. 40; for the other Lucan modifications, see ibid., pp. 40f., 195-209.

respect of sex and wealth, taking up two of the strongest impulses turning men from discipleship; to set between them a pericope saying, 'Discipleship means the Christian brings his children to be baptised', would be, to say the least, incongruous. Even if such an action could lead to persecution, there is no suggestion in our passage that Mark has this in mind.

(b) We have seen that verse 15, and probably also verse 14c, are later additions to the original pericope and they have transformed its meaning and become its climax.[51] For Mark, attention is not being directed to the need to bring children but to the requirement to be like children in receiving the Kingdom. This is appropriate to the main drive of the Gospel at this point, namely discipleship.

For similar reasons to those for our rejection of the baptismal interpretation, we must reject the view of Reploh[52] that Mark is dealing in the pericope with a problem of his own church in respect of the membership of children; the incident may at one point in its transmission have been pointed in this way but in its present setting, and with the addition of verses 14c and 15, it relates to discipleship. Likewise we must exclude from the Marcan interpretation any idea of a response to Jesus by the children;[53] even in the earliest form of the pericope the children are brought to Jesus; they are too young to come to him; they have not yet become 'sons of the Law' and are not responsible. Thus if the original pericope depicted Jesus' attitude to children, this has almost disappeared through the additions made to it and the context with which it has been provided.

What then do verses 14c and 15 mean? How do they bring a clearer understanding of discipleship? The child is clearly the model (v. 14c). But of what?

We can begin by dismissing that interpretation which takes

[51]   Cf. Légasse, Jésus et l'Enfant, p. 38.

[52]   Op. cit., p. 190; cf. K. Weiss, 'Ekklesiologie, Tradition und Geschichte in der Jüngerunterweisung, Mark 8:27–10:52', in *Der historische Jesus und der kerygmatische Christus,* ed. H. Ristow and K. Matthiae (Berlin, 1961), pp. 414–38.

[53]   Cf. Beasley-Murray, op. cit., p. 327.

παιδίον as the direct object to δέξηται, [54] 'whoever receives the kingdom of God as he reeives a child'; this makes the child the model of the Kingdom. Certainly it is a possible meaning grammatically and it can be argued that it accords with Jesus' reception of the children in verses 13f. and is similar in outlook to 9:37. It necessitates, however, that we understand verse 15 in a different way from its parallel in Matthew 18:3, where this interpretation is impossible; Matthew presumably did not read Mark 10:15 in this way or he would have retained it, since it would then have been no longer parallel to his 18:3; equally, John 3:5 does not reflect this interpretation of Mark 10:15. These facts suggest that in the original meaning of the saying the child was not the model of the Kingdom. Within the Marcan context verse 14c blends more easily with verse 15 on the assumption that the child is the model for reception, which is the generally accepted interpretation. Lastly, in the ancient world children were not esteemed and their reception would not be indicative of the honour and respect with which we would expect the Kingdom to be received.

Ambrozic appears to provide a variant to this interpretation. He takes the pre-Marcan meaning of verse 15 to relate to the child as one who needs instruction: whoever would be a 'follower of Jesus must admit that he is unwise in matters of the Kingdom, and that his only way into the Kingdom consists in his acceptance of its mystery'.[55] However, when he comes to discuss the verse in its Marcan context, he appears to shift ground and interprets it: 'Whoever does not joyfully subject himself to the hidden kingdom offered by a hidden Messiah, by accepting it as a free gift of God, will not be allowed to share in its present and future blessings.'[56] He justifies this by paralleling the argument in 10:32-45 to that in 9:33-7, and from the latter he deduces that Mark's child is the 'one who is the last of all and expected to subject himself to others'[57] – and the disciple must

[54] Cf, W. K. L. Clarke, *New Testament Problems* (SPCK, London, 1929), pp. 36-8; F. A. Schelling, 'What means the saying about receiving the kingdom of God as a little child?', in *Expository Times*, 77 (1965-66), pp. 56-8.
[55] Op. cit., p. 152.
[56] Ibid., p. 158.
[57] Ibid., p. 157.

serve even children. This appears somewhat muddled. In so far as it parallels the child and the Kingdom, it is open to the objections we made in the preceding paragraph. Additionally, while 'service' may be a parallel thought in 9:33-7 and 10:32-45, we are not dealing here with 10:32-45 and there is no necessary reason to assume that the 'child' functions in a uniform way in Mark.

We are then forced to return to some form of the traditional solution which makes the child the model for reception:[58] The Kingdom is to be received as children receive. But how does a child receive? Commentators have written variously of the innocence, simplicity, ingenuousness, receptiveness of children. All such interpretations, apart from the last, tend to romanticise the child in a way foreign to the ancient world. Légasse[59] argues strongly that the condition of becoming a disciple is following Jesus in faith (Mark 1:15), but we must beware of giving too theological a connotation to faith when children are being spoken of. A child trusts[60] adults; he has confidence in them; he receives from them what they offer. So the disciple is to trust God and receive the Kingdom. The Kingdom is not a place or a thing; it is God's active rule; the disciple has therefore to allow God to rule in his life. This is not something which is completed once and for all in the act of becoming a disciple, but something which takes place continuously; hence the appropriateness of our pericope to a context of discipleship.[61] In the second half of the verse the kingdom of God is used of the future eschatological

[58] And if Ambrozic is correct in tracing the earlier meanings given to the saying (op. cit., pp. 139ff.), then there is no violent change in the meaning of the saying in its present context.

[59] Op. cit., pp. 189ff.

[60] This is the theme which Professor Barclay highlights in *Mark* (Daily Study Bible, St Andrew Press, Edinburgh, 1954), p. 251.

[61] This interpretation is not far removed from that of McDonald (art. cit.), who argues on the basis of Jewish parallels for the 'teachability and complete obedience of the child as he learns to receive the Kingdom'. 'Trust' and 'obedience' are linked terms. The slightly different emphasis we have given the concept arises, perhaps, from its present Hellenistically coloured atmosphere; McDonald was thinking of the original Jewish context of Jesus' words.

Kingdom (this is the more normal Marcan usage[62]) into which the disciple enters; that it is the future meaning which is intended is seen from 9:47; 10:17, 21, 23, 25, 30. Thus both present and future aspects of the Kingdom appear in the one verse: receptiveness of the rule of God now ensures membership of the future Kingdom. This might appear to be a kind of prudential ethic, yet the way in which receptiveness is understood in parallel to the receptiveness of the child takes away from this conclusion.

While at the beginning we said that Christology does not bulk large in this pericope, we may draw one negative conclusion. Sometimes the pericope is used to argue that we should treat others, in particular children, as Jesus treats these children. This would yield an implicit *imitatio Christi* Christology. This understanding of the story, even if it was once present in it, has disappeared through the addition of verse 15. Jesus is not just on the same plane as the disciples; he provides the teaching and understanding through which they become disciples.

[62] Cf. Best, *The Temptation and the Passion,* Society for New Testament Studies, Monograph Series, 2 (Cambridge University Press, London, 1965), pp. 64-8, and references given there; see also now Ambrozic, op. cit., *passim.*

Chapter 7

The Role of the Disciples in Mark*

While traditional Christian thought has honoured the disciples, they have since Wrede been increasingly regarded as bearing the brunt of Mark's animus. This paper is a new examination of the role they play in Mark's thought. It is not inappropriate to present it at a meeting of the Society in the U.S.A., where so much original and fascinating work on the place of Mark as author has been advanced in recent years. It may be that Mark did not conceive of the disciples as playing any particular role. In the tradition their lives were too closely intertwined with that of Jesus for Mark to have been able to omit them from his account. Given their necessary presence he might have regarded them purely as background, an ineradicable part of the scenery but of no importance in themselves and having no essential function in what he wrote. We will not dispute this now, but all that is argued later about the disciples indicates that they were not mere scenery; Mark gave them a definite role in his book. But what role? This is a legitimate question and needs to be asked once we abandon the view that Mark is writing pure biography.

It would perhaps be better to re-phrase our question in terms of roles rather than of role for, apart from a possible lack of consistency in role which might come from differences between the tradition and the redaction or from the failure of Mark to think logically through his own position, he may have deliberately chosen and used them to fulfil more than one role, or he could have allotted different roles to different groups within the whole number of the disciples: the Twelve may not be the same group as the disciples and may have been differently used by Mark; within the Twelve smaller groups, e.g. the Three, or

98

individual members, e.g. Peter, may be used in different ways.

The role played by the disciples is naturally linked to the purpose of the book as a whole. If we view it as a polemical writing we may envisage Mark putting either the disciples or their views under attack; if we consider it to be a sermon we may see the disciples, or their views, used as examples of behaviour and doctrine and as examples either to be followed or avoided or even both of these in different sections. Our choice is of course not restricted to a polemical writing and a sermon; the book may partake in part of both elements, and it may also have a historical purpose, i.e. be intended to convey information about Jesus and the disciples or to show that Christian faith is anchored in actual events. Sermons, moreover, can have different purposes: to instruct, console or exhort the hearers, or to bring them to a point of decision – or may include a number of these elements.

While it is clear that we cannot fully solve the question of the purpose of the gospel apart from a consideration of the role of the disciples, yet other factors do assist us in forming a general view of its purpose; it is therefore necessary to give some account of my overall approach in this matter. I do not think the gospel was written with either a simple polemical or historical end in view. Few scholars today would regard Mark as intended primarily to supply historical facts either about Jesus or about the disciples. There are however a number who appear to regard it as polemical.[1] Certainly the New Testament contains polemical writings, but the tendency to take almost all of it as polemically orientated seems wrong. In approaching any writing in order to understand it the interpreter will have some question or questions in mind. One such question can be 'Against whom or against what is this written?' (There is a distinction between these two; views can be attacked without people being attacked and people can be attacked without their

---

[1] This view has been put forward most thoroughly and consistently by T.J. Weeden in 'The Heresy that Necessitated Mark's Gospel', *Z.N.W.* LIX (1968), 145-58, and *Mark: Traditions in Conflict* (Philadelphia, 1971). Cf. J.B. Tyson, 'The Blindness of the Disciples in Mark', *J.B.L.* LXXX (1961), 261-8; J. Schreiber, 'Die Christologie des Markusevangeliums', *Z.T.K.* LVIII (1961), 154-83; W.H. Kelber, *The Kingdom in Mark* (Philadelphia, 1974).

views being placed at issue.) I doubt whether this is the best question with which to approach many of the New Testament books. It is certainly the natural question with which to open up Galatians. It also seems to be a natural question for many twentieth-century scholars who from the safety of their academic ivory towers occupy themselves with scoring points off one another, an attitude made particularly acute by the continual need to produce new papers and doctoral theses based on a paucity of original documents in order to procure or secure position, advancement or reputation. The present paper is a good example of this practice. But while the question 'Aginst whom or what?' naturally comes into scholars' minds when they look at a new book or article, their situation hardly parallels that of the first century, and a question appropriate to the understanding of a twentieth-century academic exercise may be wholly misleading if used to open up a first-century church situation. I do not therefore conceive of Mark's gospel as primarily polemical but as written to help his congregation in their situation. This is confirmed by the fact that we know it by the name 'gospel'. It was written to encourage with good news those who were finding the Christian way difficult. If the view that the book is primarily polemical is rejected that does not mean that it may not contain a polemical element and be written in part against certain opinions or certain people.

What then was the situation of those for whom it was written? Without writing a book, or perhaps a series of books, it is clearly impossible to justify what is now said and many will disagree with some or all of it, but it is important to state a general position even if space forbids the giving of reasons; these eventually come from the gospel itself set in the context of first-century Christianity. The only justification that can be offered is a belief that what I say about the role of the disciples in the gospel is not clearly contradictory to what I think about the book as a whole. I pick three factors. (i) Mark was written at Rome around A.D. 70 after the church had suffered some persecution and while it believed more persecution was imminent. (ii) The writer and readers (we must assume some common ground) expect the return of Christ but do not necessarily believe it is just about to take place; he has therefore to counsel his readers how they will live until that day comes; there would have been little point in writing in the way he does if the parousia were expected at once. (iii) The readers, or at least some of them, do not understand the place of the cross in their faith; whether this should be attributed to a 'divine man' christology[2] or not is another matter; the failure to accept a theology of the cross has been endemic among Christians; it was already present in Corinth (see Paul's argument in 1 Cor 1-4).

I

There are a number of possible roles that the disciples could have played in the gospel:

(1) They could signify themselves, the original disciples, no more and no less; this would be a purely historical position. Mark might approve of them or disapprove.

(2) They could signify a group claiming to continue the position of the original disciples, and Mark might either favour or oppose the group.

(3) They could signify some other contemporary group: (a) the church as a whole, or (b) a part of the church, e.g. its officials, or a group of heretics.

(4) They could occupy a purely informatory role, i.e. Mark might believe that past history should determine the present and we should learn from the past.

We must of course realize that they may occupy more than one of these roles. There is no reason why Mark should have confined himself to using them in only one way.

II

Is there then an attack on the original disciples as a group or on any sub-group of them? If Mark's purpose was to attack the original disciples this might explain why he chose to write a gospel rather than a letter. By means of a historical account he could show their disloyalty and lack of understanding of their leader. On the other hand if his purpose had only been to set

[2] So Weeden, *op. cit.*; Schreiber, *art. cit.*

forth true Christian behaviour then like Paul he could have done this as easily by writing with direct reference to the problems of his community. However such an explanation of the origin of the gospel makes it ultimately dependent upon the disciples and not upon Jesus. This is highly unlikely.

If there is an attack on the original disciples or any of them, then it is most likely that this attack would have been made on the Twelve or on Peter. We must therefore examine how Mark uses the tradition about the Twelve and about Peter. We begin with the Twelve.

In an as yet unpublished paper I have attempted to show that where the Twelve appear in his gospel in the majority of cases they came to Mark from the tradition.[3] On at least one occasion what was said in relation to the Twelve in the tradition obtains a wider reference through Mark's redaction: at 4:10 those termed οἱ περὶ αὐτόν are joined with the Twelve and at 4:34 the combined group is termed 'the disciples'. This widening of the reference probably also takes place at: (a) 9:35, where in 9:33f., which Mark composed, the material from the tradition in 9:35a which mentions the Twelve is given a wider reference to the disciples generally, and (b) 10:32, where those who go up with and follow after Jesus to Jerusalem are equated with the Twelve and the latter term comes from the tradition. In addition to this, as we shall see later, we ought to note that Mark uses 'the disciples' redactionally much more regularly than he does the Twelve. It thus appears that Mark is not deliberately drawing attention to the Twelve and that he is not concerned to identify the Twelve and the disciples in such a way that when the disciples are mentioned we are to understand him to mean the

---

[3] 'Mark's Use of the Twelve'(infra pp. 131-161). The view that the Twelve are redactional in Mark may not have been proposed first by R. Bultmann, *The History of the Synoptic Tradition* (Oxford, 1963), p. 345, but because of his advocacy it is now widely accepted. On the place of the Twelve in Mark see also G. Schmahl, 'Die Berufung der Zwölf im Markusevangelium *T.T.Z.* LXXXI (1972), 203-13 and *Die Zwölf im Markusevangelium* (Trier, 1974); K. Kertelge, 'Die Funktion der "Zwölf" im Markusevangelium', *T.T.Z.* LXXVIII (1969), 193-206; S. Freyne, *The Twelve: Disciples and Apostles* (London, 1968); K. Stock, *Boten aus dem mit-Ihm-Sein* (Analecta Biblica 70; Rome, 1975).

Twelve and only the Twelve.[4] It is, rather, the other way round: the Twelve is normally to be understood as signifying the wider group, the 'disciples'. This is confirmed when we examine what the gospel says about the Twelve.

(i)   They are recipients of private instruction (4:10-13; 9:35; 10:32).

(ii)   They are implicitly rebuked for their failure to understnd (9:35; 10:41-5 – though the ten only are mentioned in this latter passage we may assume that the ultimate reference is to the Twelve).

(iii)   They are with Jesus in the events of his last few days (11:11; 14:17; and by implication 14:10, 20, 43).

(iv)   They are to be with Jesus (3:14).

(v)   They are given authority to exorcize and to preach (3:14f.; 6:7).

So far as the functions of the Twelve in the first three categories are concerned we find that Mark also uses 'disciples', οἱ μαθηταί, and that in each case there are more frequent instances of the redactional use of 'disciples' to convey these ideas.

(i)   4:34; 7:17; 9:28f.; 10:10, 23, etc.

(ii)   6:35-7; 6:50, 52; 7:18; 8:14-21 (cf. 8:10; 6:52); 10:14; 10:23ff.

(iii)   11:14; 14:12, 13, 14, 16, 32; 16:7.

The sole reference to the Twelve as those who are to be with Jesus (iv) is never developed in the gospel though the reference to the authority given them to exorcize and preach (v) is. We may assume the former was unimportant to Mark. He does of course show the Twelve as present with Jesus at various points in his story, but he presents the disciples even more frequently as present.

The final point – the commission of the Twelve to exorcize and preach – is not found explicitly in material about the disciples. Those termed 'disciples' do indeed exorcize, or attempt to exorcize (9:18, 38f.), but within the lifetime of Jesus they are not portrayed as preaching. Yet they are given a duty to care for those outside the community (9:29, 36f., 49f.; 10:21) and

[4]As does C.H. Turner, 'The Twelve and the Disciples', *J.T.S.* XXVIII (1927), 22-30.

Peter and Andrew are bidden to follow Jesus and fish for men (1:16-18); the latter passage is an example of a call of two disciples rather than of a call of two of the Twelve, but there is no formal commissioning. 3:13-19 and 6:6b-13 thus provide an exception to the equivalence of the Twelve and the disciples. As 6:30[5] shows, the activity of the Twelve in respect of this authority is successful. It is only at those points where the activity of the Twelve and of the disciples is the same that they are seen to fail. This implies that the Twelve as distinct from the disciples cannot be regarded as the object of an attack by Mark. In turn, since the Twelve is a much more historically concrete group than the disciples, this means that the actual disciples of Jesus' own time are not being attacked as a group. This does not exclude the idea that Mark may be attacking a contemporary group through the historical disciples or named individuals among the historical disciples. Of named individuals the most likely is Peter, and we turn now to examine Mark's use of Peter.

Strands of anti-Petrine polemic have been detected in Gal 2:11-14, but much of the New Testament evidence sustains the alternative view that Peter occupied a recognized position of importance (1 Cor 9:5; 15:5; Gal 1:18; 2:9); however, evidence from other parts of the New Testament cannot decide the issue in respect of Mark and we must briefly examine the places in the gospel where he is singled out for special attention.[6] Sometimes where the tradition spoke only of Peter, Mark has introduced the other disciples alongside him, with the result that attention is no longer focused on him alone. This is so in: (a) 1:30, where at 1:29, under the influence of 1:16-20, the two sets of brothers are introduced by Mark; (b) perhaps at 1:36, where οἱ μετ' αὐτοῦ reads like a Markan addition, and where we note also that the question with its implied rebuke to Jesus is asked by the Four and not by Peter alone; (c) at 8:33, where Mark introduces the other disciples into the tradition and they consequently become partial recipients of Jesus' rebuke; (d) perhaps at 9:2-8, where certainly Peter belongs to the basic story and where though he may

[5] Here they are called 'Apostles'; by this Mark seems to identify them with the Twelve as a group.

[6] I hope shortly to publish a paper treating more fully the role of Peter in Mark's gospel (infra pp. 162-176).

already have been featured in the tradition as failing to understand, Mark's addition of 6b, ἔκφοβοι γὰρ ἐγένοντο (note the plural as against the singular of v.6a) draws in James and John (Mark may indeed have introduced the reference to the sons of Zebedee at 9:2);[7] (e) in the Gethsemane account Peter belonged to the tradition (witness the use of the name Simon) but Mark has widened the original rebuke which is in the singular of v.37 into the plural of v.38, and perhaps introduced James and John into the account in v.33; (f) to the prediction of Peter's denial, which belongs to the tradition, Mark has added the final clause of 14:31, ὡσαύτως δὲ καὶ πάντες ἔλεγον, which associates the other disciples with Peter's affirmation of bravery, and, even if he did not add the theme of their running away, he added the Scriptural quotation of v.27b which emphasizes this theme; (g) in the story of the denial itself, where Peter obviously belongs to the tradition, Mark may have softened the attack on him by omitting (14:71) the direct object after ἀναθεματίζειν ; this was presumably the name 'Christ'.[8]

So much for the way Mark used the tradition about Peter. What about the places where he has introduced him into the story? (a) at 10:28a[9] his loyalty to Jesus is mentioned and he acts as a foil to Jesus by questioning him and drawing out his teaching; (b) it may be that Peter is introduced by Mark at 11:21 since the verse may be redactional; no slur is cast on Peter's character here; he only acts as spokesman (cf. 1:37a); (c) Simon's name lay in the tradition of the list of the Twelve; the clumsy grammar of 3:16 suggests that the reference to him as Peter arises from Mark's combination of another strand of tradition with the list; he has therefore drawn deliberate attention to the special name given to him by Jesus. Most interesting of all are the references (d) to Peter weeping after the threefold denial,

---

[7] For a discussion of the role of the disciples in the Transfiguration see my paper 'The Markan Redaction of the Transfiguration' delivered at the Oxford Congress on Biblical Studies (1973), and due to appear in *Studia Evengelica* (infra pp. 206–225).

[8] So H. Merkel, 'Peter' Curse', in *The Trial of Jesus* (ed. E. Bammel; London, 1970), pp. 66ff.

[9] See Best, 'The Camel and the Needle's Eye (Mark 10:25)', *Exsp.T.* LXXXII (1970–1), 83–9, and the references given there (infra pp. 17–30).

which indicates repentance, and may be Markan, and (e) the message given at the empty tomb to the women to tell Peter and the other disciples about Jesus' resurrection;[10] the insertion of this at this point is certainly Markan.[11]

If we take all this together we see that wherever there were references to Peter in the tradition which showed him in a bad light Mark has weakened them in some way or other, and where Mark has introduced Peter into the tradition he has done so either to show him as a spokesman who acts as a foil to Jesus in drawing out his teaching or to show the probability of his repentance from his denial and of his ultimate acceptance by Christ after the resurrection.

Although the evidence is slight a case might be made out for an attack on John. Leaving aside references to the Three and the Four, John is mentioned with his brother James at 10:35 and by himself at 9:38. In the former case the rebuke to the brothers at 10:38-40 is widened into a rebuke to the remaining Ten at 10:41-5, and since Mark has probably brought together the units of tradition contained in vv.35-40 and vv.42-5[12] we cannot see this as a deliberate attack by him on James and John. Also the reference to the brothers in vv.35-40 is pre-Markan[13] The reference to John at 9:38 is also from the tradition; note that John says 'We forbade him, ἐκωλύομεν' (plural); his protest is really that of one from the disciples as a whole.

If then Mark was not attacking the historical Twelve or the

[10] I take 14:28 and 16:7 to refer to the resurrection and not to the parousia; cf. Best, *The Temptation and the Passion* (SNTS Monograph Series 2; Cambridge, 1965), pp. 173 ff.; R.H. Stein, 'A Short Note on Mark 14:28 and 16:7', *N.T.S.* XX (1973/4), 445-52; G. Stemberger, 'Galilee – Land of Salvation?', an appendix in W.D. Davies, *The Gospel and the Land* (Berkeley and Los Angeles, Calif., and London, 1974), pp. 409-38.

[11] See E. Linnemann, *Studien zur Passionsgeschichte* (FRLANT 102; Göttingen, 1970), p. 89; R.H. Fuller, *The Formation of the Resurrection Narratives* (London, 1972), p. 53; C.F. Evans, *Resurrection in the New Testament* (London, 1970), pp. 78 f.; T.J. Weeden, *op. cit.* pp. 45-51, 111-17; L. Schenke, *Auferstehungsverkündigung und leeres Grab* (Stuttgart, 2nd edn 1969), pp. 45 ff.

[12] Cf. S. Légasse, 'Approche de l'Épisode préévangélique du Fils de Zébédée (Marc 10:35-40 par.)', *N.T.S.* XX (1973/4), 161-77.

[13] *Ibid.*

historical Peter it is improbable that he was attacking the historical disciples as such. But he may have been using the actual disciples in order to launch an attack on some contemporary group, either within or outside his own community. We go on then to consider how Mark uses the disciples. As we do so we shall ignore the possibility that in his use of them he was attacking them in their historical role. But if, as we shall conclude, he was not attacking a contemporary group through them, it is highly improbably he was attacking the historical disciples themselves.[14]

III

In the accompanying two tables[15] we attempt to clarify the functions which Mark gives to the disciples, the Twelve, the Three, the Four, John and Peter. In the first table we take the passages which come from the tradition and in the second those which can be traced to the redaction. Naurally there are many passages of which we cannot say with any certainty whether they derive from the tradition or the redaction. However, there is a sufficient number of texts of which we can be sure for a clear pattern to emerge. We need to note that certain references in the

[14] Weeden, *Mark: Traditions in Conflict*, holds the view that Mark attacks both the historical disciples and through them a contemporary group in his own community, or threatening his own community; he sees continuity between these two groups because they hold similar views (pp. 50 f., 69, 148); cf. Kelber, *op. cit.* pp. 22, 64, 69, 82, 114-16, 136, who includes the family of Jesus with the disciples as the core of opposition centred in Jerusalem. On the possible clash between Mark and the family of Jesus see J.D. Crossan, 'Mark and the Relatives of Jesus', *N.T.* XV (1973), 81-113; J. Lambrecht, 'The relatives of Jesus in Mark', *N.T.* XVI (1974), 241-58; E. Best, 'Mark 3:20, 21, 31-5', *N.T.S.* XXII (1975/6), 309-19 (infra pp. 49-63).

[15] Some references are in parentheses or have a question mark either because doubt exists whether they belong to the tradition or redaction or because as we have the material it is impossible to determine which group (disciples, the Twelve, etc.) was involved, but Mark's editing or context suggests a group; in most of these cases the context does determine clearly the group which Mark envisaged as present. In the case of the Twelve at least one of 14:10, 20, 43 is traditional and the others are formed from it; and in the case of Peter's denial, while some of the references may be redactional they derive ultimately from those of the tradition.

redaction arise because the form of the pericope coming from the tradition already referred to a particular group, and Mark was compelled to introduce this into the 'seams' or 'continuity' verses which he supplies; it is difficult to know whether we should attribute these to the tradition or the redaction. Necessarily also in the classification the same verse may appear more than once because the group fulfils more than one function. We detect the following ways in which the disciples or any group of them are depicted.

(a)   They act as a foil to Jesus, giving him the opportunity to teach and act.

(b)   They are the recipients of private instruction from Jesus.

(c)   They journey with Jesus.

(d)   They are amazed at what Jesus says or does.

(e)   They are afraid at what he says or does or at what may happen to them.

(f)   They fail to understand what Jesus says or does.

(g)   They are rebuked by Jesus.

(h)   They are told not to disclose information.

(i)   They are given a position in the post-resurrection period.

(j)   They fail in action.

(k)   They are mentioned or implied as present without their presence being in any way exceptional.

(l)   They are defended by Jesus from criticisms made against them.

(m)   They mediate in some way beween Jesus and others.

(n)   They act for or on behalf of Jesus.

(o)   They are called by Jesus.

We now need to examine our classification in more detail.

The disciples already appeared in the tradition as a foil to Jesus (a); Mark has greatly increased the number of times in which they or some one of them or some group of them so function. Nothing in such a function implies that they are to be regarded as standing for those who oppose Jesus. It was customary in material from that period which concerns a teacher and disciples for the disciples to ask questions and to perform actions which elicit instruction from the teacher.[16] Indeed, since it is natural

[16] Cf. the Platonic Dialogues.

that on many occasions it should be their failure to understand or to act which drew out the teaching of the Master, it may be that much of that failure (*f*) is natural and implies no hostility towards the point of view represented by them; hostility might be implied only if there was a unified theme running through their failure, and to this we shall return.

While again the tradition had reference to private instruction (*b*) it was mostly private instruction of the Twelve. Mark has greatly increased the number of instances and related it not only to the Twelve but to the disciples and to the Three and the Four.[17] There is nothing exceptional in such private instruction of disciples; it is found in other master/disciple situations. In and of itself private instruction does not imply that a false view is being corrected. This would only follow if that instruction were a correction of, or supplementation to, previously given adequate teaching which had been provided for a wider group of followers or disciples; this is hardly so in the case of the gospel.

Apart from the passion account the journeying of the disciples (*c*) with Jesus is largely a Markan creation[18] arising from his overall plan for Jesus' activity which takes Jesus from Caesarea Philippi to Jerusalem; it is unlikely that the oral tradition would have preserved such detail of his movements. To draw attention to the journeying of the disciples with the Master would not suggest that they or their views were being attacked unless it could be shown that after journeying with him for a time they abandoned him, as John Mark might be said to have abandoned Paul and Barnabas (Acts 13:13; 15:37-41). But is this not what happens in Mark when Judas betrays Jesus, Peter denies him and all the other disciples flee at his arrest? However, in 16:7, a verse from the redaction, Mark specifically points to the reinstatement of Peter and the disciples. Mark received from the tradition the account of Judas' failure and does nothing directly to mitigate it. But unlike Matthew and Luke he does not recount Judas' death and so leaves open the possibility of his repentance; curiously Judas is not excluded from the message of 16:7.

[17] As 9:9, 11.

[18] Cf. the Lukan Travel Narrative, which is Luke's construction.

Table 1. *From the tradition*

	Disciples	The Twelve	The Three and the Four	John	Peter
(a)	6:35 8:27b 14:12	10:41 (the Ten)	9:11(?)	9:39 10:35-9	8:29
(b)	—	4:10 9:35 10:32-4 10:41-5 14:17(?)	14:33(?)	—	—
(c)	—	10:32 11:11(?) 14:17	—	—	—
(d)	—	—	—	—	—
(e)	(6:49)	—	9:6(?)	10:37	9:6
(f)	5:31 (6:37) 8:4 9:18f.	(6:37)	—	—	—
(g)	— 10:13f. (14:27)	9:35-7 10:41	— —	9:39 10:40	8:33 14:29, 31, 54(?), 66, 67, 70
(h)	—	—	—	—	—
(i)	—	—	—	—	—
(j)	9:18 14:50(?)	—	14:37(?)	—	—
(k)	8:27a, b(?)	14:10(?) 14:20(?) 14:43(?)	—	—	—
(l)	2:18 2:23f. 7:2, 5	—	—	—	—
(m)	6:41 8:6 10:13	3:14f. 6:7-13	—	—	—
(n)	11:1 14:13, 14, 16	—	—	—	—
(o)	—	—	1:16-20 (cf. 2:14)	1:19f.	1:16-18

The amazement of the disciples (d), though entirely redactional, is not heavily emphasized; the crowds are also amazed (θαυμάζειν, [19] 5:20; θαμβεῖσθαι, 1:27; ἐκθαμβεῖσθαι, 9:15;[20] ἐκπλήσσεσθαι, 1:22; 6:2; 7:37; 11:18); it is a not unexpected trait in disciples if the teaching or activity of their master is in any way new.

It is when we turn to the fear of the disciples (e), their failure to understand (f), and Jesus' rebukes to them (g), that there may be strong grounds for suspecting on Mark's part a hostile attitude towards them. In the tradition the subjects which arise in relation to these three functions concern Jesus' power in miracle (5:31; 6:37, 49; 8:4; 9:18f.), the disciples' own exclusiveness (10:13f.; 9:38f.), their desire for personal honour (9:35-7; 10:37, 42ff.), and their attitude to the Cross (8:32f.; 14:27a, 29-31a, 66-72). Some of these themes reappear in the material from the redaction, especially in relation to the power of Jesus (4:41; 6:2; 8:17-21; 9:6), and in the attitude of the disciples to the cross (8:33(?); 9:32; 10:32).[21] In fact this latter attitude on their part arises as much from Mark's arrangement of the material as from his explicit statement. He sets their failure to understand the cross in relation to Jesus' own statements about it and within the journey which Jesus makes to Jerusalem and the cross. We should note how much of the material in this area (e), (f), (g) refers to the power of Jesus; the disciples cannot be said to fear, be rebuked by Jesus, or be blind only in relation to a failure in respect of the cross.[22] But if the power of Jesus is to be properly understood this can only be done in the light of the weakness of man; if Mark wishes to show Jesus' power he must show the weakness of his disciples. Again, it is perfectly natural that if Mark wishes to explain the true meaning of the cross he should present the disciples as those who misunderstand. It is also worthy of note that where the tradition

[19] Used of Pilate in 15:5, 44 and of Jesus in 6:6.

[20] Used of Jesus in 14:33 and of the women in 16:5, 6.

[21] Verse 17 of ch. 7 is hard to classify but probably respresents a failure on the part of the disciples to understand the cleansing powers of the new religion.

[22] Indeed it can be said that Mark's hardest words (6:52; 8:15-21) refer to the failure of the disciples to realize the might of Jesus and not to the necessity of his or their suffering.

Table 2. *From the redaction*

	Disciples	The Twelve	The Three and the Four	John	Peter
(a)	2:16 7:17 (8:17) 9:28 9:33 10:10 (11:12) 12:43 13:1	—	9:11 13:3	—	10:28 11:21
(b)	4:34 (4:36–41) 7:17 (8:15–21) 9:29 9:31 10:11f. 10:23ff. 12:43	14:17(?)	9:9 13:3 14:33	—	—
(c)	3:7, 9 6:1 6:45 8:10 8:27 9:30 9:33 (10:32) 10:46 (11:1)	9:11(?) 14:17(?)	—	—	—
(d)	10:24, 26 (10:32)	—	—	—	—
(e)	(4:41) 6:45, 50 9:32 (10:32) 16:8 (the women)	—	9:6	—	—
(f)	6:52 7:17 (8:17–21) 9:32 (14:31)	—	(9:6(?)) 14:33	—	(8:32(?))

	Disciples	The Twelve	The Three and the Four	John	Peter
(g)	—	—	—	—	(14:29, 54, 66, 67, 70)
	(8:15–21)	—	14:33	—	14:72
	(8:33)				
	(9:33–7)				
(h)	8:30	—	9:9	—	—
(i)	16:7	—	9:9	—	—
(j)	14:50(?)	—	14:37(?)	—	—
(k)	2:15	14:10(?)	1:29–31	—	—
	3:7, 9	14:20(?)			
	6:1	14:43(?)			
(l)	—	—	—	—	—
(m)	—	—	—	—	—
(n)	—	—	—	—	—
(o)	—	—	—	—	—

showed a rebuke as offered to a particular individual Mark has often in preserving this rebuke widened it so that all the disciples are brought in.[23] If some of the material about the blindness and fear of the disciples comes from Mark then this is easier to accept if Mark is using the behaviour of the disciples in order to draw lessons for his own community than if he is deliberately attacking the original disciples. In the latter case in manufacturing evidence he would be adopting a standard of conduct which would be, and is, universally condemned in political circles, quite apart from being wholly at variance with the way of the cross which he is setting out as the way for Christians. It is true that the conduct of men does not always harmonize with their ideals, yet if such a wide divergence is implied this must be taken into account in assessing probabilities in interpretation.

The instruction not to talk about Jesus to outsiders (h) is entirely Markan. It is part of a wider theme: Jesus tells those whom he heals not to speak (1:44: 5:43; 7:36; 8:26) and commands the demons to keep quiet (1:25, 34; 3:12). The power which those

[23] Cf. the cases of Peter and John; see above.

who are healed experience is real, and the confessions which the demons make are true. In presenting the instructions to silence Mark is therefore making no comment upon the character of those to whom the instruction is given. They could be either good or bad.

The role of the disciples in the post-resurrection period (i) does not come from the tradition. Doubtless they did have a role, but it is by what he himself writes that Mark draws the attention of readers to it. It may also be that 14:28 represents in Mark's eyes the commission of the disciples to go and preach. Whether this is so or not it is clear that Mark sees the original disciples as having a positive role in the post-resurrection period; he would hardly therefore attack their views. We could only accept this if he explicitly showed them as unfaithful in that period.

The failure of the disciples in action (j) belongs to the tradition but is extended by Mark. Such a failure cannot have been other than a frequent experience with Christians in Mark's church, and to learn that the disciples also failed but were restored, as their post-resurrection function implies, would not make his readers think ill of the disciples but rather give them hope for themselves when they had failed.

For Mark the disciples are clearly much more a part of the general framework of the narrative than they were for the tradition (j).

Mark received accounts in the tradition of the way in which the disciples were defended by Jesus from attacks by outsiders (l); he retains these but he does not extend them. He may not have wished to extend the evidence, but even if he did he may not have done so or been able to do so because: (i) he had no material in which he could develop this aspect; (ii) the theme would hardly be relevant to his own community, whose members could not expect to be verbally defended by Jesus; (iii) that Jesus does defend believers though in other ways is expressed in the incidents on the lake and in the Gethsemane account.

Mark received in the tradition those passages which show the disciples mediating between Jesus and the crowds (m); they appear as some kind of 'ministers' or 'officials'. His failure to extend the evidence implies that he does not see them as officials in the sense of a heretical group of leaders and that he does not wish to stress them as 'officials' over against a greater number of laity.[24]

Mark received in the tradition instances where the disciples acted for or on behalf of Jesus or the other disciples (*n*); he does not extend these references.

That Jesus called the disciples is derived entirely from the tradition (*o*); Mark, however, by the position which he gives these calls at the beginning of his gospel and by the way in which he makes them resemble one another (especially ii. 14) shows that he considers them important. Since the disciples have been called by Jesus they are to be highly regarded.

We have examined the tradition prior to Mark, and Mark's redaction of it; we must briefly examine the course of the tradition after Mark. We can see at once that those elements in Mark in which he may be said to speak adversely of the disciples have been toned down by Matthew and Luke. The evidence has been examined many times, both in commentaries and systematically;[25] it is therefore unnecessary to take this up in detail. The disciples continue to appear as companions of Jesus while he travels about, as foils to him so that through them he teaches, they are still amazed at what is said or happens, they are told not to talk,[26] they fail in action,[27] they are attacked by outsiders and defended by Jesus,[28] they act as some kind of 'officials' mediating between Jesus and the people[29] and they act

---

[24] See below for further discussion.

[25] Most recently by Weeden, *op. cit.* pp. 29-32, 35-8, 39 f.

[26] Mark 8:30 has parallels in Matthew 16:20 and Luke 9:21. Mark 9:9 has a parallel in Matt. 17:9; the passage disappears in Luke.

[27] Mark 14:50 has a par. in Matt. 26:56 but none in Luke. Mark 9:18 has par. in Matt. 17:16; Luke. 9:40. Judas remains as betrayer in Matthew and Luke, Peter still denies Jesus, the Gethsemane account still appears.

[28] Mark 2:18 has par. in Matt. 9:14; Luke 5:33. Mark 2:23 f. has par. in Matt. 12:1 f.; Luke 6:1 f. Mark 7:2, 5 has par. in Matt. 15:2 but no par. in Luke. Mark 6:41 has par. in Matt. 14:19; Luke 9:16. Mark 8:6 has a par. in Matt. 15:36 but no par. in Luke. Mark 10:13 has par. in Matt. 19:13; Luke 18:15.

[29] Mark 6:41 has par. in Matt. 14:19; Luke 9:16. Mark 8:6 has a par. in Matt. 15:36 but the passage disappears in Luke. Mark 10:13 has par. in Matt. 19:13 and Luke 18:15.

on behalf of Jesus and the other disciples.[30] On the other hand
there is in Matthew and Luke a certain lessening of the Markan
emphasis on the disciples as recipients of secret instruction and
also less on them as fearful, as failing to understand, and as the
objects of rebuke by Jesus; that is to say, those elements which
are generally recognized as Markan are played down by
Matthew and Luke. They probably do this because their
christology is less 'epiphanic' than Mark's and can therefore be
more easily understood; for that reason they do not need to
stress the wonder and belief and fear of the disciples in the same
way. Thus the altered role of the disciples arises not from a
changed view of the disciples themselves but because the
christology has changed. We can sum up: the elements which
seem to show the disciples in a bad light existed to some extent
in the pre-Markan tradition, appear to reach their peak in Mark
and again decrease thereafter.

IV

We now take up some more general considerations.

If Mark were attacking the disciples or using them as characteristic of a certain group within his own community then we should
expect to see them set over against some other group of which he
approved. The only possible candidate for this position as background 'good' group is the crowd. We therefore turn to an
examination of the role of the crowd[31] in the gospel. Mark always

---

[30] Mark 11:1 has par. in Matt. 21:1; Luke 19:29. Mark 14:13, 14, 16 has
no par. in Matt. or Luke.

[31] On the 'crowd' cf. B. Citron, 'The Multitude in the Synoptic
Gospels', S.J.T. VII (1954), 408–18; A.W. Mosely, 'Jesus' Audiences in
the Gospels of St Mark and St Luke', N.T.S. X (1963–4), 139–49; E.
Trocmé, 'Pour un Jésus public: Les Évangélistes Marc et Jean aux prises
avec l'intimisme de la tradition' in OIKONOMIA (Festschrift für O.
Cullmann; Hamburg-Bergstedt, 1957), pp. 42–50; K. Tagawa, Miracles
et Évangile (Paris, 1966), pp. 57–63; P.S. Minear, 'Audience Criticism
and Markan Ecclesiology' in Neues Testament und Geschichte (Oscar
Cullmann zum 70. Geburtstag; Zürich und Tübingen, 1972), pp. 79–89;
Freyne, op. cit. pp. 115–17.

uses the singular[32] indicating that he thinks of the crowd, ὁ ὄχλος, as a unified sociological entity. As well as actual references to the crowd there are a number of places where we find either an indefinite plural implying people in general[33] or the use of 'many'.

We begin with those passages which come from the tradition:

(a) At times they are a necessary background to the story: 2:4; 7:33; 9:14, 17 (9:15 probably arises redactionally from 9:17); 5:21, 24, 27, 30, 31; 10:46 (this though redactional arises from the later part of the story); 2:18; 3:1, 2, 4; 5:14; 15:8, 35.

(b) The crowd as the group who are taught: 3:32(?); 10:1(?).[34]

(c) The crowd as fed by Jesus: 6:35ff.: 8:1ff.

(d) The rulers fear the crowd: 11:32.

(e) Crowds are attracted to Jesus: 11:8f.

(f) The crowd as hostile to Jesus: 14:43; 15:8, 11, 15 (though possibly some of these could be redactional); 13:9-11 (if the verbs are not to be taken as 'passives').

(g) They bring sick to Jesus to be healed: 2:3 (assuming 'the Four' is the subject).

(h) They have erroneous views of who Jesus is: 6:14f.; 8:28.

If we now examine the passages which come from the redaction we find the following.

(a) 3:9, 20; 9:25; 12:41. 5:21 and possibly 5:24 follow here, but they really depend on 5:27, 30, 31, all of which belong to the story in the tradition.

(b) 2:13; 8:34; 10:1; 2:2; 3:23; 3:32(?)

(c) 6:34.

(d) 12:12; 14:2[35] (though this is possibly from the tradition).

(e) 3:7, 8; 1:45; 6:31, 35 (both 'many'; ὄχλος in 6:34); 6:55.

---

[32] Except 10:1. Matthew and Luke regularly use the plural as well as the singular.

[33] Some of the indefinite plurals represent passives but some seem to be more general; cf. C.H. Turner, *J.T.S.* XXV (1923-4), 377-86; J.C. Doudna, *The Greek of the Gospel of Mark* (JBL Monograph Series XII; Philadelphia, 1961), pp. 5-8, 66-70. The genuine passives appear to be 2:3 (?); 7:32; 8:22; 10:13; 12:13 (if not governed by 12:12); 15:27 (though possibly it is governed by 15:16). Probably 13:9-11, 26 and 14:2 are also to be classed here.

[34] The unusual plural 'crowds' may indicate tradition.

[35] ὁ λαός is used.

(f) –

(g) 1:32; 6:55f.[36] (cf. 6:13).

(h) –

(i) The crowd serves as a background which Jesus leaves in order to be alone with his disciples: 4:36; 6:45; 7:17.

(j) The crowd is the group from whom disciples are chosen: 2:13.

(k) The crowd is the group to whom parables are told: 4:1a, 1b; 7:14; 12:12 (? the presençe of the crowd during the telling of the parable is implied).

(l) The crowd are those who react with wonder or joy to Jesus' teaching: 11:18; 12:37; 1:22, 27; 2:12 (possibly from tradition); 6:2 ('many'); cf. 7:37 of the astonishment at the healing of the deaf mute.[37]

When we examine the respective roles of the disciples and the crowd we find, in comparison with the disciples (including the Twelve and oher groups), that: the crowd never acts as a foil for Jesus; they are not the recipients of private instruction from Jesus; they do not journey with Jesus (the only exceptions are the times when Jesus feeds them in the wilderness); they are not represented as afraid at what Jesus says or does; they are not set out as those who fail to understand what Jesus says, though they must have dones this;[38] they are not told not to disclose information, though individual sick persons who have been healed are told not to talk about their healing; they are not given a position in the post-resurrection period; they are not pictured as failing in action, and this is natural since they are not given particular duties; they are not defended by Jesus from criticism made against them; they do not mediate in some way between Jesus and others; they do not act for or on behalf of Jeus; if they are called by Jesus then they either respond and become disciples or they reject the call. It is not surprising that both the disciples and the crowd are at times amazed by what Jesus says and does, or that there are times when

[36] Turner, art. cit., takes these as passives, but I doubt this. There is always a vague crowd somewhere in the neighbourhood of Jesus except where he is presented as alone with the disciples.

[37] There are also a few places where Mark uses πάντες: 6:41, 42 (c); 1:37 (i); 13:13 (f); 5:40 (i); 5:20 (h).

[38] That the disciples are taught in private implies that there are things which the crowd cannot be expected to understand.

both are present with him as background without particular emphasis. It is true that the disciples are taught whenever the crowd is taught, presumably that they were fed when Jesus fed the crowd, that the disciples have erroneous views of who Jesus is (but they are different erroneous views from those of the crowd), but the crowd never receives private instruction. The crowd however is distinct from the disciples in that it can be hostile to Jesus, brings sick to Jesus to be healed, is the group which Jesus leaves in order to be alone with his disciples,[39] and is the group from which the disciples are called. The very many and contrasting roles, in part at least arising from the differences between the tradition and the redaction, show that the crowd possesses no unitary role in the gospel; had it been given a unitary and postive role then this might possibly have been used to suggest it represented the church for Mark.

In respect then of the disciples and crowd the total impresssion is of two separate groups, and not of one group which is a sub-group of another, i.e. the disciples are not part of the 'crowd' but a separate group, although, originally drawn from the crowd. This suggests that the crowd is the vague amorphous mass of men which is the object of evangelization,[40] from which disciples are chosen, which may be hostile (especially when stirred up by the rulers)[41] but which is often friendly towards Jesus and the disciples. It is in keeping with this that Mark generally refrains from using ὁ λαός of the crowd;[42] this is a 'religious' word[43] and Mark's crowd is not 'religious' but the group from which those who will be religious are called. With particular relevance to our present problem the crowd is never presented as a 'good' group over against which the disciples appear as a hostile group. When the disciples are rebuked the crowd is not praised.

[39] At times they are shaken off by Jesus, 6:46; 4:36.

[40] The father of the epileptic boy does not cry 'I believe', as he would if he were a member of the community, but 'I believe, help my unbelief' (9:24).

[41] D.J. Hawkin, 'The Incomprehension of the Disciples in the Marcan Redaction', *J.B.L.* XCI (1972), 491-500, working from 4:11f., takes the crowd to be representative of Israel in Mark's time. This seems unnecessarily restrictive.

[42] At 7:6 it appears in an OT quotation; at 11:32 it is not the true reading; it appears in general narrative at 14:2 on the lips of the Jewish leaders in respect of their own people.

[43] Freyne, *op. cit.* p. 115.

There is, however, one point at which Mark may attack a disruptive group. It is found in the Little Apocalypse and implies a group within the church as is shown by its interest in the parousia, for this is a Christian interest.[44] Its members may have set themselves up as 'divine men' (13:5f., 22).[45] But those who are criticized here cannot be identical with the disciples, for when we examine the context it is the disciples, in the persons of Peter, Andrew, James and John, who are warned against these opponents, and the introduction of the Four at 13:3 comes from Mark himself. The evidence from ch. 13 does not then support the idea that the disciples represent enemies of Mark's church.[46] Incidentally this warning to the Four also militates against the identification of the disciples as 'divine men'.[47]

If a group were being attacked through the disciples, then we would expect that there would be some easily identifiable centre to their views, whereas if the disciples were being used as examples in order to attack various false views there would be no necessary coherence in the attacks made on them, because the false views would not be held by one group but by different members of Mark's church. If then we examine the views which are attacked in Mark as held by disciples and also the matters on which they are given special instruction we see that these are wide-ranging and without inner coherence; the mystery of the Kingdom, which appears to relate (cf. 4:14ff.) to the retention of a place in the Christian community, the danger of wrong thought, speech and activity (7:17-23), the power of Jesus in his mighty works (6:52; 8:14-21; perhaps we should also include

[44] Cf. Kelber, op. cit. pp. 114-16.
[45] Cf. Weeden, op. cit. pp. 73 ff. Trocmé, op. cit. pp. 120, 209, believes that it is James, the brother of Jesus, and a group associated with him who are attacked.
[46] Ch. 9, vv. 38 f. has been seen as a defence of Paul and an attack on the Jewish leadership of the Church; cf. J. Weiss, Das Älteste Evangelium (Göttingen, 1903), p. 258. John and Paul, however, would be strange opponents. Mark in his editing of the incident makes it apply not just to 'leaders' (i.e. the Twelve) but to the community ('disciples'); it is not then for him an attack on contemporary leaders.
[47] Trocmé, op. cit. pp. 121 ff., using 8:27 – 9:8, sees an attack in Mark on those who defend a christological orthodoxy and spend their time in vain contemplation.

4:38; 6:50), the meaning of the cross (8:31-3; 9:32) and the resurrection (9:10), exorcism (9:28f.), discipleship as seen in the light of the cross, and in particular the need for service and humility in discipleship (9:33 ff.; 10:41 ff.), marriage without divorce (10:10-12),[48] the dangers of possessions (10:17-27), the nature of true fellowship (10:28-30). This runs across such a wide spectrum that it is difficult to see what one group could have been involved in all these points. In particular if it is supposed that the disciples are attacked as 'divine men' then some of these do not fit easily into the 'divine man' concept, e.g. the references to marriage, wealth and cutting off one's hand, and the temptations implied in 4:14-20.[49] Rather the views attacked are false. Though in the gospel the disciples either hold them or require special instruction against holding them, it is the views and not ultimately the disciples who are being attacked.

A clear distinction does exist between the place of the disciples in the gospel and that of the scribes, rulers and Pharisees.[50] Apart from Judas none of the disciples seeks the death of Jesus; in varying degrees the scribes, rulers and Pharisees do (3:6; 10:33 f.; 11:18; and all through the Passion account). A failure to understand the death of Jesus is much less serious than the attempt to bring it about. These Jewish opponents wish the law to be preserved and observed (2:15-17; 2:23 – 3:6; 7:1-23)[51] They do not merely fail to understand Jesus' miracles, they refuse to acknowledge his power to work them and desire him to repeat them before their eyes to prove himself (8:11-13; 9:14; cf. 6:1-6); they criticize him for forgiving sins (2: 6 f.), regard him as possessed by demons (3:22-7) and doubt his authority and ability (10:2-9; 11:27-33). The disciples are warned against them (8:11-13). It is against the background of these dark shadows

[48] The attack is not on sexual immorality as such, which is what we would expect if the opponents were proto-gnostics, antinomians or 'enthusiasts'. Instead what we have is a church rule or a statement of church practice in relation to divorce.

[49] Weeden, Z.N.W. LIX (1968), 149f. omits some of these; in this way he is able to obtain a consistent picture.

[50] On the role and opposition of these groups see Trocmé, op. cit. pp. 92ff.

[51] These passages could be directed against Judaizing Christians (cf. Trocmé, op. cit. pp. 113-15); if so Mark views them as outside the Church.

that the role of the disciples must be judged and, when we do this, they appear in a brighter light.

The total structure of the second half of the gospel supports a positive evaluation of the role of the disciples. Jesus and the disciples move together to Jerusalem; they are fearful as they learn of the cross but Jesus still continues to lead and teach them. They forsake him when when he is arrested, but their desertion is seen to be part of God's plan (14:27);[52] it is then that their failure is described as 'scandal', i.e. a rejection of Christ; but it is also at this moment that they are given hope, for 14:28 is the promise of restoration, of new beginning,[53] which is reinforced by 16:7. To a lesser degree we find the same phenomenon in 14:32-42. Here Mark has edited the tradition so that alongside the pericope's original stress on Jesus' attitude to the cross there has been added considerable emphasis on the failure of the disciples,[54] but at the same time he has inserted v.38 which shows disciples how through watchfulness and prayer they may avoid failure.[55]

What now of the relation of teachers and pupils in the ancient world? Then as now a teacher was held responsible for the behaviour of his pupils;[56] Socrates was charged with corrupting the youth of Athens. If then Mark attacked the disciples of Jesus he ran the risk of being thought to attack Jesus. Possibly he could be excused this on the ground that he argues that the

[52] The attempt to discover the relative sections of tradition and redaction in 14:27-72 is fraught with great difficulty and no clear agreement has emerged: cf. Linnemann, op. cit..; G. Schneider, Die Passion Jesu nach den drei älteren Evangelien(München, 1972); L. Schenke, Studien zur Passionsgeschchte des Markus (Würzburg, 1971); W. Schenk, Der Passionsbericht nach Markus (Gütersloh 1974); J.R. Donahue, Are You the Christ? The Trial Narrative in the Gospel of Mark (SBL Dissertation Series 10, Missoula, 1973). We assume that the denial of Peter and the flight of the disciples was not created by Mark but belonged to the tradition, though Mark has drawn more attention to them and offered some kind of theological evaluation of them.
[53] Schenke, op. cit. pp. 433-5.
[54] Mark may well have created the threefold scheme of Jesus' departure, prayer and return to find the disciples sleeping.
[55] 14:38b may even serve as an excuse for the disciples – they are only human.
[56] D. Daube, 'The Responsibilities of Master and Disciples in the Gospels', N.T.S. XIX (1972/3), 1-15.

disciples misunderstood Jesus; but there must have been some group in his own lifetime which did understand him, otherwise his true teaching would never have reached Mark. We should then expect a group of understanding disciples to be depicted so that it could be seen that Mark had the true tradition from the teacher, but their is no such group. Moreover Jesus defends his disciples (2: 15-17, 23-8; 7:1 ff.) from attack from outside. This was part of his duty as teacher[57] and it implies that he approved of them. That he approved would have been the conclusion drawn in the ancient world.

In the educational system of the Greco-Roman world, when pupils were instructed in the classics one of the objects of that instruction was the derivation of moral lessons from the characters depicted.[58] It might seem that this has provided the example for Mark, who then has used the disciples as material for deductions intended to benefit his own congregation, but the situations of a school and of an early Christian community are quite different; we would not necessarily expect that what holds for one would be true of the other. Further, while the teacher drew moral lessons from the literature he was using, Mark's basic purpose is not to draw moral lessons but lessons about God – the weakness of the disciples shows the strength of Christ, their self-importance is contrasted with his humility. Finally, while the ancient educator used the people about whom he taught to instruct his students in morality he did not intend to attack the characters he used from history and literature. If he wished to draw out bad characteristics and warn his students against them then he used acknowledged villains or enemies of his nation.[59] The disciples were not such acknowledged villains or enemies of the church.

A closer parallel in the secular world would be the lives of

---

[57] *Ibid.*

[58] Cf. Weeden, *op. cit.* pp. 12ff.; H.I. Marrou, *The History of Education in Antiquity* (ET London, 1956), pp. 160–70, 277–81; P.G. Walsh, *Livy: His Historical Means and Methods* (Cambridge, 1961), pp. 20ff., 82ff.

[59] Thus for an example of the love of luxury which he deplores Livy uses an enemy of the Romans, Hannibal (cf. Walsh, *op. cit.* pp. 77f.); Livy is not actually attacking the character of Hannibal but using him because his readers will automatically class him as bad, as one from whom a moral lesson of what to avoid can be drawn.

famous teachers with the way their followers functioned in the reports about them.[60] Most intersting is Apollonius of Tyana. At one moment Damis, his disciple, appears to understand his master and at another appears totally uncomprehending.

> Throughout the *vita*, Damis functions like Peter in Mark's Gospel, the first and most cherished of the disciples who nevertheless consistently misunderstands. Like Peter, the last scene we have of Damis is a betrayal (7:15) – and, like Peter, we have only the tradition that later reflection led to his final understanding.[61]

We find the same lack of understanding on the part of those who are recipients of revelation in the Hermetic literature.[62]

It was also a characteristic of the contemporary Jewish scene that characters from the Old Testament were used to teach religious and moral lessons; this is apparent even within the New Testament in Hebrews 11 and in the examples of Abraham, Rahab, Job and Elijah in James 2:21-6; 5:11, 16-18; Rahab is even termed a harlot. The Old Testament itself was not slow to draw lessons about God from the failure of its principal heroes. David's sin against Bathsheba and Uriah is not glossed over but is emphasized to demonstrate the forgiving mercy of God. Thus those who are on the whole to be reverenced may have their weaknesses used to teach lessons about God.

All this means that we cannot argue that in his use of the disciples Mark is attacking some group within or outside his own community and seeking to warn his readers against that group and its views, and of course this implies that he was not attacking the historical disciples.

V

If then the disciples have not been cast in the role of a heretical

---

[60] Cf. J.Z. Smith, 'Good News is No News! Aretalogy and Gospel', in *Christianity, Judaism and Other Greco-Roman Cults* (Studies for Morton Smith at Sixty; ed. J. Neusner; Leiden, 1975), part 1, pp. 21-38.

[61] *Ibid.* p. 27. We may note other similarities with the disciples in Mark: Damis' amazement (1:19), his failure to understand (1:23 f.; 7:37), his stupidity (2:22), his fear (6:25, 7:31); in 7:26 he is reprimanded by Apollonius.

[62] Cf. C.H. Dodd, *Historical Tradition in the Fourth Gospel* (Cambridge, 1963), pp. 319-21.

group it may be that they are to be understood as representative of the ministry of the church. The historical disciples would be the precursors of the ministers and their behaviour would provide the clue for the behaviour of ministers within Mark's own community. The strongest evidence for this view comes from the feedings with their eucharistic symbolism, from the call of the Twelve and the way they are set out (3:14f.; 6:6b-13, 30) and from the secret instruction which is given to the disciples at many points in the gospel.

We should note, first, that while the third area of evidence, secret instruction, seems largely due to Mark, the other two areas of evidence lay in the tradition and have not been much extended by Mark. If the feedings are taken as eucharistic then the disciples could be considered to represent the celebrants and the crowd the remainder of the church. It is not, however, clear if Mark attributes eucharistic symbolism to the feedings.[63] Whatever the earlier tradition may have held about them it is more probable that Mark thinks of Jesus as feeding men with his teaching; thus the disciples appear as teachers, but not necessarily of the church; they could be teachers of those outside. This would harmonize with the way in which the Twelve are sent out as 'missionaries'; in so far as they are given a commission and sent to carry out their commission they are presented in these passages as 'ministers' to the unevangelized rather than to the Christian community itself.[64] It is unlikely that the call of the two sets of brothers in 1:16-20 is intended by Mark to represent a call to the ministry, for in 2:14 where Levi is called his call is expressed in terms very similar to those of the sets of brothers, and Levi was not one of the Twelve. Moreover the brothers are commissioned to be fishers of men, which fits in with the idea that they are sent to the world outside rather than to the church itself.

[63] See Best, *The Temptation and the Passion* (SNTS Monograph Series 2; Cambridge, 1965), pp. 76-8; P.J. Achtemeier, 'The Origin and Function of the Pre-Marcan Catenae', *J.B.L.* XCI (1972), 198-221, argues that Mark de-emphasizes the existing Eucharistic elements in the Feeding Stories in order to present a less 'divine man' view of Jesus.
[64] See 'Mark's Use of the Twelve' (n. 3 above). Trocmé, pp. 197 f., also speaks of the missionary work of the disciples in this connection, though he assumes that the feeding miracles represent eucharists.

The parable of the doorkeeper in 13:33 ff. might appear at first sight to be instruction to ministers in that they are to guard the community within and watch for the coming of the Lord to it. Whatever meaning the parable possessed in the tradition we should note that Mark's addition[65] of v.37, 'And what I say to you I say to all: Watch', shows that he intends this to be addressed to all his readers and not merely the four who were present during the discourse of ch. 13. To each church member has been given a responsibility. Thus the reference to the doorkeeper is generalized and we should not think of it in Mark as restricted to officials.

While some of the secret instruction which is given to the disciples might suggest that they were a special group within the larger group of the community this is not the most obvious solution, and clearly portions of the secret instruction can only have been intended for the community as a whole: the warnings against failure in receiving the word (4:14-20), the need for faith in time of storm and stress (4:35-41; cf. 6:45-52), the explanation of the saying about what goes out of a man as defiling him (7:17-23), the rejection of divorce (10:10-12), the warning about the dangers of wealth (10:23-31). All the instruction about the necessity of the cross for Jesus and about the nature of discipleship in the great central section of 8:27-10:45 is most naturally understood as instruction for the church and not for some sub-group of ministers within it.

On the other hand, when we examine the teaching given to the crowd we see that it is not inappropriate for those outside the community: they are told parables but not given their interpretation (4:1-9; 7:14 f.); they are invited to become disciples (8:34) and instructed only about the essential nature of discipleship (3:32, 35); they are taught about the forgiveness of sin (2:4-11);[66] they are given the basic biblical reasoning about divorce (10:1-9) but not given the rule which governs church members in respect of it (10:10-12); they are told the identity of Jesus (12:35-7) in a

[65] Cf. R. Pesch, *Naherwartungen: Tradition und Redaktion in Mk. 13* (Düsseldorf, 1968), p. 202; J. Lambrecht, *Die Redaktion der Markus-Apokalypse* (Analecta Biblica 28; Rome, 1967), p. 248; A. Weiser, *Die Knechtsgleichnisse der synoptischen Evangelien* (München, 1971), p. 144.
[66] Often what the crowd is taught is left unspecified, e.g. 2:13.

veiled form, but the disciples alone are given it in full and true form (9:7). Then again, as we have already seen, the crowd is sometimes hostile to Jesus,[67] and it is from the crowd the disciples, not just the Twelve, are called (2:13f.;cf.10:17-22). The sick appear to come from the crowds (3:10-12; 5:21-34; 9:14-29) and it is to the sick that the Twelve are sent as 'missionaries', i.e. to those outside the church.

If the disciples were being sent to be ministers of the church then we should expect that another group would be clearly portrayed as the church. Our examination of the use of the crowd by Mark does not support such a conclusion,[68] and there is no other possible group.

Perhaps, however, Mark thinks of the Twelve as ministers whereas he thinks of the disciples as the church. On the whole Mark does not distinguish between the Twelve and the disciples except in the case of the commissioning of the Twelve, and this he has drawn from the tradition. In Mark the Twelve are normally absorbed into the disciples rather than remaining a sub-group of the disciples.[69] Disciples are not restricted to the

[67] It must be allowed that the references to the hostility of the crowd probably arise from the tradition and not from Mark.
[68] Minear, art. cit., believes that the crowd represents the church. It is unnecessary to examine his arguments in detail; we need only look at two passages (3:32; 4:10) on which he lays considerable weight. In 3:32 the crowd is in the house with Jesus; at 3:34 he points to them and says, 'Here are my mother and brothers!', thus apparently identifying the crowds with the Christian community. But in 3:32 the use of ὄχλος is redactional and 3:35, and not 3:34, is the operative conclusion for Mark, whatever may have been the earlier conclusion in the tradition; 3:35 is put conditionally and states the nature of discipleship; its purpose is not to identify who are Christians but to say how Christians should live. In 4:10 Minear takes οἱ περὶ αὐτόν to be the crowd mentioned in 4:1 and the Twelve to be the disciples; but the disciples are not limited to the Twelve for Mark and because of the change of audience implied between 4:1 and 4:10 it is easier to identify the total group of 4:10 with the disciples of 4:34, a Markan verse. Thus the crowd are οἱ ἔξω.
[69] Verses 35-7 of ch. 9 might appear to indicate a power struggle between the members of the Twelve, i.e. the ministry. But we note that by writing vv. 33, 34 Mark has widened the audience so that it is the disciples as a whole, i.e. he has the church and not just its leaders in mind. Observation of groups shows that there is no need to restrict feelings of self-importance and jealousy to appointed leaders.

number of the Twelve. What is said of the Twelve, with the exception of their missionary activity, is said of the disciples, and vice versa. Various ministerial functions, preaching, teaching, healing, are recognized as existing and being exercised by disciples, but Mark does not appear to have any interest in a group of 'ministers' who exercise these functions within the community.[70] The only group he could be said to be interested in is the group which succeeds the Twelve as 'missionaries' to the world outside the church.

We cannot then say that the disciples represent the 'ministers' within the community. But we must recognize that Mark may not use the disciples in a unitary way. While they may generally represent the community as a whole there may be times when as the Twelve they represent missionaries to the world.

VI

It is now time to draw together the threads of this discussion. Mark is not attacking the reputation of the historical disciples. He is not using the disciples as representatives of a group of heretics of his own time, either inside or outside his own community. With the one exception of their role as 'missionaries' he is not interested in disciples as 'ministers'. Generally speaking the disciples comprise the whole community.

In so far as the disciples appear in a bad light it is because Mark wishes to use them as a foil: their failure to understand is sometimes introduced in order to allow Jesus to give further and fuller instruction;[71] their fearfulness is brought out in order that Jesus may show them the sources of calm and courage; their desire for positions of importance is stressed in order that Jesus may teach them about the meaning of service. Any apparent

[70] J. Delorme, 'L'Évangile selon Marc' in Le Ministère et les Ministères selon le Nouveau Testament (ed. Delorme: Paris, 1973), pp. 155–81, says that Mark has no real interest in setting out a 'ministry', though some of the duties of officials, e.g. preaching, teaching, healing, exorcism, are mentioned.

[71] Fuller instruction is not always given; the disciples are rebuked about their blindness in respect of the feeding miracles (8:14–21) but the meaning of the two miracles is not clearly supplied; cf. W. Nützel, Die Verklärungserzählung im Markusevangelium (Würzburg, 1973), p. 200. It may be that Mark thought that in this case the meaning was sufficiently apparent and did not need driving home, unlike that of the cross.

attack on them normally ends, not in the negative side of their failure, but in positive teaching on the part of Jesus which will assist Mark's community. As we have seen, it is not unusual to find characters in literature, especially in the Old Testament, being used in this way.

But was Mark not wrong to blacken the character of the disciples like this? Some of their misunderstanding and self-seeking lay in the prior tradition. He does not then create their failure but emphasizes it, and does so with the intention of helping his own community. He is not primarily interested in their character; it has often been noted how rarely he psychologizes them; there is no direct attack on their motives; rather he is concerned above all in the Christian viability of his own community. The failure of the disciples shows God's love and strength. This can be a source of great comfort to his readers. As Christians down the centuries have failed in action and understanding and in turn been consoled by stories of the failures of the disciples, since they knew that in the end the disciples had triumphed, so must Mark's fellow believers; if they had not, the church would have been strangled at birth.

On the whole so far we have contested other views, but there are within Mark positive indications that he did not intend the disciples to be devalued, and that he views them as the church. The place where the disciples are most regularly given their private instruction is the 'house', and references to the 'house' are almost always redactional. The early church thought of the house as a suitable place for a church to meet. When the disciples are instructed in the house Mark's community will think of themselves as being instructed in their own house-churches[72] and instructed by the gospel itself. Verses 13-19 of ch. 3 represent Mark's acknowledgment of the commission given to the historical apostles; had he wished he could have omitted this and so have suggested more easily that the disciples were interlopers and their views erroneous. When the Twelve return to Jesus after they have been sent by him to preach and heal they tell him of their success and he bids them come apart with him for rest; this surely implies his approval of their missionary activity. After the transfiguration Jesus instructs them to tell no

[72] Cf. Trocmé, *op cit.* pp. 162 f.

one what they saw until the Son of Man has risen from the dead; the fact that the transfiguration story is known implies that they fulfilled this commission and were faithful in it. The instruction to the women at the empty tomb to tell Peter and the disciples (16:7 is a Markan verse), though it does not recount the actual restoration of Peter and the disciples, surely implies it. Mark regularly fails to tell his readers the sequel of events which he recounts; the fulfilment of the promise that Jesus would baptize with the Holy Spirit is never recounted because the readers know it happened; that Jesus successfully overcame Satan in the temptations is not narrated but can be deduced from what follows. The Christians of Mark's own day knew that the disciples had begun to tell the story of Jesus and so they were aware that their failure in the pre-crucifixion period was overcome and was not to be held against them.[73] The threat to the disciples that they would be scattered at the time of the Passion is followed by the promise that Jesus will go before them to Galilee; this implies acceptance of the disciples, and Mark's readers must have realized this. In Gethsemane the rebuke to Peter is in the singular but is immediately widened into the plural, 'Watch and pray that you (pl.) may not enter into temptation'; Mark is using Peter with James and John as examples for his own community. That this is his general approach appears most significantly at the end of the last section of systematic instruction given to the disciples (13:37) 'What I say to you I say to all'. Jesus' teaching as Mark views it was not primarily intended for the few, Peter, James, Andrew and John who were sitting or standing around Jesus, but was intended for all who would be his followers; the role of the disciples in the gospel is then to be examples to the community. Not examples by which their own worth or failure is shown, but examples through whom teaching is given to the community and the love and power of God made known.[74]

[73] Even if it is held that Mark believed that the women did not tell the disciples (16:8) then this would provide the disciples with an adequate excuse for failure and Mark would be inconsistent in attacking them.

[74] Since this lecture was prepared I have read H. Räisänen, *Das 'Messiasgeheimnis' im Markusevangelium* (Helsinki, 1976), and am happy to see that from an entirely different approach he has come to a somewhat similar view (see pp. 119ff.) to that propounded above.

Chapter 8

Mark's Use of the Twelve

Bultmann[1] may not have been the first to suggest that most of the references to the twelve in Mark come from Mark himself, but his assertion that they are redactional has been very influential and a reference to the twelve in a verse or clause has often been taken as an indication that Mark has been at work at that point. This acceptance of the twelve as redactional was probably an over-reaction to attempts to find a twelve source in Mark.[2] All hypotheses need to be re-examined from time to time and we propose to undertake this now in respect of the hypothesis that Mark is responsible for most of the references to the twelve in his Gospel. We are not however interested in determining their place in the community prior to Mark and certainly not in inquiring whether they had a pre-Easter position.

It may immediately be objected to the suggestion of any re-examination that Mark names the twelve more often than do the other evangelists (Mt. 9; Mk 10;[3] Lk 8; Joh 4; Act 1; 1 Cor 1; Rev 1). This of itself does not prove Mark was especially interested in them; it could equally indicate that the high point of

---

[1] *Die Geschichte der synoptischen Tradition*, Göttingen[3] 1957, 369f. This view has almost become a part of orthodox redaction theory; cf. T.J. Weeden, *Mark: Traditions in Conflict*, Philadelphia, N.J. 1971: 'It is hardly necessary in the present stage of Markan reserach to state that Mark has a particular interest in the twelve' (23).

[2] E. Meyer, *Ursprung und Anfänge des Christentums*, Berlin 1921, I, 135-147. W.L. Knox, *The Sources of the Synoptic Gospels,* Vol. I, Cambridge 1953, 17-31. Meyer's view is criticised by C.H. Turner, *JThS* 28, 1927, 22-30.

[3] Or 11 if the word is read at 3:16.

interest lay prior to Mark and that beginning with Mark successive evangelists gradually cut down the number of references. The figures themselves are not quite accurate. We should also add in the references to the eleven and the ten. When we do so the figures for the Gospels are 11-11[4]-10- 4. But since we are concerned not only with the terms but also with the concept and since in the Gospels[5] the twelve and the apostles are the same group[6] if we add in the references to the apostles the figures become 11-12[7]-15-4.[8] If, indeed, the disciples and the twelve are identified in Matthew's eyes[9] then the interest shown by Mark in the twelve is not so exceptional; it is only his use of the term which is.

In the light of the fact that it is impossible to argue that Mark created the concept of the twelve since it appears in 1 Cor 15:5 as a recognised grouping and since it was also a part of the double tradition as Mt 19:28 Lk 22:30 show[10] and so was present in the Jesus tradition apart from Mark there are a number of obvious questions:

(i)   Where was the term present in the tradition used by Mark?
(ii)   Where did he introduce the term and why did he do so?
(iii)   Is there any evidence that he omitted the term where it was already present in the tradition?
(iv)   Did he introduce any other term at those places where we

---

[4] Or 12 if 'twelve' is read at 3:16.
[5] This may not necesarily be true of the tradition contained in 1 Cor. 15:5,7; cf. G. Schmahl, *Die Zwölf im Markusevangelium*, TThS 30, Trier 1974, 20ff.
[6] In respect of Luke see G. Lohfink, *Die Sammlung Israels*, München 1975, 63ff.
[7] Or 14 if 'twelve' is read at 3:16 and 'apostles' at 3:14.
[8] Because Schmahl, op.cit. fails to do this his table on p. 16 is misleading.
[9] Cf. G. Strecker, *Der Weg der Gerechtigkeit*, FRLANT 82, Göttingen 1966, 191ff.; S. van Tilberg, *The Jewish Leaders in Matthew*, Leiden 1972, 112; Schmahl, op.cit., 17; contrast R. Schnackenburg, »Ihr seid das Salz der Erde, das Licht der Welt«, in *Schriften zum Neuen Testament*, München 1971, 177-200.
[10] Whatever original form underlies these two passages that form will have pre-dated Mark and contained an actual or implicit reference to the twelve.

might have expected him to introduce the twelve if it was his favourite term?

We begin with the last of these questions. There are three terms which may be used for the associates of Jesus: the disciples, the twelve, the apostles. Of these the last appears only once (6:30),[11] and the twelve is found ten or eleven[12] times at 3:14(16?); 4:10; 6:7; 9:35; 10:32; 11:11; 14:10,17,20,43.[13] The first, the disciples, is by far the most frequent and is used forty-two times of the associates of Jesus.[14] We have then, not only to examine the occurrences of 'the twelve' to see if they come from Markan redaction, but we also need to look at his use of 'the disciples,' which on the face of it is the Markan favourite,[15] and ask whether that use is traditional, redactional or a mixture of both. Only after we have done this can our examination of the use of the twelve have meaning.

There are some clear instances where 'disciples' came to Mark as a term in the tradition, viz: 2:15,16 (though one of these may be redactional and dependent on the other),18,23; 5:31; 6:41; 7:2,5; 8:4,6; 8:27b; 10:13; 11:14; 14:13,14,16 (though if this incident is in whole or in part a Markan construction none or only one of vv.13,14,16 may be traditional),32. There are also clear instances where the use of 'disciples' is redactional, but could be held to depend on an existing use of the word in the tradition 7:17 (cf. 7:2,5); 8:1,10 (cf. 8:4,6); 8:27a (cf. 8:27b); 9:14 (cf. 9:18); 10:10,24 (if 10:23 is pre-Markan); 14:12 (cf. 14:14,16). But in almost all these cases Mark could have used the twelve (the nine at 9:14; cf. the use of the ten at 10:41). There are also a considerable number of places where Mark uses 'disciples' in redactional passages where its use does not depend on a pre-Markan usage in the surrounding context: 3:7; 4:34; 6:1;

---

[11] See the discussion of 3:14 below.

[12] 10 times if it is not read at 3:16.

[13] See also 6:43; 8:19; 10:41.

[14] It is used four times of the disciples of John and the Pharisees.

[15] A word which appears more regularly in Mark than in any of the other Gospels is not necessarily a Markan favourite unless it can be shown that its use derives largely from him and not from the tradition.

8:33,34; 9:28,31; 10:24,46; 11:14; 12:43; 13:1;16:7. Probably 3:9; 6:35,45; 10:23 should also be classified under this heading. The text at 14:4 is uncertain. In each of these cases Mark was free to use the twelve or the apostles, but has chosen to use 'the disciples'. In particular we should note that Mark introduced the disciples into the crucial section 8:27–9:1.

I

We now turn to Mark's use of the twelve.[16]

(I) 3:14; 6:7. In 3:13–19 Mark has drawn from the tradition the list of the names of the twelve though he has probably added the 'nicknames' as the grammatical difficulties suggest. The precise reference, ἐποίησεν δώδεκα,[17] could be Markan or it could have originally headed the list of names in the pre-Markan tradition.[18] If the latter then Mark has moved its position to an earlier point in the pericope (v. 14), perhaps introduced vv.14b,15 and then may also have retained it in its original position at the head of the list. Whether he did the latter or not depends on the reading in v. 16, into which we do not need to enter. In any case the reference is pre-Markan. If the clause did not precede the list of names it is a natural deduction from it in

[16] That a reference to the twelve is found within a redactional passage does not prove that the reference itself is redactional as is apparently suggested by B. Rigaux, 'Die "Zwölf" in Geschichte und Kerygma' in *Der historische Jesus und der Kerygmatische Christus* (ed H. Ristow and K. Matthiae), Berlin 1960, 468–486; Rigaux, of course regards the twelve as a pre-Markan group.

[17] δώδεκα lacks the article only here in the Gospel. Here 'twelve' are appointed; thereafter they are 'the twelve'. This has no bearing on the question whether the twelve derive from the redaction or the tradition. They were in any case a known group and the article would be used with them as in 1 Cor 15:5. In 3:13–19 the number which is chosen is given and so the article would be inappropriate.

[18] G. Schmahl, 'Die Berufung der Zwölf im Markusevangelium'. *TThZ* 81, 1972, 203–213, argues for the introduction which is found in Mt 10:2, but this lacks a reference to the activity of Jesus and is therefore more biographically oriented in respect of the twelve. In his book, pp. 49ff., he allows that the Markan phrase is derived from the tradition.

view of the known existence of the twelve as a group.[19] The
commission of vv. 14f. probably did not previously go with the
list of the twelve; its difficult grammar suggests that its basis was
pre-Markan.[20] In the tradition it must have been associated with
some group; there are three possibilities: the twelve, the
apostles, a vague reference to disciples; there is no reason to
suppose that it was originally attached to the list of the three
(Peter, James, John). If in the tradition the commission of
vv. 14f. was connected to the list of the twelve, the reference to
the twelve is pre-Markan, but if it did not and Mark united the
commission with the list the problem remains. It might appear
at first sight that since the reference in the text of v. 14 to the
apostles is uncertain we should neglect this possibility, but the
appearance of the reference to the apostles in some texts of v. 14,
while it probably arose through harmonisation with Lk 6:13,[21]
could possibly be due to some scribe's memory of an earlier
connection in the tradition of the commission with the apostles
which the scribe then re-inserted. The sole clear reference in
Mark to the apostles is 6:30 and its context (6:6b-13) makes it
clear that for Mark the apostles are the same group as the twelve.
If, therefore, the tradition connected the commission with the
apostles it is not surprising to find it attached to the twelve by
Mark. If we reject an original reference to the apostles in v. 14 we
are still left with the question whether Mark took a commission
with a vague reference in the tradition ('the disciples') and
applied it concretely to the twelve. On the whole it would have

[19] The textual evidence for its inclusion ($\aleph$ B C* Δ 565) is by no means
weak but it could have arisen through dittography from v. 14 or from
the need for some clause to pick up the stream of thought after the
commission of vv. 14f. or from the memory that it preceded the list of
the twelve in the tradition.

[20] ἔχειν ἐξουσίαν breaks the easy association of κηρύσσειν and ἐκ-
βάλλειν and in view of Mark's interest in demonic exorcism is
probably due to his redaction. It is much easier to assume that Mark
inserted it clumsily than, as has sometime been maintained, that he
wrote vv. 14b, 15 clumsily (e.g. W. Burgers, 'De instelling van de
twaalf in het evangelie van Marcus', *EThL* 36, 1960, 605-654), for he
managed to express himself clearly at 6:7.

[21] Cf. Taylor, *Mark* ad loc., W. Schmithals, *Das kirchliche Apostelamt*,
FRLANT 79, Göttingen 1961, 62, etc. It has perhaps been inserted to
create an 'office' after ἐποίησεν.

been quite possible for οὓς ἤθελεν αὐτός [22] to have been followed in the tradition by the ἵνα clause giving the commission.[23] When Mark combines elements of the tradition he tends to combine their introductions;[24] hence probably the somewhat roundabout form of vv.13, 14a. This creates the strong possibility that the pre-Markan tradition of the list already contained an explicit reference to the twelve. Mark may then have deliberately attached the commission to the twelve if it was not referred to them in the tradition, and this would also be true if he deduced the reference to the twelve from the list. He would then be deliberately presenting the twelve as 'missionaries'. We conclude that Mark is not responsible for the appearance of the twelve in chapter 3, a conclusion which is reinforced if the reading in v.16 which refers to them is original, though he may be responsible for emphasising their role as missionaries.

In 6:7 the reference to the twelve is introduced by the same verb προσκαλεῖσθαι as in 3:13; and it is again used differently from Mark's normal usage.[25] On the other hand most of v.7 appears to be Markan: the use of ἄρχεσθαι as an auxiliary verb, and of ἐξουσία in relation to exorcism, and the choice of 'unclean spirits'[26] rather than demons. It is probable, therefore, that Mark composed v.7 using material from 3:13-15 and he may then himself have introduced the reference to the twelve at

---

[22] We take v.13, up to and including this phrase, to be from the tradition; προσκαλεῖσθαι is used in a non-Markan way; the mountain (the article is used) is introduced as if already known; see Reploh, *Markus, Lehrer der Gemeinde,* Stuttgart 1969, 43f. W. Schmithals, 'Der Markusschluß, die Verklärungsgeschichte und die Aussendung der Zwölf', *ZThK* 69, 1972, 377-411, uses the reference to the mountain as an indication that the call of the twelve originally formed part of the tradition of the resurrection appearances of Jesus.

[23] προσκαλεῖται οὓς ἤθελεν αὐτός implies some kind of choice and ought to be followed by either an identification of those chosen (this comes in vv.16-19) or a statement of the purpose for which they are chosen (ἵνα ὦσιν κτλ.). The two brief clauses, καὶ ἀπῆλθον πρὸς αὐτόν and καὶ ἐποίησεν δώδεκα, linked paratactically to what precedes and follows, suggest Mark's hand.

[24] Cf. 4:10; 9:35; 10:32 as discussed below.

[25] See n. 22 above.

[26] Mark alone of the evangelists (2-10-6-0) uses this redactionally (1:27; 3:11,30) though it does also occur in the tradition (1:23,26; 5:8).

this point but vv.8–11 must have had some introduction. They may have originally been united with 3:13-15 and the tradition have contained a reference to the twelve; if so when Mark split them he retained the reference; if it did not, he introduced it. If they were not united with 3:13-15 in the tradition they will have been addressed to the twelve or to the disciples; in the latter case Mark changed the address to the twelve. In either case the use of the twelve at 6:7 is redactional, but it almost certainly depends on its prior use in 3:13-15.[27] 6:30 is generally taken to be Markan; if so, he has introduced the term 'apostles' in relation to the twelve. The use of this term in the N.T. is complex but in its present context where the cognate verb is used in 3:14 and 6:7 it needs to be viewed in the light of the verb[28] rather than of the developed theological ideas of other parts of the N.T. It emphasises the concept of the twelve as those who are 'sent'.

(II) In 4:10 there are four possibilities:[29] (1) Mark created the whole phrase οἱ περὶ αὐτὸν σὺν τοῖς δώδεκα; (2) he found οἱ περὶ αὐτόν in the tradition and added σὺν τοῖς δώδεκα;[30] (3) he found a reference to the twelve and added οἱ περὶ αὐτόν adapting the existing reference to its present form; (4) he found both οἱ περὶ αὐτόν and the reference to the twelve in different strands of the tradition and himself produced the combined expression. We assume that both the parable (vv.3-8) and its interpretation (vv.14-20) were united in the pre-Markan tradition and that the logion of vv.11f. was also existing tradition

---

[27] If this argument is correct, the connection of the twelve with missionary activity pre-dates Mark. This does not necessarily conflict with Schmithals' view (op.cit., 57f.) that they were not originally missionaries but makes it more difficult. That they had a role as witnesses of the resurrection (ibid., 60) does not exclude a missionary role.

[28] Cf. Schmahl, op.cit., 78f.

[29] The reading οἱ μαθηταὶ αὐτοῦ (D W Θ Φ it sy^s) arose out of the inherent difficulty of Mark and under the influence of the Matthean and Lukan parallels.

[30] So A. Schulz, *Nachfolgen und Nachahmen,* München 1962, 51f.; Schmahl, op.cit., 82-87; J.M. Nützel, *Die Verklärungserzählung im Markusevangelium,* Bamberg 1973, 106f., attempts to argue that the use of σύν here is Markan but the amount of supporting evidence is too sparse to permit such a conclusion.

which Mark introduced here[31] Whether Mark also introduced
v.9 and how much of v.13 he wrote or modified do not concern
us.

It is unlikely that the first of these four possibilities is correct
since the total phrase is so clumsy; we shall not therefore
consider it further. If however Mark did compose it it is clear
that he did not wish the private instruction which is given at this
point to be confined to the twelve.

In the pre-Markan *Vorlage* there must have been some
connecting clause between the parable and its interpretation; it is
probable that this is still to be found in v.10. In v.10 the plural
τὰς παραβολάς does not fit the single parable of vv.3-8 and
we assume Mark modified it from a singular in view of the
logion he was introducing in vv.11f. and his attempt to offer a
general theory about the purpose of parables, although if there
was a pre-Markan collection of parables the plural may have
been used in it. κατὰ μόνας is not found elsewhere in Mark; in

[31] For analysis of Mark 4:1-34 see e.g. J. Jeremias, *The Parables of Jesus*
(E.T.) London, 1963, 13-18, 77-79, 149-51; W. Marxsen, 'Redaktions-
geschichtliche Erklärung der sogenannten Parabeltheorie des Markus',
ZThK 52, 1955, 255-271; C. Masson, *Les Paraboles de Marc IV*,
Neuchâtel and Paris 1945; H. W. Kuhn, *Ältere Sammlungen im
Markusevanglium*, Göttingen 1971, 99-146; C. E. B. Cranfield, 'St.
Mark 4:1-34', *SJTh* 4, 1951, 398-414; 5, 1952, 49-66; G. H. Boobyer,
'The Redaction of Mark IV: 1-34' *NTS* 8, 1961/2, 59-70. With special
reference to vv. 10-13 see B. Lindars, *New Testament Apologetic*, London
1961, 17ff., 159ff.; G. Minette de Tillesse, *Le secret messianique dans
l'évangile de Marc*, Paris 1968, 173-9; R.P. Meye, *Jesus and the Twelve*,
152-6 and 'Mark 4.10: "Those about Him with the Twelve"', *Studia
Evangelica II*, TU 87, 1964, 211-18; J. Gnilka, *Die Verstockung Israels:
Isaias 6:9-10 in der Theologie der Synoptiker*, StANT 3, München 1961;
Reploh, op.cit., 59-61; A. Schulz, op.cit., 51f.; A.M. Ambrozic, *The
Hidden Kingdom*, CBQ Monograph II, Washington, D.C. 1971, 47ff.;
H. Räisänen, *Die Parabeltheorie im Markusevangelium*, Helsinki 1973; J.R.
Kirkland, 'The Earliest Understanding of Jesus' Use of the Parables:
Mark IV 10-12 in context', NT, 19, 1977, 1-21. A few scholars take
4.10-12 to be pre-Markan, e.g., Räisänen, 48ff.; E. Trocmé, *The
Formation of the Gospel According to Mark*, E.T.; London, 1975, 160, n.2.
The latter (177, n.1) does envisage the possibility that while the
reference to the twelve is pre-Markan, 'those about him' may be a
Markan addition. Our argument is not affected if vv.11f. were united
with vv.3-9 and 14-20 prior to Mark since it would still be true that the
two audiences of v.10 could originally have been separately linked to
vv.11f. and vv.14-20.

other places he expresses the same idea with κατ' ἰδίαν(4:34;
6:31,32; 7:33; 9:2,28; 13:3; all of these appear to be redactional);
the phrase is thus traditional.[32] It must therefore have referred to
Jesus as absolutely alone or as alone with some group; the
former would be pointless and so we assume the latter. it is
probable that this group survives in the text as either
οἱ περὶ αὐτόν or as 'the twelve'. Thus the connection of its
interpretation to the parable would have been something like
either 'when he was alone those around him asked[33] him about
the parable and he said', or 'when he was alone with the twelve
they asked him about the parable and he said', and this would
have led into v.14; v.13b is probably redactional.[34]

The logion of vv.11f., which we assume to be pre-Markan,[35]
must also have had a defined audience because within it there is a
group (ὑμῖν) which is addressed and which is distinguished
from those outside it (τοῖς ἔξω).) Although καὶ ἔλεγεν αὐτοῖς
is probably[35] Markan there must have been some original
introduction of the type 'Jesus said to . . . "To you is given
. . ."'. Again this group could have been either τοῖς περὶ αὐτόν
or τοῖς δώδεκα; the latter might seem more probable since the
logion in v.11 is theologically developed and, therefore, would
require a more precisely defined group like 'the twelve'[37] than
'those around him', but οἱ περὶ αὐτόν contrasts very effectively
with τοῖς ἔξω.[38] In addition σὺν τοῖς δώδεκα runs on easily
after κατὰ μόνας. Whichever we choose it looks as if both the

---

[32] γίνεσθαι in the sense of 'to be' is also unusual in Mark (cf. Stock,
op.cit., 71) and Mark prefers the compound ἐπερωτᾶν to the simple
verb (cf. Schmahl, op.cit., 83); the latter only appears elsewhere twice,
7:26; 8:5, and both of these are from the tradition.

[33] See preceding note.

[34] Cf. Stock, op.cit., 72. Räisänen, op. cit., 70f., considers it redactional
though it bears no signs of Mark's hand.

[35] There is nothing particularly Markan about the phraseology apart
from the plural 'parables'; it could have been this plural which led Mark
to use the logion. On the other hand μυστήριον and οἱ ἔξω are not
found elsewhere in Mark but were regular terms in use in the early
church (for the second see 1 Cor 5:12f; Col 4:5; 1 Thess 4:12).

[36] H.W. Kuhn, op. cit., 130f.

[37] E. Meyer, op. cit., 138f. attributes this verse to his 'twelve' source.

[38] περὶ αὐτόν in 3:32, 34 also carries the contrast between those who
are with Jesus (and on his side) and those who are outside (and not his).

components come from the tradition, and neither is due to Mark.[39]

4:34b appears to be Markan[40] because it accords with 4:11, but not with 4:33; Mark was free here to define the group to which the secret of the kingdom is made known and he defines it as 'the disciples'. But even if v.34 is from the tradition[41] by his failure to alter the reference to the disciples Mark equates them with the group of v.11. Thus οἱ περὶ αὐτὸν σὺν τοῖς δώδεκα as a combination of phrases means 'the disciples' and is not to be understood as either 'the crowd' or 'the twelve'. Mark will probably have understood σύν as 'inclusive', i.e., 'those around him including the twelve'[42] rather than as 'exclusive', i.e., 'those around him together with the twelve'.[43] In either case the twelve is only a part of the group which is told the mystery of the parables and the twelve are therefore a smaller group than the disciples (v.34).[44]

(III) 9:35. Vv.33f. and v.35a form an unnecessary double introduction to the set of logia, 9:35b–50.[45] Mark has either

---

[39] S. Freyne, *The Twelve: Disciples and Apostles,* London 1968, 111, says of 4:10 that 'there is little in the vocabulary or style that is typical of Mark apart from the single reference to the twelve', but if he had not begun with the assumption that the twelve was redactional he would not have made this exception.

[40] κατ' ἰδίαν is Markan terminology; see above.

[41] Note the unusual τοῖς ἰδίοις μαθηταῖς and singular usage in Mark of χωρίς and ἐπιλύειν: cf. Gnilka, op.cit., 59ff.: Weeden, op.cit., 143.

[42] Because Mark has taken both phrases from the tradition we do not see this as a genuine duplicate expression in which the second phrase determines more precisely the meaning of the first (F. Neirynck, *Duality in Mark,* Leuven 1972, 45ff.). If Mark had intended this he would not have expressed the idea with σύν

[43] R.P. Meye, art.cit., takes the unusual view that σύν means "included in "; those around Jesus are a small inner intimate group who belong to the twelve. Liddell and Scott do not attest this meaning of σύν ; the only examples Meye offers are Lk 24:24 and Acts 14:4 but neither is a genuine parallel.

[44] There seems no reason to conclude from this verse that the twelve were nearer to Jesus than the disciples; see J. Delorme 'L'Évangile selon Marc' in: *Le Ministère et les Ministères selon le Nouveau Testament* (ed. J. Delorme), Paris 1974, 155–181, at 164.

[45] It is unnecessary to determine whether vv.35b–50 existed as a unit in the pre–Markan tradition.

written both introductions, written one and drawn the other from the tradition, or drawn both from the tradition. Of these possibilities the first and the last are least likely. The first is unlikely because of the difficulty created by the initial identification of αὐτούς and ἀλλήλους of vv.33f. with the disciples in the preceding context and by its later identification in v.35 with the twelve; if Mark had written both he would have put τοὺς δώδεκα in place of αὐτούς in v.33. The last solution is improbable because, as we shall argue, Mark composed vv.33f. If it was true it would have arisen because Mark in compiling (if he compiled it) the sequence of logia in vv.35b-50 combined the existing introductions to some of the logia; it would, of course, imply that 'the twelve' was from the tradition.

There are clear signs of Mark's hand in vv.33f. Capernaum usually appears in the Gospel in the material which introduces pericopae; while there is no reason to doubt that the name belongs to the tradition about Jesus (only in Mt 11:23 = Lk 10:15, and possibly in Lk 4:23, is its appearance essential to the material) place names are quickly lost in oral transmission; there is no necessary connection of the present set of logia with Capernaum. Mark knew it as a town in Galilee where Jesus taught and adopts it to increase the verisimilitude of a journey.[46] If it is redactional so also must be the whole of its clause. In the next clause the 'house' motif is Markan, as is the use of ἐπερωτᾶν.[47] In the question ἐν τῇ ὁδῷ is redactional,[48] and διαλογίζεσθαι is used regularly by Mark.[49] The use of ἐπερωτᾶν and the reference to the journey takes us back to vv.30-32 which apart from its logion is a Markan construction.

---

[46] A house, Peter's, was already connected with Jesus and Capernaum (1:29) and this possibly gave Mark the idea for using Capernaum here. On the other hand to name Capernaum where Jesus was known does make the idea of a secret journey more difficult; Mark, however, was probably not seeking for consistency on a point like this. Luke omits Capernaum, Matthew transfers it to the beginning of the incident about the temple tax; it is appropriate there since it is on the edge of the Sea of Galilee and Peter is instructed to go and fish.

[47] 8-25-17-3.

[48] Cf. 8:27; 10:32,52. This argument is not affected if with A D it^pm syr^s it is omitted from v.34, since it is certainly read in v.33.

[49] 3-7-6-0; its use is certainly redactional at 8:16,17.

If then the question of v.33 belonged to the tradition it must have had some setting, now lost, and we must ask why Mark dropped it. It is easier to assume that he himself composed the question of Jesus; in this way he has created dramatic tension: the disciples discuss but are afraid to ask Jesus (v.32); he asks them (v.33).[50] Matthew and Luke both omit this verse; Luke retains διαλογισμός from it; Matthew loses the connection between his parallel to 9:36 and the passion prediction by his insertion of the pericope about the temple tax (17:24-27). If v.33 is redactional in Mark then that part of v.34,[51] and that means almost all of it, which refers back to it will be also, i.e., the references to the silence of the disciples and to their discussion.[52]

The redactional nature of vv.33f. is confirmed if, alternatively, we suppose that it is from the tradition and that v.35 is redactional. At first sight this might appear reasonable because v.35 is omitted by Matthew and Luke and because v.35b may have been an isolated logion (it reappears in variant form at 10:43f.). But if we omit v.35 there is no easy movement from the question in v.34, 'Who is greatest?', to the reception of the child in vv.36f. Jesus is not saying in vv.36f. that a child is as important as a disciple and that therefore greatness is unimportant, i.e. the disciple should behave as a child.[53] If Mk 10:15 came here (and many commentators think it would be more suitable at 9:37) then this could be the sense; unfortunately for this argument it does not. So we conclude that vv.33f. are Markan whereas v.35a is from the tradition.[54]

V35a also contains internal signs that it comes from the

---

[50] On the redaction of v.33b. see W.G. Thompson, *Matthew's Advice to a Divided Community: Mt. 17.22-18.35.* AnBibl 44, Rome 1970, 123.
[51] σιωπᾶν is again a Markan favourite word (2-5-2-0).
[52] Schmahl, op.cit., 89 points out that we have here the only Markan use of διαλέγεσθαι and that therefore we have pre-Markan material; presumably, however, he has varied the verbs between v.33 and v.34 for stylistic reasons. The form of v.34b as a γάρ clause is Markan.
[53] This is Matthew's argument for he connects 18:1 and 18:3f. through the reference to the Kingdom of Heaven; Luke does the same by his addition of 9:48b. Codex Bezae omits v.35; perhaps Matthew and Luke knew Mark without it, but it is more likely that D harmonises with Matthew and Luke.
[54] Cf. P.S. Minear, *Commands of Christ*, Edinburgh 1972, 86f.

tradition. Φωνεῖν is not a Markan word; when he presents Jesus as summoning men for instruction he prefers to use προσκαλεῖσθαι.[55] καὶ λέγει αὐτοῖς is usually pre-Markan.[56] Mark does not emphasise Jesus' use of a sitting position when teaching,[57] though this was the position regularly adopted by Jewish teachers; in itself this suggests pre-Markan material.

Thus the reference to the twelve is derived in 9:35 from the tradition and does not come from Mark. This is confirmed when we observe that the twelve appear in the variant forms of the saying of v.35b at 10:43 (cf. 10:41) and Lk 22:26. Finding the reference in his source Mark preserved it according to his usual custom,[58] but his editorial work serves to turn the emphasis from the twelve to a less determinate body, the disciples. If Mark had wished to stress the twelve or if their appearance in his Gospel derives from him then he could easily have put τοὺς δώδεκα instead of αὐτούς in v.33. Finally there is nothing in v.35 to suggest that Mark sees the twelve as a sub-group of the disciples.

(IV) 10:32. Apparently three groups are referred to in this verse: (i) those at whose head Jesus walks and who are astonished; (ii) those who follow him and are afraid; (iii) the twelve whom Jesus tells what is about to happen to him. The

[55] Cf. 3:13,23; 6:7; 7:14; 8:1,34; 10:42; 12:43. Stock, op.cit., 115, notes the unusual nature of φωνεῖν but nowhere discusses what is redactional and what traditional, with the result that his explanation for its use is contorted (116).

[56] Cf. Kuhn, op.cit., 131; contrast Räisänen, op.cit., 104, who however argues that Mark has united two pieces of tradition (vv.33f. and vv.35ff.) with it.

[57] The verb καθίζειν is used by Mark in a parallel situation in 12:41, but the sitting is not closely related to the summoning or to the teaching; he uses the synonym καθῆσθαι at 3:32 where it is probably not redactional and it is only implied that Jesus was sitting, at 4:1 where Jesus sits in a boat but the connection between teaching and sitting is not clear (it is difficult to stand steady in a small boat), and at 13:3 whch is the only occasion where Jesus is said to sit to give formal instruction.

[58] Cf. Best, 'Mark's Preservation of the Tradition' in: L'Evangile selon Marc; Tradition et rédaction (ed. M. Sabbe), BEThL 34, Gembloux and Leuven 1974, 21-34 (infra p. 31-48). W. L. Knox, op. cit., 17ff., attributes v. 35 to Mark's use here of the 'twelve-source'. We would make no such claim but would argue that the collection of logia which follows began with a reference to the twelve.

textual tradition has attempted to solve the difficulty[59] here either by omitting one group[60] or by clearly identifying two of the groups.[61] Neither solution has sufficient support; both are too obviously corrections. More recently commentators have supposed a primitive corruption of the text,[62] a marginal gloss which later came to be interlopated,[63] or a misunderstanding of a supposed underlying Aramaic *Vorlage*.[64] Of these the first two suggestions are notoriously difficult to justify and the third falls because v.32 is largely Markan and therefore had no Aramaic *Vorlage*. The difficulty is much more likely to have been created through Mark's redaction.

The redactional nature of most of v.32 can be easily shown.[65] ἦσαν (or ἦν) δέ introduces a piece of new and important information for what follows, a new step in the story;[66] ἐν τῇ ὁδῷ, omitted as usual by Matthew and Luke, is, as we have seen, Markan;[67] ἀναβαίνοντες εἰς Ἱεροσόλυμα repeats in a Markan manner[68] material from the tradition in v.33; the periphrastic imperfect, ἦσαν . . . ἀναβαίνοντες;[69] ἐθαμβοῦντο,

[59] Both Matthew and Luke avoid the difficulties by omitting most of the verse.

[60] So D K it^{a,b}.

[61] καί is read for οἱ δέ by A fam^{13} it^{l,q} vg syr^{p,h}.

[62] C.H. Turner, *The Study of the New Testament*, Oxford 1920, 62 conjectures ἐθαμβεῖτο.

[63] E. Haenchen, *Der Weg Jesu*, Berlin ²1968, 363.

[64] C.C. Torrey, *Our Translated Gospels*, London, n.d., 151-3. *The Four Gospels*, London, n.d., 302.

[65] See now R. McKinnis, 'An Analysis of Mark X 32-34', *NovTest* 18, 1976, 81-100.

[66] Cf. 2:6; 5:11; 8:9; 10:32; 14:1,4; 15:7,25,40. The sentence so introduced is not necessarily parenthetical as suggested by M. Thrall, *Greek Particles in the New Testament*, Leiden 1962, 64. 5:11; 14:1,4 are not parenthetical.

[67] See n.48.

[68] Cf. 2:18; 3:31f. 6:1,4; 7:2,5 (vv.3f. are parenthetical); 10:46; cf. J. Sundwall, *Die Zusammensetzung des Markusevangeliums*, Acta Academiae Aboensis, Humaniora, IX, 2 Åbo 1934, 69.

[69] Cf. Taylor, *Mark*, 45; J.C. Doudna, *The Greek of the Gospel of Mark*, JBL Monograph Series 12, Philadelphia 1961, 46.

both the word and the theme are Markan;[70] προάγων; [71] ἀκολουθοῦντες;[72] ἐφοβοῦντο, the theme of fear;[73] ἄρχεσθαι as an auxiliary;[74] πάλιν.[75] The weight of this evidence falls in the first two-thirds of the verse and the first two groups (if they are distinct groups) are thus Markan creations. The pre-Markan tradition would then have begun 'Jesus (took the twelve and) told them (the twelve) what was about to happen[76] to him'. Of these the simpler form is preferable since Mark uses παραλαμβάνειν in editorial passages in reference to the disciples at 14:33 and, probably, at 9:2.

Such a clause can have served in the tradition only as in introduction to some saying of Jesus; this was probably the passion prediction of vv.33f. This prediction is fuller than those of 8:31 and 9:31; there are some grounds for believing Mark did not compose it but received it from the tradition. That it follows the Markan passion account fairly closely is no reason to assume it was composed by him in the light of that account; the Markan passion account was that of the Roman church; this prediction could also have been part of the tradition of the Roman church; thus the two would have been brought into harmony prior to Mark. Certain differences between it and the Markan passion narrative can be accounted for most easily if the prediction came from the tradition: (i) 10:33f. omits the ill-treatment of Jesus by the Jewish authorities (14:65), and this suggests its formation in a milieu in which blame could be freely laid on the Romans, perhaps in a Jewish Christian community.[77] (ii) The false witnesses who appear to be important for Mark are missing from 10:33f. (iii) The elders are not mentioned though Mark refers to them at 14:53; 15:1. (iv) κατακρίνειν is used with the

[70] Mark is the only evangelist to use θαμβεῖσθαι: 0-3-0-0 (cf. ἐκθαμβεῖσθαι: 0-4-0-0). See also K. Tagawa. *Miracles et Évangile*, Paris 1966, 99ff.; G. Minette de Tillese, op.cit., 264ff.
[71] 6-5-1-0. Four of Matthew's uses are drawn directly from Mark.
[72] Cf. 1:18; 2:14(*bis*),15; 6:1; 8:34; 9:38; 10:21b,28,52.
[73] Cf. 4:41; 6:50; 9:6,32; 16:8b; cf. Tagawa, op.cit., 99ff.
[74] Cf. Taylor, *Mark*, 48, 63f.
[75] 17-28-3-43.
[76] For συμβαίνειν cf. Gen 42:4,29; 44:29; Est 6:13, 1 Macc 4:26; Job 1:22; Lk 24:14.
[77] Cf. E. Schweizer, *Markus*, ad loc.

dative; there is a different construction at 14:64.[78] One other factor points in the same direction: the double use of ἀναβαίνειν (vv. 32, 33).[79] While it is possible Mark used the word twice, it is one of his regular practices when composing seams or introductions to an incident from the tradition to draw words from the incident itself for the seam or introduction.[80] In v. 33 the verb is used in the first person plural whereas the content of the prediction is in the third person singular with the Son of man as subject. If we assume that both the verb and its form in v.33 pre-date Mark this implies that the prediction of vv.33f. was used as narrative and not as confession.[81] The absence of scriptural determination as in 9:12; 14:21,27; or of a word expressing divine necessity as in 8:31 together with the use of future tenses[82] and the presence of considerable detail would be appropriate to a narrative context. But how would this brief narrative have been used in the early community? While part of the tradition strongly emphasises the predeterminate nature of Jesus' death there must also have been some recognition that it did not come as a surprise to himself, and therefore some statement attributed to Jesus announcing his intention to go to the cross would have been necessary for apologetic purposes. Such a statement would naturally have fallen into narrative form but it **would probably not have begun 'Behold! We are going up . .' but would have had some preface: 'Jesus said to . . . (for the moment we leave the group unspecified) "Behold! We are going**

[78] Other differences from the Markan narrative exist but do not help us in determining whether 10:33f. is formed from it, e.g., ἀποκτείνειν is used instead of σταυροῦν but this may be due to the influence of 8:31 and 9:31; παραδοθήσεται (10:33) is used instead of ἀπήγαγον (14:53) but the former is a regular word in the theological vocabulary of the passion.

[79] It is the correct word to use for a journey to Jerusalem and arguments about it as Markan favourite or non-favourite are irrelevant.

[80] See above n.68.

[81] 8:31 and 9:31, because of their simpler form, would be more likely to have been used confessionally. This does not exclude the view of McKinnis, art.cit., that the portion from κατακρινοῦσιν onwards has hymnic form. Some of the evidence for the non-Markan origin of vv.33f. lies in the words prior to the 'hymn'. McKinnis is compelled to suppose that 'after three days...' did not belong to the hymn.

[82] There are none in 8:31; 9:12 and only one in 9:31.

up . . . ".' It would not be inappropriate if this group were the twelve for the earlier forms of the passion narrative probably spoke of the twelve rather than of the disciples;[83] and vv.33f.is the fullest prediction of the passion.

Are we still left with two groups in v.32, both stemming from Mark's work? It is probable that Mark does not intend to depict separate groups, for: (I) He likes duplicate expressions of which the second amplifies or redefines the first.[94] (II) δέ in οἱ δὲ ἀκολουθοῦντες could be taken as continuative rather than adversative.[85] (III) The actual content of the two clauses suggests that the same group is intended for προάγων is neatly balanced by ἀκολουθοῦντες. (IV) Elsewhere Mark has stressed separately the fear and astonishment of the disciples;[86] it is fitting that he should now bring those qualities together on the occasion of the last passion prediction.[87] Thus we translate the second clause 'and as they were following they were afraid'.[88]

Consequently as in 9:33-50 Mark has introduced a piece of teaching, which the tradition had presented as addressed to the twelve, with a reference to a group whose membership is identified no more closely than by a vague αὐτούς. The result, as in 9:33-35a, is a twofold introduction and, as there, there is no obvious sign that Mark wishes to distinguish the twelve from a larger and more indefinite body of disciples; rather his composition of v.32 shows that he wishes to widen what was said to the twelve so that it becomes relevant for all disciples, i.e., all his community. We can confirm that Mark attaches no particular

[83] See below.
[84] Cf. Neirynck, op.cit., passim.
[85] Cf. Thrall, op. cit., 51f. The references which she gives to δέ continuative relate to its use with the article acting as a demonstrative pronoun. There are many more instances; it is only the context which enables us to decide whether it is used in continuation or adversatively. 10:50 provides a clear example of continuative use in which as in 10:32 we have article, participle and finite verb. See also R.P. Meye, Jesus and the Twelve, Grand Rapids, Mich. 1968, 162f.
[86] 'Fear' and 'amazement' cannot be clearly distinguished in Mark; see especially 16:5-8.
[87] Schmahl, op.cit., 9, suggests that the two verbs have a climactic effect.
[88] For no very apparent reason, Stock, op.cit., 131, identifies αὐτούς with the twelve and envisages those who follow as a second group.

significance to the use of the 'twelve' here by observing that the earlier two predictions (8:31 and 9:31) were addressed to disciples (clearly stated in 9:31; at 8:31 an inference from 8:27 and 8:33). [89]

(V) 10:41. Strictly speaking the twelve are not mentioned here but the 'ten' are and therefore the concept of the twelve is envisaged. The ten complain about the request of James and John for seats of honour. 10:35-40 and 10:41-45 were probably not joined together in the pre-Markan tradition. [90] Vv 41,42a bear signs of Mark's hand: ἄρχεσθαι is employed as an auxiliary and a participial form of παρακαλεῖν is used with a verb of saying. [91] Vv.42b-45a are found in another form in Lk 22:24-27 and are therefore a pre-Markan logia sequence. Such a sequence must have had some form of introduction: either 'Jesus said' or 'Jesus said to . . .'. In view of the second plural in vv.43f. it is probable that some group was identified and this would have been either the disciples or the twelve. Since we find the ten in v.41 it is easier to assume it was the twelve. The mention of the ten in v.41 is not strictly necessary for Mark could have made his point as easily by writing 'the other disciples'. In support of the view that the original logia sequence was addressed to the twelve we note that the independent but parallel piece of tradition in Lk 22:24-27 has them as its audience (cf. 22:30) and that 9:36f., which also deals with the issue of importance within the community, had originally the twelve as its addressee in the pre-Markan tradition. Thus the explicit reference to the ten in v.41 and the implicit reference to the twelve are pre-Markan. [92]

---

[89] Stock, op.cit., 132, 133, regards the third prediction as addressed only to the twelve. His suggestion (134f.) that the first plural (here in the verb ἀναβαίνωμεν) is used only of the twelve and Jesus is not true of 9:40 (the implication of our earlier discussion is that the disciples are in mind); 14:15 ('disciples' is the nearest referent); 4:35. At 1:38 and 10:42 we have smaller groups.

[90] Cf. S. Légasse, 'Approche de l'Épisode préévangélique du Fils de Zébédee (Marc X. 35-40 par.)', NTS 20, 1973/4, 161-177.

[91] Cf. 3:23; 7:14; 8:1,34; 12:43 (all in redactional passages with the possible exception of 12:43). Schmahl, op.cit., 94, argues that the sentence structure of v.41 is Markan.

[92] It has often been supposed that 10:42b-45a and 9:35-7 were related in the tradition; if they were the twelve was a common factor.

But is it not the implication of vv.42-44 that some are in authority in the church and that these are the twelve? Rulers exercise authority over their people (v.42), so some Christians will exercise authority over other Christians(vv.43f).[93] But vv.43f. do not necessarily imply that any Christian should exercise authority. Those who *wish* (expressed conditionally) to exercise authority are to be servants and slaves, and servants and slaves do not exercise authority. Moreover the ὑμῶν of v.43 implies that those who are to have authority belong to the same group as those who aspire to authority exercised over them, i.e., the 'you' of vv.43f. cannot really be restricted to the twelve but is intended to apply to all disciples or all Christians, or else it applies to authority exercised by one member of the twelve over other members of the twelve; the total context in Mark seems too general for the last suggestion to be the case.

(VI) 11:11. This verse contains both redaction and tradition.[94] Even if the tradition set the cleansing of the temple on the day after the entry into Jerusalem and Mark did not alter the tradition in this respect he has certainly created the sandwich which consists of the cleansing surrounded by the two halves of the account of the cursing of the fig tree. He had thus to create a new link and this is 11:11. It would accordingly seem that he was free to put 'with his disciples' rather than 'with the twelve'. On the other hand the twelve were a traditional feature of the passion narrative[95] and Mark may have thought it wise at this point to refer to them or, more probably, they already formed a part of the tradition which he used in compiling our verse. Since Bethany and the 'evening' both belong to the tradition the twelve may have belonged with them also in the pre-Markan material or Mark may have brought forward, as he often does,

---

[93] Stock, op.cit., 139f., suggests this but does not push it.

[94] περιβλέπεσθαι: 0-6-1-0; ὀψία: 7-5-0-2 (ὀψέ: 1-3-0-0); a compound verb followed by the preposition of the compound is frequent in Mark; all these suggest redaction. But Mark elsewhere has ὀψίας with γενομένης (1:32; 4:35; 6:47; 14:17; 15:42) and not οὔσης and the phrase is usually unqualified. If the variant ὀψέ is read this also goes with γίνεσθαι at 11:19 (13:35 is irrelevant). It could be that ὀψίας ἤδη κτλ. belonged to the tradition which related Jesus' overnight departure to Bethany.

[95] See below.

material which came from the traditional introduction to the
account of the cleansing; as it stands this is very vague, 'and they
came to Jerusalem', and reads like redaction; the introduction
which lay in the tradition may thus be preserved in v.11 and
have read 'and he entered into Jerusalem with the twelve'; Mark
transferred it to v. 11 when he inserted vv. 12-14. We should
also note that we find 'the disciples' at v.14b. This brief sentence
is a Markan comment.[96] Mark, now free from the tradition, uses
his favourite expression for the followers of Jesus. 'The twelve'
are thus to be understood as 'the disciples' and the lessons taught
are not to be restricted as if they were instruction for the twelve
alone. All the church is to hear.

(VII) *The Passion Narrative.* If we take the Passion narrative to
begin at 14:1 there are four references within it (14:10,17,20,43)
to the twelve, three of them being associated with Judas
(14:10,20,43). Before we examine them it is important to recall
that there is independent evidence for an association of the
twelve with the Passion. 1 Cor 15:5 contains an early tradition
relating them to the resurrection. Lk. 22:30, whether this is the
original position of the logion or not, shows that Luke assumed
that the twelve were the group with Jesus at the Last Supper and
Luke's tradition about the Last Supper is so different from that
of Mark that we can conclude some independence here on his
part.[97] Lk 24:10 which is certainly independent of Mark,
indicates that Luke thought of the apostles, and for him these are
the same as the twelve, as the group concerned in the event of
the cross and resurrection. Lk 22:14 may not be independent of
Mark, but if it is it provides further confirmation.

14:43a may be Markan, the link with which he resumes the
main story of the passion report which in its pre-Markan form
lacked the accounts of the Last Supper and Gethsemane; if
so 14:44ff. would have been probably joined to 14:10 or

---

[96] Note the imperfect ἤκουον and the regularity with which Markan
pericopae conclude with a brief sentence which appears to come from
him (12:12,17,34,37; 13:37; 14:11,31,50,72).

✓ [97] Cf. V. Taylor, *The Passion Narrative of St.Luke*, SNTS Monograph
Series 19, Cambridge 1972, 61ff.; J. Jeremias, *The Eucharistic Words of
Jesus* (E.T.), London 1966, 97ff.; H. Schürmann, *Quellenkritische
Untersuchung des lukanischen Abendmahlsberichtes Lk. xxii, 7-38*, Münster
1953-7, *passim.*

14:11[98] and the reference to Judas as one of the twelve in v. 43 would be redactional, though its precise form would be dictated by 14:10; the crucial verse is then 14:10. If, however, the immediate pre-Markan form of the passion narrative included the accounts of the Last Supper and Gethsemane then the phrase probably came from the tradition.[99]

There seems no reason to doubt the association of Judas with the tradition in the pre-Markan stage since he is also associated with it in the Johannine account (Joh 18:1ff.)and in the independent traditions of Mt 27:3-10; Act 1:16-20.[100] If Luke had a separate source for his account of the arrest[101] this provides further verification of Judas' place. 14:1f.,10f. or at least the parts of them relevant to the discussion, are widely accepted as tradition[102]; Mark has used them to form a sandwich with

[98] See E. Linnemann, *Studien zur Passionsgeschichte*, FRLANT 102, Göttingen 1970, 44ff.

[99] Jeremias, op.cit., 89ff. G. Schneider, *Die Passion Jesu nach den drei ältern Evangelien*, München 1972, 43ff., takes vv.43-46 to have been a pre-Markan unity.

[100] This is not to make any claim that Judas belongs to the genuine Jesus-tradition.

[101] Cf Taylor, op.cit., 72ff. It is increasingly accepted that Luke had a special source for his passion account; in addition to the references in n.97 see T. Schramm, *Der Markus-Stoff bei Lukas*, SNTS Monograph Series 14, Cambridge 1971, 50f.; F. Rehkopf, *Die lukanische Sonderquelle*, Tübingen 1959.

[102] See the evidence as presented in Linnemann, op.cit., 148f.; W. Schenk, *Der Passionsbericht nach Markus*, Gütersloh 1974, 44ff.; D. Dormeyer, *Die Passion Jesu als Verhaltensmodell*, Münster 1974, 66-72. L. Schenke, *Studien zur Passionsgeschichte des Markus: Tradition und Redaktion in Markus 14:1-42*, Würzburg 1971, 12-66, 119-150, takes them as wholly Markan, but we should note in 14:10 the following non-Markan characteristics: ἀπέρχεσθαι πρός (only also at 3:13; elsewhere he uses εἰς with the verb: 1:35; 6:32,46; 7:24,30; 8:13; cf. Schenke, 127); the mention only of the High Priests (contrast 14:1,43,53,55; 15:31; they are by themselves at 15:3,10,11; at an earlier stage the tradition may have referred to them alone; so Dormeyer op.cit., 69-71); the use of αὐτόν for Jesus without an easy reference back at this point suggests the passage once stood in a larger context; the use of παραδίδοναι with Judas is pre-Markan (Dormeyer, op.cit., 83). 14:1,2, while perhaps composed by Mark, must be based on tradition; if in the tradition the Jewish authorities were held in any way responsible for the death of Jesus and if Judas belongs to the tradition, the tradition must have brought them together at some point. Finally we should note that Mark's sandwiches are usually created from existing material.

14:3-9. Granted the traditional nature of the reference to Judas did Mark add 'one of the twelve'?[103] Those who begin with the assumption that the appearance of the twelve in Mark is a sign of redaction would naturally draw this conclusion; for us to do so would be to beg the question. Schenk[104] who takes 'twelve' to be a favourite term with Mark and assumes its redactional nature here also supports his conclusion by alleging that the references to the twelve in 14:17 and 14:20 are Markan. His argument in the case of 14:20 is defective; he says this ought to read 'one of you'; while this may be allowed,[105] he does nothing to show that it was Mark and not the preceding tradition which made the modification, i.e., he again assumes any reference to 'twelve' must be Markan and this is the point at issue[106]. On the other hand, positively in support of the traditional nature of the reference to Judas as one of the twelve in 14:10 is the use of the article with the phrase, which may suggest a known formula, i.e., a formula known in the passion report to Mark's

[103] Matthew stresses the phrase by altering the order of the words; cf. D.P. Senior, *The Passion Narrative According to Matthew*, Leuven 1975, 43.
[104] Op.cit., 149f., 185f.
[105] K. Kertelge, 'Die Funktion der »Zwölf« im Markusevangelium', *TThZ*, 78, 1969, 193-206, does not allow it but argues that the known formularly character of 'one of the twelve' forced the change on Mark, or on the preceding tradition.
[106] We assume that 14:18-21 is not a Markan creation, for: (i) the 'amen'-saying of v.18 is probably traditional; (ii) v.20b with its knowledge of passover custom and unusual words is also probably traditional and is paralleled in the independent traditions of Joh 13:21-30 and Lk 22:21 (cf. Taylor, op.cit., 59-61 and references there); (iii) In Mark we should expect ἐμβαπτόμενος . . . ἐν since it is his custom to repeat the preposition from the verb. We note that ἤρξαντο here means 'begin' and does not have the auxiliary sense it normally has in the Markan redaction. Matthew's elimination follows his normal habit of removing one-half of Mark's double expressions (Senior, op.cit., 72). For these reasons we necessarily also reject the view of Schenke, op.cit., 204ff., that 14:18-20 is Markan. Most of his argument is of the of the form 'x' could possibly be Markan, therefore it is Markan. His arguments for dissociating vv.18-20 from vv.12-16 and from vv.22ff. are much stronger. Dormeyer, op.cit., 94-100, argues that vv.18ab,19,20 are pre-Markan but because he assumes the twelve is Markan redaction argues that Mark inserted 'one of the twelve' into the tradition of v.20. The assumption is gratuitous.

community. Schmahl[107] argues for the traditional nature of the formula from a comparison of εἰς ἐξ ὑμῶν in v.18 and εἰς τῶν δώδεκα in v.20. If v.20 is an insertion then we should expect εἰς ἐξ τῶν δώδεκα; the known formula forces the use of the form we have.

The analysis of the pre-Markan form of the passion account is very difficult as is shown by the variety of solutions propounded. If, as is very probable, 'one of the twelve' in relation to Judas belonged to the tradition then we may never be finally certain whether it was original in all of 14:10,20,43 but can be sure that it belonged to at least one of them, or perhaps even two of them. If it only belonged to one Mark has transferred it as a fixed formula to the other two because of his desire to emphasise the heinousness of the offence of Judas; he may have wished to preserve his own community from being too sure of themselves; if someone who was present at the Last Supper could betray Jesus then any church member who attended the Eucharist could, if he was not careful, betray another church member in time of persecution. The phrase does not then suggest for Mark membership of the twelve as much as closeness to Jesus.

The fourth reference to the twelve in the passion narrative appears at 14:17. ὀψίας γενομένης is redactional[108]; this combined with the historic present in v.17 suggests that that verse is Markan and accordingly he will have provided the reference to the twelve.[109] The nature of the narrative compelled him at this point to make some reference to those who ate the Last Supper with Jesus; v.18 depends on the group named in v.17. There were apparently four possibilities: 'the ten', 'the apostles', 'the disciples', 'the twelve'. The first of these would appear to be the logical statement since Jesus had already sent on two of the twelve to make preparations and this would be particularly pertinent if Mark identified the twelve and the disciples, but logic does not always determine matters. 'The apostles' is not a normal Markan designation. The disciples have been mentioned regularly in the preceding pericope (vv.

---

[107] Op.cit.,102.
[108] See n. 94.
[109] Cf. Schenke, op.cit., 199ff.; Dormeyer, op.cit., 88f.

12,13,14,16),[110] though in v.16 this refers to the two whom Jesus sent on ahead; if Mark had used 'the disciples' in v.17 this might have been misunderstood as referring back to these two. These considerations are negative. Was there anything which would have compelled Mark to use 'the twelve' here? We have already indicated that 'the twelve' were part of the tradition of the passion narrative and so the use of δώδεκα in v. 17 was probably forced on Mark by the tradition and though his insertion of v.17 is redactional the reference to the twelve is thus created by the tradition. (Its use also helped to prepare for the reference to Judas as 'one of the twelve' in v.20[111]). Possibly it may be due to his desire to associate the twelve with the Eucharist.

Stock[112] draws out a possible alternative or additional explanation. In v.18 we find ὁ ἐσθίων μετ' ἐμοῦ where we ought to have ὁ ἐσθίων τοὺς ἄρτούς μου (LXX) and we have a similar use of μετ' ἐμοῦ in v.20. Stock relates these to the μετ' αὐτοῦ of 3:14 where the twelve are commissioned to be with Jesus. This explanation has difficulties. Stock does nothing to show that the use of μετ' ἐμοῦ in vv. 18,20 is Markan and not pre-Markan; it is a perfectly normal phrase to use; it is used with a reference other than that of the twelve at 4:36; 5:18; 5:40; 14:33. The phrase serves to emphasise the position of Judas as an immediate follower without any direct reference back to 3:14.

The variation between the use of 'disciples' in vv.12–16 and of the twelve in 14:17 probably arises on the one hand from Mark's loyalty to the tradition that only the twelve were with Jesus at the Last Supper and on the other from his desire to indicate that participation in the Eucharist is for all disciples and that even though a disciple has participated yet this does not ensure that he will never become an apostate; the question each of the twelve asks Jesus implies the answer 'No!' yet has some doubt in it, or it would not be asked. The disciple can never be wholly confident of himself. In conformity with this desire to use the twelve as examples to contemporary Christians and not as a 'college' is

[110] Dormeyer, op.cit., 84–94, argues strongly for the traditional nature of 14:12–16.
[111] Cf. Schenke, op.cit., 201.
[112] Op.cit., 152f.

Mark' use of 'disciples' at 16:7 where, as is generally agreed, he adds a logion from the tradition; in his own mind he thinks of them as disciples.[113]

(VIII) There are some passages which may be held to imply the presence of the twelve without directly referring to them. In 6:43; 8:19 we have the twelve baskets of fragments which were gathered up after the feeding of the five thousand. Variant accounts of the feeding exist (6:35–44 and 8:1-9); thus the number twelve in the feeding of the five thousand may not itself be original. 8:14–21[114] is generally taken to be a Markan construction and the reference in 8:19 to the twelve baskets must be Markan. But the reference to the feeding of the five thousand could not be made there in the way it appears without introducing the number twelve; consequently its use is not significant for an appreciation of Mark's role in building up the concept of the twelve. Is then the reference to twelve at 6:43, on which 8:19 depends, from the tradition or from Mark? There is nothing distinctively Markan about 6:43 in language or style. In the independent account of John[115] we again find the twelve baskets. We see no reason to doubt that the twelve baskets belong to the tradition, but do they necessarily imply a reference to the twelve? Those who gathered the fragments need not even have been disciples of Jesus. In the feeding of the four thousand seven baskets are used. Therefore, the number twelve cannot have been the only significant number; in other words the

[113] The suggestion of Stock, op.cit., 171f., that he uses 'disciples' in 16:7 because he does not know the concept 'eleven' hardly bears consideration; since he knows 'the ten' at 10:41 it would not have been beyond him to say 'Peter and the ten' at 16:7 (strictly 'the eleven' never enter into the matter).

[114] See the unpublished thesis in the University of St.Andrews of Dr. Earl S. Johnson, Jnr., *The Theme of Blindness and Sight in the Gospel According to Mark;* cf. Taylor; Schweizer, *ad loc.;* Best, *The Temptation and the Passion,* SNTS, Monograph Series 2, Cambridge 1965, 78; T.A. Burkill, 'Mark 6.31-8.26; The Context of the Story of the Syrophoenician Woman' in Burkill, *New Light on the Earliest Gospel,* Ithaca and London 1972, 50; Reploh, op.cit., 76f.; Q. Quesnell, *The Mind of Mark,* Rome 1969, 103ff. Some, including Johnson, attribute much of the content of the verses to Mark; others, e.g., Taylor, regard them as a Markan amalgam of largely traditional material.

[115] Cf. C.H. Dodd, *Historical Tradition in the Fourth Gospel,* Cambridge 1963, 199f.

twelve in relation to the feeding cannot be of great importance.

Yet it can be argued that by the position he gives to the feeding of the five thousand Mark has tied it to the mission of the twelve.[116] While the use of 'apostles' at 6:30 may be pre-Markan, vv.31-34 are largely his construction and he has thus created the link. Thus the twelve could be said to be those who ministered the food to the people, and consequently the ministers of the Eucharist to the church. Against such a conclusion we would point out: (1) It is by no means clear if Mark intends the feedings to be understood eucharistically; there are good grounds for believing, whatever is true of the pre-Markan or post-Markan interpretation, that he understood them of the appropriation of Jesus' teaching.[117] (2) Where else would Mark have set the feeding accounts? He may have received them as already part of a catena of miracles, or as parts of two catenae[118], and this would in part determine their position, or if they were isolated pericopae he may have decided to place them prior to 8:27-30 because they can be used (cf. 6:52; 8:14-21) to emphasise the lack of understanding of the disciples. They would also have to be placed reasonably late so that this failure on their part would be perceived as a failure in the light of the possibility of knowledge.

One further possibility is open to examination: the pre-Markan tradition may have contained a reference to the twelve which Mark has changed to 'his disciples' (v.35). The original introduction might have run 'the twelve came to him and he said'. Certainly the twelve would seem the appropriate group in view of the number of baskets.[119]

---

[116] Cf. Stock, op. cit., 106-112; Delorme, op.cit., 171; Schmahl, op. cit., 108.

[117] Cf. Best, op.cit. 76-78, 104f. P.J. Achtemeier, 'The Origin and Function of the Pre-Markan Miracle Catenae', *JBL* 91, 1972, 198-221, argues that Mark inserted 6:1-33 prior to the feeding account in order to de-emphasise the eucharistic significance of the latter; his insertion stresses Jesus and his disciples as teachers rather than miracle workers *(theioi andres)*.

[118] Cf. Achtemeier, art.cit., and 'Towards the Isolation of Pre-Markan Miracle Catenae'. *JBL* 89, 1970, 265-291.

[119] To understand 'disciples' in v.35 as governed by 'apostles' in v.30 and this in turn as governed by 'the twelve' in vv.6b-13 is difficult, especially since the apostles are presented in 6:30 as 'missionaries' rather than as 'officials' or members of a fixed group.

II

We must now return to our initial questions and seek to answer them:

(i) οἱ δώδεκα was present in the tradition used by Mark at 4:10; 6:43; 9:35; 10:32, 41; in at least one of 14:10, 20, 43; probably in 3:14.(16?); 11:11.

(ii) Mark introduced the term from the tradition at 6:7; 8:19; the remainder of 14:10, 20, 43; 14:17; and possibly in 3:14, 11:11.

(iii) There is no clear evidence that he omitted the term where it was already present in the tradition, but this is a possibility at 6:35. This is clearly a question which it is very difficult to answer since any omission of the term would leave no trace of its original presence.

(iv) Mark regularly introduced 'the disciples' in places where we might have expected him to introduce 'the twelve', if the latter was his favourite term.

Mark[120] distinguishes to some extent between the twelve and the disciples,[121] the latter being the wider group. Thus the twelve together with those about Jesus (4:10) are identical with the disciples (4:34) and the twelve are part of a smaller group than those who received secret instruction in 9:33–35 and 10:32; Levi is a disciple but not one of the twelve; 3:13 is most easily understood as the selection of the twelve from a larger group whom Jesus had summoned to himself; 2:15 implies that there were many disciples; 15:40f. (the women) implies the existence of a wider group than the twelve;[122] in 3:34f. everyone who does the will of God is Jesus' brother and brotherhood implies discipleship. Yet Mark makes little distinction in the way in which he uses the twelve and the disciples;[123] the same role is attributed to them; the sole exception is in relation to the twelve depicted as missionaries. Thus Mark takes up and uses the

---

[120] Luke sees a distinction between the twelve and the disciples (cf. Lk 6:13,17), the disciples being the wider group. His use of μαθηταί throughout Acts indicates that he wishes the disciples in the Gospel to be understood as representative believers.

[121] Pace Burgers, art.cit.

[122] Note the use of the discipleship word ἀκολουθεῖν in 15:41.

[123] Cf. Best, 'The Role of the Disciples in Mark', NTS 23 (1977) 377–401 (infra pp. 98–130).

material from the tradition which referred to the twelve and does not change the term, but when he himself wishes to refer to followers of Jesus he calls them 'disciples'. He is not basically interested in the twelve. He is able easily to replace the twelve by the disciples and to identify the functions of the two groups because at no point does he give a reason why their number should be twelve and not some other number (cf. Mt. 19:28).

Turning now to 3:14 and 6:7 we have seen that in these two passages there is a common theme, that of the sending out of disciples. The twelve appear here as 'missionaries';[124] this word denotes a function rather than a status. In 3:14 they are formally instructed in how they are to carry out their commission. It is important to note that the term 'disciples' is never used in connection with this formal commission; Mark could have introduced the term at 6:7. Disciples, however, either as a group or as individuals, are also given an outward or missionary function towards those outside the community, but this is incidental and informal rather than formal: Peter and Andrew are called to be fishers of men (1:17); exorcism is not restricted to the twelve (9:28, 38f.);[125] care for the more material needs of others is implied by 9:36f. and 10:21; 14:28 and 16:7 probably represent Mark's general commission to the church to be active in mission work.[126]

In the light of this evidence it is best to think of the twelve in these two passages as representing those who are engaged in more or less full-time missionary activity.[127] We note that it is

---

[124] G. Schille, Die urchristliche Kollegialmission, AThANT 48, Zürich 1967, 121, appears to see the origin of the concept of the twelve in the mission of the church, but this is to go too far.

[125] If Mark is specially conscious of the twelve and not the disciples at 9:35 then 9:38f. would be an indication that exorcism is not restricted to the twelve.

[126] On 14:28 16:7 as a general missionary commission for Mark see C. F. Evans, 'I will go before you into Galilee'. JThS 5, 1954, 3-18; G. Stemberger, 'Galilee – Land of Revelation?' in: W. D. Davies, The Gospel and the Land, Berkeley and Los Angeles, Calif. and London 1974, 409-438.

[127] Mark never indicates the group to whom the twelve are sent; had he suggested they were sent to Israel (cf. Mt 10:5 and Luke's distinction between the twelve and the seventy) this would have limited their application to his own time. There is nothing to suggest that he does not think of the sending of the twelve as historical but nothing to indicate he thinks this to be the sole reason for his account.

only in connection with this missionary activity that Mark terms
the twelve 'apostles' (6:30); whether he derived the term from
the tradition or introduced it himself its use here indicates that
for him it still carried its verbal significance – the ones who are
sent.[128] They are sent to mission and are instructed (6:8-11) how
they should carry it through. We should note that though the
commission refers to authority it is not to authority exercised
within the community but to authority exercised outwith the
community over unclean spirits.[129]

Although the twelve are commissioned to be with Jesus this
does not imply a special relation between them and Jesus. We
note that the phrase was part of the tradition in relation to the
commission which came to Mark and that when in 6:6b-13 he
spells this out he does not refer to their relation to Jesus;
moreover throughout the Gospel 'the disciples' are equally set in
relation to Jesus as recipients of secret instruction and as those
who must go after him on the way of the cross and the
resurrection.

Do the twelve have any special function other than that of
full-time missionaries? At 4:10; 9:35; 10:32 they appear as
recipients of special teaching. At 9:35 by his addition of 9:33f.
Mark shows that he intends that what the tradition addressed to
the twelve should also be seen as addressed to the disciples. At
4:10 and 10:32 by his combination of material he shows that he
regards the instruction given there as imparted to a group wider
than the twelve. Special instruction is also given to 'disciples' in
4:34; 9:31; 10:10; 11:14 (cf. 3:7; 6:1); all these are clearly
redactional passages. Mark cannot therefore be held to regard

[128] Cf. Roloff, *Das Kerjgma und der irdische Jesus* (Göttingen, 1970) 141f.
[129] J. Coutts, 'The Authority of Jesus and of the Twelve in St.Mark's
Gospel', *JThS* 8, 1957, 111-118, argues for a wider authority given to
the twelve, but he fails to observe Mark's preference for the use of
'disciples'. Consequently his argument falls that 13:34 must refer to the
twelve because of its generalisation beyond the four in 13:37; if
authority is being given at this point it is being given to all Mark's
community (Mark added 13:37). Nor is the reference back in 11:23-25
(authority in prayer) necessarily limited to the twelve because of 11:11;
in 11:14 we find a Markan redactional reference to the disciples. Apart
from this we doubt if Mark really was thinking of the imparting of
authority even to disciples in 11:23-25 or 13:33-37.

the twelve as exclusive recipients of Jesus' special instruction.

The twelve as such are not then the link between Jesus and the post-resurrection church in the transmission of his teaching, though it is possible that the disciples, including the twelve, fulfil this function. Schmahl has a variant of this argument in that he sees the twelve as a group of the past[130] who carry on the same activities as Jesus [131] and so are the necessary link between him and the church. This might be easier to accept if the equivalence between the twelve and Jesus had been made clearer by Mark. At 3:14 and 6:30 Mark says that the disciples preach and teach but does not give the content of what they say; only at 6:12 is this given and it is repentance. The only other places where Mark connects preaching and repentance are 1:4 which refers to John and 1:14f. where repentance apparently precedes belief in the Gospel and is not its content. At 1:38f. Jesus' preaching is undefined. Preaching the gospel (undefined in nature) is the implied task of the church at 13:10; 14:9. At 5:20 (a redactional passage) the healed demoniac preaches what Jesus had done (certainly here there is continuity but it is not the twelve who are involved); at 7:36 preaching is used absolutely of those who have witnessed the healing of the deaf and the dumb man. Since according to Schmahl[132] Mark composed 3:14f. and 6:12 it is remarkable that he did not either make the preaching of the twelve resemble more closely that of Jesus or specified Jesus as the content of their preaching, which would have made them the bearers of continuity; this could have been done easily by saying that they preached the Gospel as Jesus was said to do in 1:14 and at the same time leaving open the idea that they preached Jesus through Mark's close association of Jesus and the Gospel (8:35; 10:29). Mark much more often refers to Jesus as teaching than as preaching so if Mark created 3:14 and 6:12 and wished to stress continuity we should have expected him to use διδάσκειν rather than κηρύσσειν. He certainly does use the former word at 6:30 but 6:30 represents the completion of what the twelve have done and not something they are to do. Their mission is complete within the life of Jesus and if we take them

[130] Op.cit., 65, 128.
[131] Ibid., 66, 80, 143.
[132] Ibid., 54-60.

as a group of the past there is nothing to suggest that they, and not the disciples as a whole, have a future task. We should expect a post-Easter commission; if 14:28 and 16:7 represent such a commission it is not given to the twelve but to the disciples as a whole, i.e., the church. Moreover the twelve function as examples to Mark's church rather than as a group of the past in 9:32; 10:32; 10:41 and probably also at 3:14 and 6:7 if our interpretation of these passages as relating to full-time missionaries is correct.

As we have already seen Mark does not make anything of the number twelve in relation to the twelve, nor does he connect the number twelve to any of the Old Testament 'twelve' concepts, nor does he attempt to relate the appointment of the twelve to any of the calls of groups of twelve in the Old Testament[133]; Judaism is not helpful here in understanding Mark. It cannot then be said that the twelve are set out as the new Israel, nor does it appear that they are the core or kernel around which the disciples are built. Both the twelve and the disciples are grouped around Jesus; there is no idea of concentric circles with the twelve as an inner circle and the disciples as an outer circle, for the twelve and the disciples are often interchangeable terms.

[133] Stock, op.cit., 37ff.

Chapter 9

Peter in the Gospel According to Mark

For a long period scholars assumed that Mark was Peter's "interpreter";[1] today many completely ignore any possible connection between Peter and the gospel. It is not the purpose of this paper to discuss whether Peter was Mark's source of information but to inquire instead after the role of Peter in the Gospel itself, and, in particular, to examine whether Mark in any way attacks Peter or through him a Peter-party.[2]

The earliest strands of tradition were not entirely pro-Petrine. Paul argues against Peter in Gal 2:11-14 and tells how he rebuked him;[3] in the Fourth Gospel the beloved disciple is preferred to Peter. On the whole, however, most of the NT gives him an important position. While all the material about him in the earlier chapters of Acts may not be wholly historical, there is sufficient to imply his central position within the primitive Jerusalem Christian community; he may be said to have some importance as first witness of the resurrection (1 Cor 15:5); Paul

---

[1] A review of the present position in relation to this is to be found in R.P. Martin, *Mark:Evangelist and Theologian* (Exeter: Paternoster, 1972) 52-70.

[2] Eusebius,*H.E..*, iii. 39, 15. Cf. R. Bultmann, *The History of the Synoptic Tradition* (Oxford: Blackwell, 1963) 258; J. Schreiber, "Die Christologie des Markusevangeliums," *ZTK* 58 (1961) 154-83; E. Trocmé, *The Formation of the Gospel According to Mark* (London: SPCK, 1975) 125-30; U.B. Müller, "Die christologische Absicht des Markusevangeliums und die Verklärungsgeschichte," *ZNW* 64 (1973) 159-93.

[3] This is not an argument for or against the primacy or authority of Peter; cf. P. Benoit, "The Primacy of St. Peter in the New Testament," *Jesus and the Gospel,* (London: Darton, Longman and Todd, 1972) 2. 121-53.

acknowledges his position in 1 Cor 9:5; Gal 1:18; 2:9. His pre-eminence is also testified by the existence of pseudonymous literature attributed to him. The earlier we place its origin the earlier we see the acknowledgement of his position.[4] Even Paul's rebuke to him at Antioch implies that the opinions of Peter were held to be important by many, otherwise Paul would not have been as eager to correct him as he was.

We shall examine first those references within the gospel in which Peter is featured by himself apart from other disciples, and shall then glance briefly at those in which he appears with others, the Three, the Four and the Twelve.

1. Peter first appears by himself in 1:30; the reference to Andrew, James and John in 1:29 is Mark's redactional introduction linking this pericope to the preceding material in which all four disciples have been named (1:16-20). The main attention focuses on Peter and his name must have belonged to the pre-Markan stage of the pericope. Mark did not then introduce him nor does he draw particular attention to him; he neither slanders nor praises him in this passage. We note that Peter is described as Simon in this incident, as he is in 1:36.

2. While within the pericope 1:35-39 vv 35a, 38b, 39 bear strong traces of Mark's hand,[5] the core of the story could be from the tradition.[6] It is possible that 1:36 may be redactional, but even if this is so Peter functions in it as the one who by his question draws out from Jesus the positive statement of v 38. Peter then acts as a foil to Jesus and is presented in neither a good nor a bad light. More accurately we ought to say that although Peter is mentioned by name it is the whole group of disciples who ask the question (the verbs are plural) and receive the implied rebuke. However, better than assuming all of v 36 to be redactional is to take only its last phrase, *kai hoi met' autou* "and those with him," as such;[7] the original pericope would have

---

[4] I take 1 Peter to be non-Petrine and to date from 80-100A.D.

[5] Cf. M. Wichelhaus, "Am ersten Tage der Woche," *NT* 11 (1969) 45-68.

[6] Luke ascribes the action against Jesus to the crowds who wish to see him as a leader; this may represent an independent form of the same tradition.

[7] Cf.2:25; 3:14; 4:36; 5:18, 24, 40; 14:33. Mark prefers *meta*, "with," to *syn*, "with."

mentioned Simon, but Mark generalizes it, as we shall see he does elsewhere, to include others. With Peter's name alone the original pericope could easily have existed by itself in the tradition; when Mark inserted it into the narrative at this point he had of course to make a reference to the other disciples because of v 29.

3. Peter is mentioned in 8:29, 32, 33.[8] It may be that 8:33b was originally linked to 8:29[9] or that 8:32b, 33b formed a brief pericope by themselves[10] and were united by Mark to 8:27-30. In either case Peter was already part of the tradition[11] and described in it as Satan, though Mark may have inserted his name in 8:32b. It has been argued that 8:32b, 33 is entirely a Markan creation making use of Peter's name because the name already appeared in 8:29;[12] but those who have argued for a Markan composition at this point have usually assumed hostility on Mark's part towards Peter as their reason for his creation of this verse; it is this hostility that needs to be demonstrated and not assumed. Note the clumsy way in which the other disciples are introduced in v 33a; this suggests that Mark is adding the reference to them to existing tradition.[13] But by their introduction he is also indicating that the rebuke to Peter is not to him

[8] For a survey of recent thought on this passage see R.E. Brown, K.P. Donfried, J. Reumannn, *Peter in the New Testament* (Augsburg: Minneapolis; New York/Paramus/Toronto: Paulist, 1973) 64-69. This book also provides a comprehensive review of Peter's place in the NT; for the latter see also R. Pesch, "Peter in the Church of the New Testament," *Concilium,* Vol.4, No.7 (1971) 21-35.
[9] E. Dinkler, "Peter's Confession and the Satan Saying: The Problem of Jesus' Messiahship,"*The Future of our Religious Past* (ed. J. M. Robinson; London: SCM, 1971) 169-202; F. Hahn, *The Titles of Jesus in Christology* (London: Lutterworth, 1969) 223-28; R.H. Fuller, *The Foundations of New Testament Christology* (London: Lutterworth, 1965) 109-11.
[10] U. Luz, "Das Geheimnismotiv und die markinische Christologie," *ZNW* 66 (1965) 9-30; R. Pesch, "Das Messiasbekenntnis des Petrus (Mk 8/27-30)," *BZ* 17 (1973) 178-95.
[11] John 6:67-69 suggests a tradition independent of Mark but parallel to 8:27-29. So Müller,"Die christologische Absicht," 163-170. Cf. Dinkler, "Peter's Confession," 188-189; O. Cullmann, *Peter: Disciple, Apostle, Martyr* (London: SCM, 1953) 24.
[12] Cf. Müller, "Die Christologische Absicht," 163-170.
[13] Cf. Dinkler, "Peter's Confession,"186

alone but concerns all the disciples, and this serves to draw some of the sting from the rebuke. Granted that Peter's name did belong to the underlying tradition of v 29, we have to inquire how Mark's editing of this incident reveals his view of Peter. Mark has set the pericope of the healing of a blind man in two stages (8:22-26) just prior to the pericope of Peter' confession. The healing is symbolical. Peter's sight is to be restored but not all at once. The first stage comes in 8:29. He has been with Jesus and seen his great works. He is now prepared to acknowledge that Jesus is unique and calls him "Christ," but he has not yet come to see that the way of salvation lies through Jesus' suffering. Mark accordingly depicts Peter at this stage as partially blind. He does not however imply that Peter never comes to full sight, or even that he loses his half sight. Full sight or understanding are to come later. It is only at 10:46-52 that Bartimaeus, recovering his full sight, goes willingly on the way with Jesus into Jerusalem. If Peter were finally rejected in the gospel, then it might be possible to argue that his eyes were never fully opened, but 16:7 implies final acceptance[14] and not rejection. It is after the resurrection that Peter receives his full sight.

4. At 9:5[15] Peter belongs to the basic story of the Transfiguration whether the reference to Peter, James and John in v 2 is Markan or not. If it is not, at least all of the second clause of v 6 is Markan, for *ekphoboi gar egenonto*, "for they were afraid," is a typical Markan *gar*, "for," clause and emphasizes the Markan theme of the fear of the disciples.[16] We note that it is plural whereas v 6a is singular. It looks therefore as if v 6, containing an original reference to the stupidity of Peter following naturally

---

[14] Bultmann's suggestion (*Synoptic Tradition*, 258-59) that the earlier tradition about Peter's confession contained Matt 16:17-19 has not been widely accepted. If Matthew were the earliest gospel, then Mark must have omitted these verses; however many of those who argue for Matthean primacy also argue for an Aramaic Matthew which probably did not contain the logion (cf. Benoit, *Jesus and the Gospel*, 135-36).

[15] Cf. the discussion of the Transfiguration in my paper "The Markan Redaction of the Transfiguration" (infra pp. 206-225)

[16] Curiously W. Nützel (*Die Verklärungserzählung im Markusevangelium* [Bamberg: Echter, 1973] 122-41) takes this as the only possible Markan clause in vv 5,6.

from v 5, has been widened by Mark into a reference to all three disciples as being afraid. Thus Mark has again turned the spotlight partly off Peter.

5. In the Gethsemane incident it is difficult to discern precisely the pre-Markan tradition; Mark may have combined two accounts of the same incident[17] or, more probably, have worked over a single account.[18] Whichever solution is correct the use of Simon rather than Peter in v 37 implies pre-Markan material, for prior to 3:16 Mark always uses the name Simon but after the statement there that Simon was given the name Peter he always uses Peter.[19] We may also note the probable Markan introduction of James and John (14:33) and of the change from the singular in v 37b to the plural in v 38.[20] This again suggests that as in the account of the Transfiguration the reference in the tradition to Peter has been widened by Mark beyond him at least to James and John, who are present with Peter, if not also to all disciples.

[17] See K.G. Kuhn, "Jesus in Gethsemane," *EvT* 12 (1952-53) 260-85, followed by T. Lescow, "Jesus in Gethsemane", *EvT* 26 (1966) 141-59 and R. S. Barbour, "Gethsemane in the Tradition of the Passion", *NTS* 16 (1969-70) 231-51.

[18] See E. Linnemann, *Studien zur Passionsgeschichte* (FRLANT 102; Göttingen: Vandenhoeck & Ruprecht, 1970) 11-40; W.H. Kelber, "Mark 14:32-42: Gethsemane–Passion Christology and Discipleship Failure," *ZNW* 64 (1973) 194-208; L. Schenke, *Studien zur Passionsgeschichte des Markus* (Würzburg: Katholisches Bibelwerk, 1971) 461-560; D. Dormeyer, *Die Passion Jesu als Verhaltensmodell* (Münster: Aschendorff, 1974) 124-37.

[19] Kelber ("Mark 14:32-42: Gethsemane," p. 184) is almost alone in thinking that the use of "Simon" represents an attack by Mark on Peter; he argues that by the use of this word Mark is suggesting that Peter has relapsed to the position he occupied before Jesus made him one of the twelve. If Mark had intended this interpretation he would have continued to call him Simon throughout the remainder of the passion, and this he does not do. A Loisy (*L'Évangile selon Marc* [Paris: Emile Nourry, 1912] 413) says that the use of Simon indicates that it is "le pêcheur Simon, et non l'apôtre Pierre" who is involved. It is possible that if we had here a Petrine reminiscence it would represent how Jesus addressed Peter; elsewhere in the passion Peter appears not as addressed by Jesus but as described in narrative and so the normal "Peter" is used.

[20] The logion of v 38 is a kind of Christian proverb which Mark could easily have drawn from the liturgical tradition and inserted at this point. The narrative reads quite satisfactorily without it.

6. There are naturally several references to Peter in the account of the denial.[21] At first sight 14:66–72 seems to be a complete story that is not easy to dismember.[22] But this illusion may have been created by Mark. The pericope possesses certain of his characteristics,[23] e.g., the use of *archesthai* (not as meaning "to begin") and the heaping up of participles (v 67); but it also has some pre–Markan material: the asseveration of v 68 can most easily be explained on rabbinic models[24] or as a mistranslation of an Aramaic phrase.[25] The reference to Jesus as the Nazarene is traditional at 1:24; 10:47; 16:6, and so is probably also here. The story may then have been rewritten by Mark (it is not unnatural for someone retelling a story to shape it into his own style; this seems to have happened with many of the Markan pericopes)[26] or Mark may have changed a single denial by Peter into a threefold denial.[27] The use of *anathematizein*, "to curse," in v 71 forms another difficulty. This verb ought to have a direct object; commentators regularly explain it as a self-cursing by Peter[28] or as indicating his use of a series of imprecations.[29] If it had been either of these there would have been no reason to omit the

---

[21] For earlier discussions of this passage see G. Klein, *Die zwölf Apostel* (FRLANT 77; Göttingen: Vandenhoeck & Ruprecht, 1961) 285–87.
[22] So Klein, *Die zwölf Apostel*, 309–11.
[23] Cf. W. Schenk, *Der Passionsbericht nach Markus* (Berlin: Mohn, 1974) 215–23 pace R. Pesch, "Die Verleugnung des Petrus. Eine Studie zu Mk 14,54. 66–72," *Neues Testament und Kirche* (Für R. Schnackenburg; ed. J. Gnilka; Freiburg: Herder & Herder, 1974) 42–62.
[24] Cf. Strack-Billerbeck, 2. 51. E. Klostermann, *Das Markusevangelium* (HKNT³; Tübingen: Mohr, 1926) 175.
[25] Cf. V. Taylor, *The Gospel According to St. Mark* (London: Macmillan, 1952) 573–74.
[26] This will be more likely to be true if either the Lukan or Johannine account is independent of Mark. Klein (*Die zwölf Apostel*, 287–94) takes the account of Luke to be independent, but Linnemann (*Passionsgeschichte*, 96–108) disagrees. C.H. Dodd (*Historical Tradition in the Fourth Gospel* [Cambridge: CUP, 1963] 83–88) argues for the independence of the Johannine account.
[27] Cf. Schenk, *Passionsbericht*, 215–23; Dormeyer, *Die Passion Jesu*, 149–55; K.E. Dewey, "Peter's Curse and Cursed Peter," *The Passion in Mark* (ed. W.H. Kelber; Philadelphia: Fortress, 1976) 96–114. For others who have held this view see Klein, *Die zwölf Apostel*, 309,n.4.
[28] So RSV.
[29] So NEB

object. Merkel[30] therefore suggests that at an earlier stage in the
tradition the object was expressed and was "Christ", he supports
this from the use of *katarasthai*, "to curse," in the Gospel of the
Nazarenes. If this is so then it may have been Mark himself who
omitted the direct object "Christ" after *anathematizein*, though it
could have been the earlier tradition. The double phrase
anathematizein kai omnynai, "to curse and swear," is characteristically Markan;[31] perhaps in dropping the object to the first verb
he introduced the second. Whatever the explanation of the
present form of the pericope there is no reason to suppose that
Mark introduced the name of Peter into the denial; and indeed, if
Merkel is correct, he may have trimmed down the horror of
Peter's action. If then the introductory words of v 66 are Markan
and the reference to Peter is also his, this is only because the
name already appeared in the story. Thus the introduction of
Peter's name in v 66 does not indicate approval or disapproval of
Peter by Mark.[32] V 54 which brings Peter to the court of the
High Priest's house may well be Markan, for its position
suggests that it is part of one of his typical sandwiches whose
outer segments relate here to Peter and whose center is the trial
of Jesus. We may thus to some extent suspect Mark's hand at
this point in the overall arrangement and possibly in the creation
of v 54; the basic material is pre-Markan but Mark needed to
create a mechanism to bring Peter to a place in which he could
deny Jesus.[33] If Mark created the threefold denial out of an

[30] H. Merkel, "Peter's Curse," *The Trial of Jesus* (ed. E. Bammel; SBT
2/13; London: SCM, 1970) 66–71. Cf. T.A. Burkill ("Blasphemy: St.
Mark's Gospel as Damnation History," *Christianity, Judaism and Other
Greco-Roman Cults* [ed. J. Neusner; SJLA 12; Leiden: Brill, 1975] 1.
51–74) who seems to end in a similar kind of view.
[31] There is not really much to say for the view of J. Behm (*TDNT* 1
[1964] 355) that Mark by omitting the object to the verb intended an
ambiguity, Peter cursing either himself or the people (E. Dewey,
["Peter s Curse and Cursed Peter," 101] claims to follow Behm but in fact has
a different ambiguity). Such ambiguities are not a Markan characteristic.
[32] G. Schneider, *Die Passion Jesu nach den drei älteren Evangelien*
(Munich: Kösen, 1973) 73–82.
[33] That its omission would lead to an uneasy connection between v 55
and v 53 (so R. Pesch, "Die Verleugnung des Petrus," pp. 44–45) is
hardly relevant. If Mark inserted v 54 he will to some extent have
adapted vv 53 and 55. Schneider (*Die Pasion Jesu,* 78) and Dormeyer
(*Die Passion Jesu,* 149–50) take the verse to be from the tradition.

existing account which contained a single denial, he probably did so in order to ensure the fulfillment of Jesus' prophecy of v 30.

Was v 30 not then created by Mark as a *vaticinium ex eventu*?[34] When we examine 14:27-31, we see that vv 27b, 28 form a Markan insertion into existing material[35] so that v 29 must be pre-Markan; therefore the reference to Peter will be pre-Markan.[36] Consequently the prophecy of Peter's denial may also be assumed to be pre-Markan.[37] Has Mark stressed it by adding v 31? There is nothing peculiarly Markan about Peter's word, though it may not be original since it makes the story end other than with a saying of Jesus (v 30) and has biographical characteristics. It is more probable that the final words of v 31, *hōsautōs de kai pantes elegon* "and they all said the same," are Markan;[38] he likes to use the imperfect tense and he regularly

[34] Bultmann, *Synoptic Tradition*, 306.

[35] Cf. Schenk, *Passionsbericht*, 225-27; A. Suhl, *Die Funktion der alttestamentlichen Zitate und Anspielungen im Markusevangelium* (Gütersloh: Mohn, 1965) 62-63; Klein, *Die zwölf Apostel*, 296; Dormeyer, *Die Passion Jesu*, 110-17.

[36] Klein (*Die zwölf Apostel*, 298-302) would support this by arguing that there is an independent tradition in Luke 22:31-32; see also his "Die Verleugnung des Petrus," *ZTK* 58 (1961) 286-328. Linnemann (*Passionsgeschichte*, 72-82) disputes his claim. Schenke (*Passionsgeschichte*, 356-460) argues that all of 14:27-31 is Markan. He fails, however, to produce sufficient evidence of Markan style and vocabulary in 14:27a (apart from the introduction), 29-31, and in the course of his analysis he brings out so many inconsistencies that it is hard to see the pericope as the creation of one author. The conclusion, v 31c, is very weak at the point where we would have expected the incident's climax; the reference to Peter in v 31ab is much more like a climax, which in a way Mark has spoiled by adding v 31c.

[37] If Mark created a threefold narrative in 14:66-72 out of an original single denial he will have added *tris* "thrice" to the prophecy of 14:30.

[38] Dormeyer (*Die Passion Jesu*, 110-17), while acknowledging that there is little characteristically Markan about the earlier part of v 31, argues that the pre-Markan pattern a-b-a of vv 27a, 29, 30 (cf. vv 18-20) would be destroyed by its presence. But: 1. pericopes do not have to follow a fixed pattern; 2. v 31 was added and did destroy the pattern (if it ever existed); there is no reason why it may not have been destroyed prior to Mark; 3. v 31c (see below and n.39) is the kind of clause Mark adds to existing material. Peter is not, as Dormeyer suggests, the spokesman of the twelve here; he speaks for himself.

adds a brief but important clause at the end of pericopes.[39] If the clause is Markan it shows Mark widening the discussion from Peter to include the remaining disciples,[40] as we have seen him do at other points. We should note finally the possible addition by Mark of v 50 which fulfills the prophecy of scattering in v 27b,[41] itself a Markan addition. If Mark did not create the theme of the running away of the disciples in v 50 then his addition of the quotation of v 27b emphasizes its presence in the tradition.[42] We can thus see that the denial story in relation to Peter belongs to the tradition, that if Mark has rewritten the account of the actual denial in vv 66-72 this was in order to show a more exact fulfillment of the prophecy of v 30, and that if he has not introduced the flight of the remaining disciples he has brought out its significance through the deliberate OT quotation of v 27b. Thus it cannot be said that Mark has deliberately drawn attention to the weakness of Peter at this point.[43] The reference to Peter's weeping[44] to some extent cancels his previous behavior as it indicates his repentance and therefore his re-acceptance. It may indeed be that Mark has himself created the reference to his weeping. As we have seen he regularly adds a brief but important independent clause at the end of pericopes.[45] Even if it came to him in the tradition, the way he has stressed it as the final item indicates the importance it holds for him.[46]

7. The passages we have examined so far come from the tradition and we can see that in none of them does Mark pay

[39] Cf. 5:20; 6:6a, 56; 9:32; 12:12, 17, 34, 37; 14:11, 31, 50.

[40] Cf. Schneider,*Die Passion Jesu*, 55-64, 73-79.

[41] Schenk, *Passionsbericht*, 225-226; Klein, *Die zwölf Apostel*, 297.

[42] Note the *pantes*, "all," which runs through vv 29, 31, 50b and holds them together.

[43] The same result follows if we accept the view of M. Wilcox ("The Denial-Sequence in Mark XIV 26-31, 66-72," *NTS* 17 [1970-71] 426-36) that the story is not primarily about Peter; see especially p. 436.

[44] The variant readings do not affect this.

[45] See n. 39 above. Many of these final clauses are connected as here by *kai*, "and," to what precedes them.

[46] The last clause of v 72 would be more certainly Markan if we accept the reading of Codex Bezae.

more attention to the position of Peter than the tradition did; attention is rather turned from him to the other disciples, either the remainder of the Three or Four, or the group of disciples as a whole.

We turn now to the passages where Peter's appearance is clearly redactional and not caused by the surrounding context.

1. 10:28a, with its use of *archesthai* as an auxiliary and the inappropriate reference of vv 29-30 to Peter who left his nets and not his fields,[47] implies Mark's redaction. Peter has thus been introduced by Mark as spokesman; Peter however does not speak for himself alone for he uses the first plural. His position in the story is neutral; it cannot be said that Mark is clearly either supporting or attacking the historical Peter by this introduction, but on balance he could be said to be supporting since nothing is introduced to rebut Peter's claim that he, and the other disciples, have left all. We cannot say why Mark chose Peter as spokesman; those holding a traditional view of authorship would say that it was because the material came to Mark through Peter; but this should not be taken in the sense that Peter told Mark he made the statement of v 28b to Jesus, for as we have seen the statement would be inappropriate on his lips and in fact the separate units of 10:17-31 have been put together by Mark.[48] It would be better to say that Mark used Peter's name because it was well known to his community or because it was the name of the disciple that was found most frequently in the tradition.

2. 11:21, in which Peter again appears as a spokesman, is probably but not certainly redactional; it only exists to drive home what had been already stated in the preceding verse, that the fig tree had withered.

3. The most interesting redactional reference is that in 16:7; as in the case of 14:28 the logion of this verse is a Markan

---

[47] Possibly the fact that wives are not mentioned would reinforce this conclusion since Peter had a wife.

[48] See Best, "The Camel and the Needle's Eye (Mk 10:25)," (infra pp. 17-30), and the references given there.

insertion,[49] but is the introduction to the saying as well as the saying itself to be traced to him?[50] The pre-Markan tradition could have ended at v 7a with, "Go, tell his disciples and Peter." Mark could have composed or introduced only v 7b and v 8;[51] the reference to the disciples and Peter fits the early pre-Pauline list of appearances (1 Cor 15:5). Against this we may argue that if 1 Cor 15:5 was being followed we should expect, "Go, tell Peter and the Twelve"; the inversion of order might then be due to Mark: "Go, tell the Twelve *including* Peter,"[52] but would he have changed "Twelve," as in the tradition according to 1 Cor 15:5, to "disciples"? "Disciples" is the word he usually inserts when he writes redactionally, but where the Twelve appeared in the tradition Mark has tended to preserve the word.[53] It is unlikely then that the whole clause is pre-Markan. The tradition could also have ended, "Go, tell his disciples," and Mark could

[49] See Linnemann, *Passionsgeschichte,* 89 for references. To these may be added R.H. Fuller, *The Formation of the Resurrection Narratives* (London: SPCK, 1972) 53; C.F. Evans, *Resurrection and the New Testament* (SBT 2/12, London: SCM, 1970) 78-79; T.J. Weeden, *Mark—Traditions in Conflict* (Philadelphia: Fortress, 1971) 45-51; 111-17; J. Schreiber, "Die Christologie des Markusevangelium," *ZTK* 58 (1961) 154-83; L. Schenke, *Auferstehungsverkündigung und leeres Grab* (Stuttgart: Katholisches Bibelwerk, 1969) 43-53. R. Pesch ("Der Schluss der vormarkinischen Passionsgeschichte und der Markusevangeliums: Mk 15:42-16:8," *L'Évangile selon Mark: Tradition et Rédaction* [ed. M. Sabbe; BETL 34; Gembloux: Duculot/Leuven University, 1974] 365-409) is one of the few who argue that v 7 was an original part of vv 1-8.

[50] There is nothing un-Markan about v 7a; cf. 6:38; 1:44; 10:21.

[51] V 8 is full of Markan themes and language; cf. Evans, *Resurrection,* 79; Schenk, *Passionsbericht,* 269-71; J. Delorme, "Résurrection et tombeau de Jésus: Marc 16 1-8 dans la tradition évangélique," *La Résurrection du Christ* (E. de Surgy *et. al.,* eds.; Paris: Cerf, 1969) 111-20. It is also possible that v 8a is pre-Markan; it would follow on easily after v 6 (So Schenke, *Auferstehungsverkündigung,* 45-53).

[52] Though his exegesis is otherwise fanciful, J.D. Crossan ("Empty Tomb and Absent Lord [Mark 16:1-8]," *The Passion in Mark* [see n.27] writes, "Peter is singled out not only as being in authoritative first place but as especially designated to receive *this* message" (p. 149).

[53] Cf. Best, "The Twelve in Mark," (infra pp. 131-161), and, more generally, Best, "Mark's Preservation of the Tradition," (infra pp. 31-48); K. Kertelge, *Die Wunder Jesu in Markusevangelium* (SANT 23; Munich: Kösel, 1970) 185-86.

have added Peter's name.[54] In either case there are good grounds for thinking that Mark stressed Peter's name here. It is however much more probable that Mark himself composed v 7a as well as v 7b. Whatever we decide, it is clear that Peter's name is retained or introduced by Mark, not in order to attack him, but in order to show special favor on the Lord's part towards him, presumably to balance the unfavorable impression created by the denial (if, of course, the reference in 16:7 is from the tradition, then it implies that this correction was already being carried out in the tradition).

4. Thus where Mark has introduced Peter into the material, he has presented him as spokesman without any clear evidence of an attack upon him; indeed, if anything, the evidence favors the idea that Mark had a good opinion of Peter.[55] This would be strongly confirmed if, as is highly probable, the reference to Peter in 16:7 is Markan.

We look now at those places where Peter's name is found in association with others.

1. At 3:16 Mark has apparently unified two pieces of tradition, one of which gives the names of the Twelve and the other the special names that according to tradition Jesus had given them. In this way he introduces the name Peter; since he does not explain this as he does in the case of Boanerges we may assume that its meaning was known to his readers and that they would have regarded it as a compliment. Moreover, unlike the name "Boanerges" which is never again used and which therefore may be considered a "nickname," the name "Peter" is used throughout the remainder of the gospel (apart from 14:37).[56] It must therefore have Mark's approval and would appear to signify that Peter's position is in some way accepted

[54] Cf. Schenk, *Passionsbericht*, 268. For Dormeyer (*Die Passion Jesu*, 224–26) the only Markan part of v 7 is the reference to Peter.
[55] Luke twice introduces Peter as spokesman (8:45; 12:41, cf. Matt 24:44-45); in the first of these he is presented as failing to understand; Luke (22:8) also identifies Peter as one of the two who go to prepare the passover. John identifies Peter as the disciple who cut off the ear of the High Priest's servant (18:10), hardly a claim to honor.
[56] Cf. K. Stock, *Boten aus dem Mit-Ihm-Sein* (AnBib 70; Rome: Biblical Institute, 1975) 28-34.

since, whether Matt 16:17-19 is historical or not, the meaning of the name would connote a good quality. A new name implies the beginning of a new life.[57] The appearance of Peter's name at the head of the list corresponds also to the number of times in comparison with the other disciples in which he is named in the Gospel, but its position there belongs to the original tradition and not to Mark's redaction.

2. There are a number of occasions when Peter's name appears with James and John ("the Three") and also with James, John and Andrew ("the Four").[58] We have the latter association in 1:16-20; 1:29 (at which we have already looked), and 13:3. 1:16-20 is clearly from the tradition, though Mark may possibly have joined together its two separate incidents. If Jesus is to call disciples then it is necessary to record some incidents in which this takes place and there is no idea of hostility towards the four or towards Peter alone in these incidents. Again in 13:3 we cannot detect an attitude towards Peter which is different from that towards the other disciples, especially since 13:3 is widened in 13:27 to all disciples. We have already looked at all the incidents where Peter appears with James and John apart from 5:37 and seen that the names of James and John were probably added by Mark.[59] In 5:37, however, the reference to "the Three" may come from Mark's redaction, but it does not in any way single out Peter. He is treated in the same way as James and John.

To sum up: Where Peter appears in the tradition in a bad light Mark normally lifts the strain off him by associating other disciples with him;[60] the only exception is the story of the denial where Mark may have increased the amount of material about

[57] Cf. Stock, *Boten aus dem Mit-Ihm-Sein*, 32.

[58] For Mark's use of "the Three" and "the Four" see G. Schmahl, *Die Zwölf im Markusevangelium* (Trier Theologische Studien 30; Trier: Paulinus, 1974) 128-40.

[59] It is much more probable that Mark took up a known unit of three from the tradition and used it for his own purposes than that he created the unit.

[60] This conclusion differs from that of Trocmé (*Formation of Mark*, 126) who speaks of a tendency on Mark's part to detract from the pre-eminence accorded Peter in the tradition.

him, perhaps turning the single denial into a threefold; but it is by no means clear that he did this in order to vilify Peter, since he probably also emphasized the flight of all the disciples. There may also be another factor: Peter's failure may be heightened in order to bring out the contrast in behavior to Jesus. Where Mark has himself introduced Peter he either presents him in a good light or, at least, neutrally; if the reference in 16:7 is Markan then this is an obvious attempt to correct the impression left by the denial. Thus there is no reason to conclude that Mark was attacking the historical Peter. If the question is asked why Mark did not omit the passages about Peter if he wished in some way to defend him, the answer must be that these passages formed part of the tradition known to his community; he cannot eliminate them and therefore he modifies them, the beginning of a process which Matthew and Luke carry further. On the other hand if Mark really wished to attack Peter's reputation there are places where he could have introduced him; 8:14–21 is his composition; its argument could have been sustained as easily by using Peter's name alone; the same is true of 6:52. 9:33–34 could also have been expressed mentioning Peter in particular. More generally, to ask the question about Mark's treatment of Peter may imply a view of Mark's purpose as ultimately biographical. But Mark does not set out to tell his community about Peter for Peter's sake but for the sake of the community. Failure occasioned by pressure from outside the community must have been all too common; if Peter's failure was eliminated he could not be seen as the proto-penitent.

It is generally allowed that in Matthew's Gospel the pressure is taken off Peter to an even greater extent,[61] though he is also introduced at some points where he is not featured in Mark. Thus he appears as a spokesman for the disciples in 15:15 (=Mark 7:17; cf. Matt 17:24; 18:21). However our evidence shows that Mark is not the high point in an attack on Peter, nor, since we have produced no actual evidence of an attack on him, the high point in which Peter appears in a bad light. This point must lie in the tradition behind Mark. Where and when did it occur? There are two obvious answers:1. Within an anti-Petrine

---

[61] See Brown, Donfried, and Reumann, *Peter,* 75–107.

faction (which could either have been pro-Paul or pro-James) during the time of the controversy about the admission of the Gentiles to the Church. 2. With Peter himself, or some other of the disciples, and going back to the time of Jesus when Peter was in some ways a failure. Since time tends to make reformed characters see their past life in much blacker colors than it really was, Peter might have blackened his own character; in any case in order to encourage Christians, the tradition might have concentrated on Peter's initial failures since everyone knew of his later Christian life.

Chapter 10

The Miracles in Mark

We do not deal here with miracles in general but only with those in the Gospel of Mark and, more particularly, only with their significance for Mark. Though the miracle stories once existed and were understood as separate pericopae they are now part of the Gospel and we examine how they are to be understood, not as individual incidents, but in the light of the whole Gospel.[1] We begin then by setting out a view of the Gospel so that within it we can see their place. The Gospel was written primarily for a Christian community, and not as a handbook for missionaries or as a pamphlet to be placed in the hands of potential converts, even less as a source book for christology. If the earlier *Sitz im Leben* of the miracle stories had been the missionary or evangelistic activity of the Church or if in the life of Jesus they had been taken as signs of the Kingdom[2] or of the Messiah,[3] this is no longer so within Mark's Gospel; and they cannot be understood in any of these ways. The Gospel was written not only for a Christian community but for a particular Christian community at a particular time and intended to meet its needs. In writing for this community Mark was not polemicizing against a definite heresy or aiming to provide information about the historical Jesus, but seeking to preserve and deepen the Christian faith of his readers. Naturally in the course of this he

[1] Cf. D. A. Koch *Die Bedeutung der Wundererzählungen für die Christologie des Markusevangeliums* (Berlin: de Gruyter, 1975), pp. 8-12.
[2] Cf. J. Kallas, *The Significance of the Synoptic Miracles* (London, SPCK, 1961).
[3] Cf. R. H. Fuller, *Interpreting the Miracles* (London: SCM, 1963), pp 46–48.

did supply information about Jesus and rebut false views, but his
main aim was to show his readers what God could do for them
through Jesus and tell them what their response ought to be;
these two would naturally be closely related. Given this pastoral
purpose, what part do the miracles play in it? It is clear that we
shall view the miracles differently if we approach them from this
angle rather than from an attempt to determine what christology
they display.

In examining them we assume that Mark was the first to
write a Gospel and that prior to his time the individual stories
existed mainly as discrete units. Some of them may have been
joined together, but it is difficult to be certain if any of the
miracle stories were already formed into a collection or a
connected narrative.[4] In the oral tradition most of the pericopae
had already lost their original data of time and place, and so
lacked within themselves the clues as to how they could be
joined together in a consecutive account. Thus the way in which
Mark has placed them tells us something about the use to which
he was putting them. Clearly Mark was not totally free in
respect of the separate incidents; insofar as some of them were
already joined together he probably did not split them up, and
insofar as certain incidents, e.g., the baptism, must necessarily
precede other incidents, e.g., the passion, he preserved their
order. For the moment all we need to note is that Mark set most
of the miracle stories in the first half of his Gospel. Other
implications of their positioning will emerge later. Secondly, we
learn something of the way in which he wished them to be
understood by the alterations he made in retelling them, and
redaction criticism allows us to trace the signs of his hand. But

---

[4]   The question of a pre-Markan collection or collections of miracles is
differently answered; cf. Koch, op. cit., pp. 30-38; H. W. Kuhn, *Ältere
Sammlungen im Markusevangeliums,* "Studien zur Umwelt des Neuen
Testaments," 8 (Gottingen: Vandenhoeck & Ruprecht, 1971), pp.
191-213; P. J. Achtemeier, "Toward the Isolation of Pre-Markan
Miracle Catenae", *Journal of Biblical Literature,* LXXIX (1971), 265-291,
and "The Origin and Function of the Pre-Markan Miracle Cantenae,"
Journal of Biblical Literature, XCI (1972), 198-221; L. Schenke, *Die
Wundererzählungen des Markusevangeliums* (Stuttgart: Katholisches Bibel-
werk, 1974), pp. 383-385; H. C. Kee, *Community of the New Age*
(London, SCM, 1977), pp. 32-38.

again Mark was not completely free, for the incidents he used
were already current in the oral tradition of his community. The
modifications he could make would then be the kind of
modifications which preachers make when they retell stories of
Jesus in order to draw out particular points from them. Those
who have preached from the same Gospel incident on a number
of occasions realize that they have at least slightly altered the
emphasis each time beacause they wished to use the story for
different purposes. Mark was free to do the same.

In this brief study we do not discuss the historicity of the
miracles nor make any attampt to trace them back to their origin
in the life of Jesus or in that of the primitive Palestinian or
Hellenistic communities. There is no reason to suppose that
Mark invented the stories he used; he employed material which
was already known to his own community. Nor is there any
reason to suppose that he doubted the truth of the stories he told.
The attitude of people then towards the "wonderful" was quite
different from that of people today. They were used to hearing
and believing stories of fantastic events in the lives of great men.
We live in a more sceptical age, and even devout Christians who
accept all the miracle stories of the canonical Gospels normally
dismiss those of the apocryphal gospels. The criteria used today
to discuss historicity would be quite different from those used in
the ancient world.[5] Without discussing what these are, it will be
sufficient if we look briefly at the last of Mark's miracles, the
cursing of the fig tree (11:12-14, 20f.). In almost all the other
miracle stories Jesus is helping people, here he destroys a tree;
does such an action cohere with what we know of him elsewhere
in the Gospels? Moreover he destroys the tree for not producing

[5]   On the attitude of the ancient world to miracle see G. Theissen,
Urchristliche Wundergeschichte, "Studien Zum Neuen Testament," 8
(Gütersloh: Gerd Mohn, 1974) *passim*; J. M. Court, "The Philosophy of
the Synoptic Miracles," *Journal of Theological Studies*, XXIII (1972),
1-15; *Miracles: Cambridge Studies in their Philosophy and History*, ed. C. F.
D. Moule (London: Mowbray, 1965); P. J. Achtemeier, "Gospel
Miracle Tradition and the Divine Man," *Interpretation*, XXVI (1972),
174-197; H. van der Loos, *The Miracles of Jesus*, "Supplements to
Novum Testamentum," 9 (Leiden: Brill, 1965). For a historical outline
of the modern theological and philosophical discussion see E. and M. L.
Keller, *Miracles in Dispute* (London: SCM, 1969).

figs at a time of the year, the spring, when it would be unnatural to find figs on it; only a fool would look for figs then. (It may be that the story's origin is Jesus' parable of Lk. 13:6-9.) Mark is clearly aware of the difficulty of the time-setting he gives the story for he says, "It was not the season for figs" (11:13), and this is his own insertion into the story. From this awareness on Mark's part we learn: (1) elsewhere in telling the miracle stories he was not aware of historical difficulties; (2) he used this story, and therefore probably others, for a purpose other than its literal factuality. When we examine where he has placed this story we see that he has created one of his typical sandwiches where one incident is set in the middle of another and they throw light on each other. Here the cleansing of the Temple is preceded by the action of Jesus in cursing the fig tree and followed by the recognition of its destruction. The fig tree is Israel, and Jesus has come to Jerusalem, the city of God, looking for the fruit which should have appeared in Israel, but as the sequel shows he finds none: God's greatest messenger is rejected in the very place, Jerusalem, where he ought to have been received.

Accepting this as its meaning for Mark, there remains a residual question for us, and it applies not only to this miracle but also to some of the others. Our attitude to the events of history is different from that of a person of the first century. A young child who believes in Santa Claus can have his conduct profoundly affected by that belief in the days before Christmas; an adult who has stopped believing will not be affected. This suggests something which needs to be considered by preachers. Can lessons be drawn from events which did not happen? It has often been inferred that Jesus can provide for all man's spiritual needs becasue he fed the five thousand; but if some people today have doubts about the literal accuracy of this event this may lead them to doubt the inference. The error in the argument lies in the deduction. It is true that Jesus satisfies all man's spiritual needs. It is not true that this depends on the accuracy of the account of the feeding of the five thousand. The latter is only an illustration of it. Mark was quite clear in 11:12-14 that he was using an illustration; when we use the miracles we must be equally clear how we are using them. The phrase "acted parable" which is sometimes applied to them is difficult. A parable is

something which might be true, but is not true; the parable of
the Good Samaritan never actually happened. There is, however, no reason to doubt that Jesus did heal the sick and exorcize
the possessed.

It is clear that Mark considered the miracles to be important,
for they occupy more than a quarter of his Gospel. We shall
confine our attention to those events which are normally classed
as miracles and which are the result of an action by Jesus;[6] this
excludes the resurrection and such signs as the rending of the veil
(15:38; cf. 15:33). If Mark had been asked what were the
wonderful events or miracles in his Gospel he might also have
included the call of the disciples (1:16-20; 2:14) which took place
without psychological preparation and as a result only of Jesus'
simple word to them; perhaps also the blinding of those outside
the church as the direct result of God's action (4:11ff.), the
transfiguration in which two figures appear alongside Jesus and
he himself is transformed (9:2-8), and the support by the Holy
Spirit of believers in time of trial (13:11). If it is argued that Mark
had no interest in the miracles but used them only because they
were already known in his community it is only necessary to
point to the summaries (1:32-34, 3:7-12; 6:53-56; cf. 8:14-21) he
wrote[7] referring to them; he did not need to draw such explicit
attention to them. Paul does not refer to them; they feature
relatively rarely in Q; they are a part of the gospel which Mark
proclaims.

Did he then use this extensive mass of material in order to
impress people with Jesus as "divine man" (*theios aner*)? There
were many contemporary healers and miracle workers; does
Mark wish Jesus to be classed among them? Against such a view

[6] Since we are concerned with "content" rather than "form" we do
not need to discuss rival views as to which stories have an approved
miracle "form".
[7] Cf. T. Snoy, "Les miracles dans l'évangile de Marc," *Revue
Theologique de Louvain*, III and IV (1973), 58-101; Koch, op. cit., pp.
160-176. Their significance is not diminished if Mark used material
from the tradition in their compilation; cf. K. Kertelge, *Die Wunder Jesu
im Markusevangelium* "Studien zum Alten und Neuen Testament," 23
(Munich: Kösel-Verlag, 1970), pp. 30-38; Schenke, op. cit., pp.
112-115; R. Pesch, *Markusevangelium* "Herders theologischer Kommentar zum Neuen Testament," (Freiburg: Herder, 1976), p. 133.

182   DISCIPLES AND DISCIPLESHIP

we note: (1) In 8:11-13 Mark uses a piece of material in which
Jesus refused to give the Pharisees a miracle or sign to assure
them as to his nature; by including this at the end of the main
section on miracles he indicates that the miraculous element
within them is not to be stressed.[8] (2) At 13:21-23 the believers
are warned against false Christs and false prophets who perform
signs and wonders; miracles, of themselves, do not certify that
the one who performs them is from God. (3) Mark emphasizes
the blindness of the disciples in respect of some of the miracles,
but when he does so it is not in relation to the extent or wonder
of the miracles, but to their true understanding of them. This is
especially clear in 8:14-21, where, in a passage which he has
himself compiled and which directly follows the refusal to give a
sign, he warns them against behaving like Pharisees who ask for
signs. (4) As we read through the Gospel we are continually
thrown forward to its conclusion in the cross and resurrection;
all the earlier parts are controlled by this conclusion. With three
exceptions all the miracles precede the main predictions of the
passion and the resurrection; we therefore move from the
miracles to the latter, and the miracles must be seen in their
light. Jesus is primarily the one who dies on the cross and rises
again and not the one who works miracles. The cross might
suggest he was powerless, but the miracles show him as the one
who can and does come in his risen power to the help of the
community. (5) When we examine the accounts it is difficult to
find in them redactional evidence that Mark has accentuated the
miraculous element. Instead, where that element was important
in the preceding tradition there follow on his part commands to
silence (1:44; 5:43; 8:26); those who have been healed are not to
go around proclaiming it. Mark 5:19 is an apparent exception,

[8] If Mark knew the logion of 8:12 in the Q form (Mt. 12:39 = Lk.
11:29) with the reference to Jonah and deliberately omitted the reference
he may have done so to insure a total rejection of signs (cf. Schenke,
op. cit., pp. 282-288); Snoy, art. cit., pp. 456-464, suggests he omitted
it because it referred to the resurrection; this might parallel his omission
of risen appearances of Jesus (assuming 16:8 to be the end of the
Gospel); the risen Jesus is to be seen everywhere in the Gospel, not just
in particular events after his death. We cannot agree with K. Tagawa,
Miracles et Évangile (Paris: Press Universitaires de France, 1966), pp.
75-78, that 8:11-13 refers to apocalyptic signs and not to miracles.

but since this is the healing of a Gentile the exception may be related to Mark's theology of the Gentiles as the new people of God replacing the Jews.[9] (6) As we go on we shall see that from each miracle Mark draws a lesson or a number of lessons and these are not related to the wonder of the miracle as past event, but to some way in which the community can be helped or instructed, or the gospel proclaimed in the present.

Yet some of the pericopae isolated from their Markan setting and without their Markan modifications could be read in a way which would suggest that they might have been used to glorify Jesus as a worker of miracles.[10] Did this derive from a deliberate attempt to depict Jesus as a divine man like the other divine men of the ancient world, or, given the miracles, was it a natural human attempt to evade the foolishness of the cross (1 Cor. 1:22-24)? It is not as certain as it is sometimes alleged that there was a clear concept of a divine man in the contemporary world;[11] even if there was, it is less clear that the early Christians would have consciously formalized their teaching along its lines. Christian history, however, shows that Christians have always tended to regard Jesus as someone who achieves things for them and to ignore the radical demands on their behavior which the cross makes. It is this natural tendency to water down the cross that Mark sets out to correct. Yet within his overall purpose he is still able to find a positive place for the miracles. Even the passion itself is interpreted through miracles: the noonday darkness (15:33), the rent veil (15:38), the empty tomb (16:1-8). The way of the cross is misunderstood (8:32; 9:30-37; 10:32-45); that does not mean Mark does not have a positive place for it. The miracles are misunderstood (6:52; 8:14-21); that should not mean they are to be rejected. They were a part of the life of the early church (2 Cor. 12:12; Heb. 2:4; Acts *passim*): what is required is their understanding and repetition. Mark does not

[9] Cf. Tagawa, op. cit., pp. 168-172.
[10] Cf. Schenke, *passim;* see especially p. 392.
[11] Cf. E. Schweizer, "Neure Markus Forschung in USA," *Evangelische Theologie*, XXXIII (1973), 533-537. Cf. D. L. Tiede, *The Charismatic Figure as Miracle Worker*, "Society of Biblical Literature Dissertation Series," 1 (Missoula, Montana: Scholars Press, 1972); W. V. Martitz, "Huiós," *Theological Dictionary of the New Testament VIII*: 338-340.

then simply replace a divine man christology with a passion christology.

In any case, Mark's theology is not one of the cross alone, but a theology of the cross and the resurrection; he emphasizes the resurrection equally with the cross. Each of the three formal predictions (8:31; 9:31; 10:32-34) concludes with a prophecy of Jesus' resurrection. Mark 9:9 implies that true perception of the glory of Christ only comes to those who realize his risen presence. In 14:28 and 16:7 Mark depicts Jesus as promising to go at the head of his disciples as they venture out on the mission and life of the Church. In 14:58 and 15:29 the promise is made of a new temple, a church, which comes into being with Jesus' resurrection. The disciples, who in Mark's understanding represent the members of his community,[12] are continuously with Jesus. They often go apart with him privately into the "house" and are taught by him just as the members of Mark's community meet and are taught in their house churches. (Mark has written little about the continued presence of God in his people through the Holy Spirit simply because he assumes the presence of the risen Christ with them).[13] In the transfiguration the disciples are commanded to listen to Jesus (9:7); when the members of Mark's community hear the words of Jesus he is present with them. Mark believes in the presence of the risen Christ with his community.[14]

If then Jesus is present in the community when his words are heard may he not also be present in his actions? His words teach; his actions continue to help. The Christians need help; they face persecution and have to meet the temptations of the world, the desire for riches, security, popularity (4:14-20). They go the hard way of the cross, but it is not a lonely, unsupported

---

[12] Cf. E. Best, "The Role of the disciples in Mark," *New Testament Studies,* XXIII (1977), 377-401 (infra pp. 98-130).

[13] Contrast Acts.

[14] *Pace,* T. J. Weeden, *Mark: Traditions in Conflict* (Philadelphia: Fortress, 1971), pp. 85-90, 101-117. For the presence of the risen Jesus in the Gospel, see E. Trocmé, *The Formation of the Gospel according to Mark* (London: SPCK, 1975), pp. 164-174. "Easter is implicit in his (Mark's) whole message," W. Marxsen, *Introduction to the New Testament* (Oxford: Blackwell, 1968), p. 141; cf. Tagawa, op. cit., pp. 121-122.

following of Jesus, but one in which they have his presence. The miracles indicate some of the ways in which his support is offered. Though they are to be understood in the light of his resurrection,[15] yet it would be wrong to say that they reveal him as the Risen One;[16] the resurrection is the presupposition of their repetition in the church and the presupposition of their proper understanding.[17]

We look now in a little more detail at some of the miracles, beginning with those in the second half of the Gospel which fall outside the main section of miracles. In these the promise of the risen Christ is not stressed. We have already dealt with the story of the cursing of the fig tree (11:12-14; 20f.). Its position brings it directly into relation with the passion and the resurrection; because there is no fruit to be found in Judaism, Jesus dies on the cross; because the Jews have failed, a new temple is created for the Gentiles (11:17).

The remaining three miracles in this part of the Gospel all relate in some way or other to the theme of discipleship.[18] The healing of the epileptic boy (9:14-29) is set firmly within the main section on discipleship (8:27-10·45). If two distinct stories are united in this account, then their union is almost certainly pre-Markan.[19] In any case verses 28f. come from Mark, as does the positioning of the account within the discipleship section. There was no original relation of the account to the transfiguration, and it is very doubtful if this relation was in Mark's mind for he has placed 9:9-13 between the two pericopae. Had he wished to draw out the relation, he would have said something in verse 14 about Jesus coming down from the mountain (cf. Lk.

---

[15] Cf. Kertelge, op. cit., pp. 193-196.

[16] Cf. Koch, op. cit., pp. 176-179.

[17] Cf. Theissen, op. cit., pp. 133-135; A. Fridrichsen, *The Problem of Miracles in Primitive Christianity* (Minneapolis: Augsburg, 1972), pp. 77-84.

[18] Attempts to group the miracles in sections so that they relate to particular themes (e.g., Theissen, op. cit., pp. 208-209) are not wholly successful.

[19] Cf. Kertelge, op. cit., pp. 174-179; Koch, op. cit., pp. 114-126; Theissen, op. cit., pp. 139-140; P. J. Achtemeier, "Miracles and the Historical Jesus in Mark 9:14-29," *Catholic Biblical Quarterly*, XXXVII 471-491.

9:37). Verse 28 stresses the failure of the disciples, but this is not used to blame them, as verse 29 makes clear; instead, their failure creates an opportunity for positive teaching on how the sick should be healed. Christians in the early church were active in healing (1 Cor. 12:9, 28; Rom. 15:19; 2 Cor. 12:12; Jas. 5:14f.; Acts 3:1ff.; 9:36ff.; 16:18; etc.). The disciples were commissioned to heal and exorcise (3.14f.; 6.7, 13); how can Christians carry this out?[20] They need divine strength and this only comes through prayer. Thus by position and redaction the story fits into the theme of discipleship, incidentally indicating again the positive attiude of Mark and the early church to miracles.

There are two accounts of the healing of blind men; these are strategically placed just before and just after the section on discipleship. In the first of these, 8:22-26, there is little Markan redaction, but the position of the incident is important. Mark 8:14-21 is a Markan construction; the disciples are accused of a failure to understand and this failure is expressed in terms of a failure to see. Sight is a widely used metaphor for understanding;[21] Mark 8:14-21 draws this out explicitly. The miracle of 8:22-26 thus represents the restoration of understanding. That Jesus' healing fails at the first attempt and only succeeds at the second represents the coming of understanding by stages.[22] In the immediately following confession of Peter at Caesarea Philippi Peter sees, but does not see clearly. He confesses Jesus as the Chrst but does not understand that Jesus must die (8:31-33). This is the stage of those who have followed Jesus up to this point in the story of the Gospel. They have heard some of his teaching and seen some of his mighty works, so they can categorize him as all-important, the Messiah. They have not

---

[20] T. A. Burkill, "The Notion of Miracle with Special Reference to Saint Mark's Gospel," *Zeitschrift für die neutestamentliche Wissenschaft,* L (1959), 33-48, argues that one reason for the preservation of the miracle stories was the church's own practice of healing and exorcism.

[21] Cf. Kertelge, op. cit., pp. 163f. The restoration of hearing in 7:31-7 has the same significance (see 8:18); cf. Kertelge, op. cit., p. 160; Schenke, op. cit., p. 279. D. E. Nineham, *Saint Mark* (Harmondsworth: Penguin, 1963), pp. 202-203, regards 8:22-26 and 7:31-37 as fulfillment of Isa. 35:5.

[22] The two stages are not intended to imply that Jesus found the miracle difficult.

yet understood his death, nor how they themselves must follow in the way of the cross.

That disciples can have full sight emerges when we turn to the second healing of a blind man (10:46-52). Again there is little Markan redaction, and again the position of the incident is important. Verse 52b comes from Mark: Jesus goes "on the way" of the cross (1:2f.; 8:27; 9:33; 10:32) and the disciple must go on the same way. The meaning of "the way" for both Jesus and the disciple has been described throughout 8:27 - 10:45; now there only remains the actual act of going by Jesus. Christians who have read and understood this section of the Gospel ought now to be ready to go with him. So Bartimaeus follows Jesus into the city; his eyes have been opened. Thus again this miracle helps us to understand what discipleship means.

This story has another theme which was probably its original climax "Your faith has made you well"(v. 52a). Although Mark has added verse 52b and so changed the purpose of the miracle he cannot have been unaware of the importance of verse 52a, for he uses the same theme elsewhere (5:34; and 9:23f.). The Greek word *sōzein* has the double connotation "save, heal." Thus 10:52 and 5:34[23] might as easily be translated "your faith has saved you."[24] Mark 5:36 again refers to faith; this may be the reason Mark was led to link the two stories of 5:21-43 (cf. vv. 23, 28); they thus reinforce each other. The centrality of faith appears again at the conclusion of the visit of Jesus to Nazareth (6:6a); there are strong indications of Mark's hand in this passage, and it owes its position to him.[25] In emphasizing faith Mark is emphasizing a trait already in the tradition. Salvation requires the believing response of the one to be saved. In contrast to many miracles from the contemporary religious world, faith is the presupposition of miracle and not its result. Faith and salvation go together; thus many of the healing miracles speak of

[23] Mark 5:34 forms the climax to the account (Kertelge, op. cit., p. 115) and is probably part of Mark's redaction (Schenke, op. cit., pp. 200-202). It incidentally corrects any false idea that the woman was healed magically through touching the clothing of Jesus.

[24] Cf. Nineham, op. cit., pp. 158-159; E. Schweizer, *The Good News according to Mark* (London: SPCK, 1971), p. 118.

[25] Cf. E. Grässer, "Jesus in Nazareth," *New Testament Studies,* XVI (1969), 1-23; Koch, op. cit., pp. 147-153.

the total saving power of God through Christ;[26] like Jairus's daughter, those dead in sin are raised to new life (Eph. 2:5f).

There are other healing stories in which Mark sets out the redemptive power of Jesus. In 1:40-45 a leper is cleansed. At times in the Old Testament leprosy is a punishment for sin (Num. 12:10; 2 Kings 5:27; 15:5); the word 'cleanse' is used both of forgiveness of sin and of healing from leprosy. Leprosy is then a type of sin. He who can heal the leper can also forgive the sinner and bring the excluded leper, i.e. sinner, into the community.[27] The same theme is continued in the next pericope, 2:1-12. Whether or not Mark joined together two stories here,[28] the connection between sin and sickness continues. He who can free into activity the limbs of a paralytic can also forgive his sins. Verses 1f. of this section are largely Markan. In them Jesus is said to speak the word, i.e., preach. There is, however, no preaching in 2:3-12, except the statement of Jesus about the healing of the sick and the forgiveness of his sins. The story thus proclaims the gospel of the forgiveness of sins.[29] The movement from physical healing to forgiveness again confirms Mark's positive attitude to the miracles; the same movement must have taken place many times in the missionary activity of the early church; miracles as such cannot then be condemned.

Another healing, 7:24-30,[30] deals with the extent of redemption rather than its nature. Note again the careful way in which Mark has positioned it. It follows directly on a dispute with the Jews, from which Jesus goes into Gentile territory and heals the daughter of a Gentile woman. This extension of his activity to include the Gentiles is also emphasized by the discussion between Jesus and the woman. Though the second feeding is set

[26] Cf. R. P. Martin, *Mark: Evangelist and Theologian* (Exeter: Paternoster Press, 1972), pp. 169-171.

[27] Cf. Kertelge, op. cit., p. 73; he is wrong however is seeing 1:40-45 as equivalent to an exorcism.

[28] Kertelge, op. cit., p. 77; Tagawa, op. cit., p. 13; and Schenke, op. cit., pp. 146-160, take their union to be pre-Markan.

[29] Cf. A. Fridrichsen, op. cit., p. 153; R. Schnackenburg, *The Gospel according to St. Mark* (London: Sheed & Ward, 1971), I:38-42.

[30] See especially T. A. Burkill, *New Light on the Earliest Gospel* (Ithaca: Cornell, 1972), pp. 48-120.

in Gentile territory, it is not said whether those who are fed are Jews or Gentiles, but perhaps we may conclude that Mark has given the miracle this context (cf. the setting of 7:31-37)[31] to show Jesus' saving help and teaching as intended for all the world. If Jesus is willing to heal Gentiles, then the church must bring to them the gospel of their redemption. The universal nature of salvation is emphasized at many points in the passion story (cf. 11:17; 12:9; 13:10; 15:38f.).

Mark 3:1-5, the healing of the man with the withered hand, though not strictly related to redemption, is used to define an element in the teaching of Jesus; and the miraculous nature of the healing is thrust almost completely into the background. Any story in which Jesus had helped a man on the Sabbath would have served Mark's didactic purpose.

In a number of the healings at which we have already looked, there was a command of Jesus to the person who had been healed to keep silent about his healing (1:44; 5:43; 7:36; 8:26). In most cases it would have been historically impossible for the healed person to have done this. (These commands to healed people should be distinguished from the commands to the exorcised demons not to confess Jesus). Redaction criticism shows that these commands probably derive from Mark's pen.[32] At 7:37 the original conclusion to the pericope (in which the spectators acclaimed Jesus' deed) has survived and it contrasts strongly with the command. But even within the command of 7:36 we already find from Mark's hand a statement that the command was not kept.[33] In 1:45, which may be Markan, the cleansed leper, though forbidden to proclaim his healing, does talk so freely about it that Jesus can no longer openly enter the town.[34] Thus Mark has an ambivalent attitude to the healing miracles:[35] the tradition had already stressed how Jesus' healing

[31] Cf. Martin, op. cit., pp. 210-212.
[32] Theissen, op. cit., pp. 146-147, 152, regards the commands within miracles as pre-Markan though he accepts passages like 1:34; 3:12; 8:30; 9:9 as Markan.
[33] Cf. Koch, op. cit., pp. 72-73; Schenke, op. cit., pp. 271-272.
[34] Mark 5:18-20 might also be adduced here but its redactional analysis is uncertain; cf. Koch, op. cit., pp. 78-84.
[35] Cf. Tagawa, op. cit., pp. 164-172.

activity drew men's attention to him, and Mark not only permits such statements to remain but intensifies them; at the same time he depicts Jesus as demanding silence about his miracles, for he is not a mere thaumaturge.[36] In two of his summaries Mark explicitly mentions the way in which the healing powers of Jesus draw people to him (1:32–34; 6:53–56), and yet he also shows Jesus as arousing antagonism through his miracles (3:20–30). What are we to make of these seeming contradictions? The healing stories in Acts suggest that often in the early church the healings drew the attention of men to the healer who was then able to proclaim Jesus (Acts 3; 14:8ff.). On the one hand, the healing narratives attract men to Jesus; on the other, they do not reveal his true nature and the real claim he makes on them; this only comes from the cross. Hence Mark's ambivalent attitude. So he retains the miracles, but sets them within the framework of a story dominated by the passion.

We turn next to the picture of Jesus as exorcist. There are four accounts of individual exorcisms, viz., 1:21–28; 5:1–20; 7:24–30; 9:14–29, though in the last two the demonic element is relatively unimportant. In addition the exorcisms are mentioned in two summaries (1:32–34; 3:11f.)[37] and one discussion (3:22–30). The summaries and to some degree the discussion show us what was significant in them for Mark: (1) there is a victoy of Jesus over evil;[38] (2) Jesus commands the demons to be silent; (3) the demons are aware of Jesus' identity. The preservation of a double reference to the authority of the twelve to exorcise together with instruction on how exorcism is to be carried out (9:28f.) shows the importance of exorcism in the life of the early church. Today we normally attribute physical illness to viruses or mental maladjustment and treat psychological disturbance with drugs and psychiatric counselling, but in the ancient world demonic evil was seen not only in physical and mental illness but

---

[36] Cf. Theissen, op. cit., p. 154; Koch, op. cit. pp. 84–85.

[37] The summary of 6:53–56 does not include a reference to exorcism suggesting that there is no longer any interest in it from this point on in the Gospel.

[38] This aspect is emphasized especially by J. M. Robinson, *The Problem of History in Mark,* "Studies in Biblical Theology," 31 (London: SCM, 1957), pp. 33–42; but cf. Tagawa, op. cit., pp. 80–84.

also in disturbances in the material world; in 4:39 the storm on the lake is rebuked as if it were a demon.

It was important to Mark's community to know that Jesus had been a successful exorcist and that exorcism was still possible; to deny this would be to deny the Holy Spirit (3:29-30).[39] The risen Jesus is present in the contemporary exorcist who contends with the powers of demonic evil. We detected a certain ambivalence in Mark where he depicted healed people as forbidden to speak about what had happened to them; this ambivalence is not present in the command to the demons to be quiet. The absence of a counter element underlines the success of Jesus in destroying demons; it may also indicate that Jesus does not require the testimony of evil to his nature.

The demons by their very nature have supernatural knowledge and recognize the true identity of Jesus; he is the Son of God. Other equivalent titles appear in the exorcism accounts, but when Mark writes freely it is this title he uses, probably because it is the main title of confession in his own community. It is used by God at Jesus' baptism and transfiguration and by the Gentile centurion at the cross. Its close relation to the cross is also seen in the parable of the vineyard where the son of the owner is killed (12:6-8); "beloved son" there and at the baptism and transfiguration is probably a play on Isaac as Abraham's only or beloved son (Gen. 22:2) whom he sacrificed. (Jewish tradition paid considerable attention to this sacrifice.) The Markan "Son of God" is thus again not the "divine man" of pagan religion. Even if the exorcisms are related through this title to the passion, they do not govern Mark's understanding of it. The cross is not for him the center of a demonic struggle between Satan and Jesus.[40] We should not, therefore, use the exorcisms to interpret the Gospel as a whole, and certainly not to interpret all the other miracles.

We look finally at the four so-called nature miracles. Mark would have been unaware of our distinction between healing

[39] Cf. M. E. Glasswell, "The Use of Miracles in the Markan Gospel" (in *Miracles,* edited C. F. D. Moule, see n. 5).
[40] Cf. E. Best, *The Temptation and the Passion,* "Society for New Testament Studies Monograph Series," 2 (Cambridge: Cambridge University Press, 1965).

and nature miracle which derives from our scientific outlook; he groups them together, but for other reasons. Strictly there are five such miracles, for the cursing of the fig tree ought to be included. The other four are the two accounts of feedings (6:35-44; 8:1-10) and the two voyages on the Sea of Galilee (4:35-41; 6:45-52). All four came to Mark in the tradition and he repeats them though with some important qualifications. He introduces, or continues where it is already present, the fear, misunderstanding, and blindness of the disciples explicitly through comments at 6:52 and 8:14-21[41] and implicitly by an insertion into the narrative at 4:40.[42] Mark intends these four miracles to be treated as a group, for the comment at 6:52, which follows directly on the second ship miracle, refers to a failure of understanding on the part of the disciples in respect to the first feeding.

Preceding the account of the feeding of the five thousand, he has introduced another important qualification. Mark 6:30-34 is a Markan compilation,[43] and in verse 34 Jesus is presented as the compassionate shepherd who feeds his flock.[44] It is commonly concluded from this that Mark depicts Jesus as continuing to feed the church with the eucharist,[45] but Mark explicitly refers to Jesus as teaching in response to the need of the people. It may be that in the earlier tradition, and certainly later in the Gospel of John, the feedings were regarded as symbolic of the eucharist; but Mark has another interpretation. Food is a regular and easily

[41] Mark 8:1-10 has been linked by Mark to 8:11-13 and through it to 8:14-21; cf. Schenke, op. cit., p. 281.

[42] Cf. Pesch, op. cit., p. 268; Schenke, op. cit., pp. 90-93; Koch, op. cit., p. 97.

[43] E.g., Koch, op. cit., pp. 99-101; Schenke, op. cit., pp. 217-222. Although Kertelge, op. cit., pp. 129-131, takes most of 6:34 to be pre-Markan he allows that the reference to the teaching of Jesus comes from Mark.

[44] J. M. van Cangh, "La Multiplication des pains dans l'évangile de Marc; Essai d'exégèse globale," in L'Évangile selon Marc, "Bibliotheca Ephemeridum Theologicarum Louvaniensium," ed. M. Sabbe (Louvain: Leuven University Press, 1974), pp. 309-346.

[45] E.g., Kertelge, op. cit., pp. 134-137, 144-145; Nineham, op. cit., p. 179. But cf. Koch, op. cit., p. 103, Schenke, op. cit., p. 235.

understood metaphor for teaching,[46] and the central element of
Jesus' teaching in the Gospel is teaching about the passion and
the discipleship which should issue from an understanding of it.
Thus, whether teaching or the eucharist is the theme, there is a
connection with the passion. Here again as with many of the
other miracle stories the element of the miraculous is not so
much directly as indirectly devalued by giving the story a new
interpretation.

Because the feeding and sea miracles are presented as a group
by Mark, it is probable that we should go on and interpret the
latter in a similar way[47] as relating to Jesus' care for the
community. The little company of disciples in the ship
represents the church of Mark's own day beset by the storms[48]
of the world (persecution, the various temptations of wealth,
sex, etc.); in such need the risen Jesus comes to them or is found
to be in their midst. It is true that the epiphanic element is
important[49] in these stories, but it is wrong to ignore the fact
that Jesus gets into the ship (6:51) and that the storm ceases. The
disciples do not understand – a pattern of the church which will
not believe that Jesus comes to help it in emergencies; by adding
6:52 Mark has turned attention away from the epiphanic
element. This may also be the significance of "he wished to pass
them by" (6:48), if this phrase is redactional[50] (cf. 7:24); the
disciples are not to spend their time in amazement at Jesus'

[46] At 8:3 the crowd is said to be likely to faint "on the way." It is "on
the way" (8:27; 9:33; 10:32, 52) that believers go after Jesus to the cross
and resurrection. It is perhaps implied that without the food of the word
disciples may faint and therefore fail through trial and temptation.
[47] Cf. P. J. Achtemeier, "Person and Deed: Jesus and the Storm-tossed
Sea," *Interpretation*, XVI (1962), 169-176.
[48] Note the demonic nature of the storm (4:39 cf. 1:25); the disciples
are delivered from a spiritual and not a physical peril; cf. A. E. J.
Rawlinson, *The Gospel according to St. Mark* (London: Methuen, 1942),
p. 88.
[49] Cf. Kertelge, op. cit., p. 148. On the partial epiphanic nature of the
sea-miracles, see Theissen, op. cit., pp. 102-111, who recognizes that
they are miracles of "deliverance" and (pp. 186-187) that Mark has
played down the epiphanic element.
[50] Cf. T. Snoy, "Marc 6:48: '. . .et il voulait les dépasser.' Proposition
pour la solution d'une énigme," in *L'Évangile selon Marc* (see n. 44), pp.
347-363.

walking on the sea. Mark 4:40, 41 depict the fear and astonishment of the disciples; "fear" is also associated with the risen presence of Jesus (16:8); he is risen and will quell storms. The questions of 4:40, 41, expressing the astonishment of the disciples, drive home what Jesus can do for them; if the church doubts, let it be reassured. Finally, we note that it is the disciples who benefit from the two sea miracles; they represent the community of Mark's own day. In the feeding miracles the crowd (= the flock = the church) again represents that community and is the beneficiary of Jesus' goodness; thus the readiness of Jesus to protect and feed his community is shown in these four miracles.

What now of the fear and blindness of the disciples? They see the miracles but are not convinced by them of Jesus' true nature: let the early church beware of presenting Jesus as a miracle worker to the world, for the world may see the miracles and not be convinced. Within the church the failure of the disciples can be represented as a failure to understand their significance for themselves;[51] believers need to grasp again what they mean, and especially in their relation to the cross and resurrection. In the same way they fail to understand the parables and thus to understand the gospel in relation to the Kingdom of God. Explanations of the parables are not withheld for those within the church (4:10-12, 33-34); so those within the church should be able to understand the miracles – in the light of the resurrection.

As we look back the way we have come, we can see that Mark has used the miracles which came to him in the tradition in different ways. He expects them to be reproduced in the life of the community (9:28f.). But also each has its own lesson to teach, and some a number of lessons. Through them Mark teaches about the Sabbath (3:1-5), the failure of the Jews (11:12-14, 20f.) and the acceptance of the Gentiles into the church (7:24-30); he stresses the need for a deep understanding of Jesus in respect of true discipleship (8:22-26; 10:46-52) and implies that Jesus himself alone gives it; he reassures his congregation that Jesus is greater and continues to be greater

---

[51] Koch, op. cit., pp. 92-93, points out that while commands to silence are linked to the healing miracles it is in relation to the nature miracles that the failure to understand is brought out.

than demonic evil (the exorcisms), illustrates the saving power of Jesus in respect to sin (the healing miracles), shows that Jesus still meets the needs of a persecuted, tempted, and spiritually deficient church. In this way he has "spiritualized" the miracles. In many of the stories, while the miracle still remains, the emphasis no longer lies on it as an outward and physical miracle but as a miracle which takes place within the inner life of the community. We should also note that there are other passages which are not normally recognized as miracles, but in which supernatural help is offered to the community for its life: in 1:16–20 the disciples are called without psychological preparation and seen unable to resist the calling; in 4:10–12 revelation is given to the community which is denied to those outside it. The lesson which the miracles teach also relates to the person of Jesus; if he saves from disease or the devil or storm, we learn something about his nature;[52] but the primary emphasis lies on what they tell us about his activity for and on behalf of men.

If Mark has spiritualized the miracles he has not, on the other hand, denied their physical reality. (It is impossible to spiritualize what has not happened; a spiritual lesson cannot be drawn from a non-existent event). He has played down the element of wonder, but has not eliminated it. He gives them their proper place as physical events; hence the commands to silence and the emphasis upon the fear and blindness of the disciples. The miracles may draw men to the church, but of themselves they do not bring them to true faith. The conclusion of the miracle stories in the tradition probably contained a statement of the fear or wonder of the by-standers; if Mark sometimes retains this (1:27), he also applies it more widely in relation to the cross (10:32, 14:33; 16:5–6; cf. 10:24).[53] The miracles must be left behind as physical events as disciples go on the way of the cross. There must have been many in Mark's community who were drawn to it by the charismatic activity of some of its members; they must be helped to understand the need to grow beyond the miracles for these alone cannot bring them to true faith. Hence

[52] Cf. Glasswell, op. cit., who in common with most commentators tends to see the lessons taught in the miracles as lessons in christology; we disagree.
[53] Cf. Tagawâ, op. cit., pp. 94–122.

the miracles taper away after 8:27. Those who have seen the miracles and got as far as 8:27 are "on the way" (8:27; 9:33; 10:32, 52), but a long and difficult path still lies before them in which they must pick up the cross and deny themselves. Peter's half sight, gained from the earlier teaching and the miraculous activity of Jesus, as he enunciates it in 8:29 is not wrong but insufficient; he must go much further. It is the same for Christians, and as they go on that further path and towards the cross and resurrection they can begin to understand the miracles more fully and realize that they do not have to travel alone and unsupported. Jesus is with them to help them grasp the meaning of their faith and assist them through the trial and the difficulties that lie before them. The miracles are not merely far-off events in the past life of Jesus but part of the present life of believers.[54]

---

[54]   The narrative "draws the reader into the story as a participant," N. Perrin, *The New Testament: An Introduction* (New York: Harcourt Brace Jovanovich, 1974), p. 165.

Chapter 11

Uncanonical Mark

Review of E. J. Pryke, *Redactional Style in the Marcan Gospel*. (Society for New Testament Studies, Monograph Series 33). C.U.P.; Cambridge 1978, pp. ix + 196.

Given that Mark took material from tradition and adapted it in various ways for his Gospel how can we distinguish what comes from his hand from that which comes from the various sources he used? Already a great deal of work has been done both on individual passages in the Gospel and on particular themes which appear in it; in consequence there is a certain amount of agreement that some passages are Markan; Can we use such agreements to distinguish other passages? Dr. Pryke has examined many of the books and articles which have already appeared and starts from the basis of what they held in common as coming from R (The Markan Redactor). He has also made use of the various stylistic features identified by previous work on Mark from Hawkins and C. H. Turner onwards. He assumes the results of form criticism, in particular the pericopal nature of the pre-Markan tradition. He lists eighteen stylistic features. Many of these had already been detected by Hawkins and C. H. Turner, but they assumed that the features appeared uniformly throughout Mark. Pryke sets out to examine this uniformity and in the end challenges it.

In his work he takes each feature in turn and examines its occurrences. Assuming the work of previous redactional critics he is able at once to say that in a certain number of cases each feature appears in clearly redactional passages. He then examines the other passages where at first sight it looks as if it may have come from the sources (S) which Mark used. Looking at the passages in their context, and introducing the additional test of characteristic Markan vocabulary, he is able to transfer from S to R many of these passages. Finally he lists one by one verses which appear to be Markan with the redactional features which enable him to identify them as such and concludes by printing the text of these verses. Because of the detailed nature of the argument which leads him to the agreed text it is impossible to reproduce it here or even to give a sample of it; it has to be seen as a whole rather than as work done on individual verses. We can, however, indicate some of his results. 'Markan usage then would support 16.8 as the genuine ending of the Gospel, and in keeping with style and literary ability.' (p. 45). Most of 1:1–8 are from R but vv. 5,7 are not. 9.31, the second prediction of the Passion, like the other predictions, is from R. Though Mark had adapted and modified many stories about Jesus he does not appear to have created any incidents; he has formulated summaries and generalising statements but he has not on the whole invented new narrative. The nearest he comes to the invention of new narrative is the healing of Bartimaeus.

Not everyone will agree with all these conclusions. For myself, I am happy to see that in contra-distinction from some American redaction critics he concludes that Mark did not invent whole pericopae of narrative nature, but I would challenge his conclusion that the predictions of the Passion are from Mark's hand. If Mark had written these I would have expected him to speak not of Jesus being killed by the Jews but of him being crucified (note that in 8.34 immediately after the first prediction of 8.31 he plays on the meaning of Jesus' death as crucifixion), to have said 'on the third day' rather than 'after three days', and to have used the normal word in the tradition for the resurrection of Jesus *(egeirein)*. Pryke seems to imply that the unusual nature of the vocabulary suggests R whereas I would take it to suggest S.

This is a valuable and important piece of work; no one who attempts to examine Mark redactionally will in the future be able to ignore it. It is a task which needed to be done and once done will not require to be done again for some considerable time because it has been carried through so thoroughly. There seems, however, to be one serious flaw, and in mentioning this, I do not intend to detract in any way from the importance of the book. Pryke does not examine what is left of the S material after he withdraws the R material. Once the R material is withdrawn from some pericopae it is not clear if what is left and regarded as S would be able to stand by itself as a unit of tradition. So little is left of 1.40–45 or 3.31–35 or 10.13–16 that it is difficult to see how these existed as units within the tradition. There needs then to be added a section on *Traditionsgeschichte* dealing with the material before Mark took it over.

The book also raises by implication some important questions. Did Mark translate the material from Aramaic into Greek, or did he put together material existing in Greek which was already known to the community in which he worked? Did he sometimes do the one and sometimes the other? If he translated material we would expect his language and style to be detectable everywhere; Pryke does not argue for homogeneity of style in the existing Gospel yet there are times when he speaks of Mark as a translator. If he retold material which was already known to his community, it is almost certain that in retelling he would not reproduce it verbally but would allow some of his own style and favourite words to enter; if that is so then we would expect evidence of the work of his hand within traditional pericopae even when he was not creating or adapting and modifying the material but merely retelling it. Everyone who retells anecdotes puts the imprint of their own style on them; clearly they will do this at some points in the material more than at others, e.g., in the introductions, but not so much in others, e.g., in the conclusions. By implicitly raising these questions this book pushes us a step forward in any consideration of the way in which Mark reacted to his material and treated it. It is important not least for this.

Because of the pattern Pryke has distinguished in the Markan use of certain stylistic features it seemed a good idea to go on and examine an alleged piece of Markan material to see if the same pattern was to be found there, viz., the section of the letter of Clement of Alexandria discovered by Morton Smith, *Clement of Alexandria and a Secret Gospel of Mark* (Harvard U.P., Cambridge, Mass., 1973), which purports to quote from an edition

of Mark (termed 'uncanonical Mark' hereinafter) otherwise un-
known to us. We reproduce below the text as transcribed by
Smith and list by page and line of his edition the places where the
characteristics studied by Pryke appear. The letters in brackets
refer to Pryke's itemisation of the tests. An English translation
(not necessarily the same as Smith's) is provided in parenthesis
for easy identification and where it might be thought helpful
examples of the characteristics are given for comparative
purposes from Pryke's lists.

II

23	(k)	'impersonals' ('they come')
24	(i)	'redundant' participle ('she coming') cf. 12.42; 14.40; 7.25
26 and III	(g)	'and immediately'

III

1	(i)	'redundant participle' ('Jesus coming') cf. 1.35; 7.24; 8.13.
2	(g?)	'immediately' cf. 1.28; 3.6; 6.45; but see 6.25; 14.45 where it may not be redactional
5	(f)	*archesthai* + infinitive
6	(n)	*gar* explanatory ('for he was rich')
7	(b)	genitive absolute ('it being evening')
9.10	(a)	parenthetical clause ('for he taught him the mystery of the kingdom of God') cf. 13.10; 8.15; alternatively this clause may be an example of (n). *gar* is a Markan favourite.
10	(i)	'redundant' participle ('rising from there') cf. 7.24; 10.1; such participles usually fall at the beginning of incidents unlike III.10 which is at the conclusion.

The Markan characteristics are thus well spread out through
the pericope whereas in canonical Mark they tend to cluster in
the seams. On the whole this suggests that the passage does not
come from Mark. We might however account for the phe-

nomena if either (a) Mark had joined together a number of incidents, or (b) if we could give a reason why he has edited the material extensively at some points. III 5-7 might represent a possible join of two incidents.

Plate II: folio 1 verso

καὶ ἔρχονται εἰς βηθανίαν καὶ ἦν ἐκεῖ μία γυνὴ ἧς ὁ ἀδελφὸς αὐτῆς ἀπέ:

θανεν· καὶ ἐλθοῦσα προσεκύνησε τὸν ἰησοῦν καὶ λέγει αὐτῷ· υἱὲ δα

25 βὶδ ἐλέησόν με· οἱ δὲ μαθηταὶ ἐπετίμησαν αὐτῇ· καὶ ὀργισθεὶς ὁ

ἰησοῦς ἀπῆλθεν μετ᾽ αὐτῆς εἰς τὸν κῆπον ὅπου ἦν τὸ μνημεῖον· καὶ

Plate III: folio 2 recto

εὐθὺς ἠκούσθη ἐκ τοῦ μνημείου θωνὴ μεγάλη· καὶ προσελθὼν ὁ ἰησοῦς ἀπ

ἐκύλισε τὸν λιθον ἀπὸ τῆς θύρας τοῦ μνημείου· καὶ εἰσελθὼν εὐθὺς ὅπου

ἦν ὁ νεανίσκος ἐξέτεινεν τὴν χεῖρα καὶ ἤγειρεν αὐτόν· κρατήσας:

τῆς χειρός· ὁ δὲ νεανίσκος ἐμβλέψας αὐτῷ ἠγάπησεν αὐτὸν καί:

5 ἤρξατο παρακαλεῖν αὐτὸν ἵνα μετ᾽ αὐτοῦ ἦ· καὶ ἐξελθόντες ἐκ

τοῦ μνημείου ἦλθον εἰς τὴν οἰκίαν τοῦ νεανίσκου· ἦν γὰρ πλούσιος· καὶ μεθ᾽

ἡμέρας ἓξ ἐπέταξεν αὐτῷ ὁ ἰησοῦς· καὶ ὀψίας γενομένης ἔρχεται ὁ

νεανίσκος πρὸς αὐτόν· περιβεβλημένος σινδόνα ἐπὶ γυμνοῦ· καὶ

ἔμεινε σὺν αὐτῷ τὴν νύκτα ἐκείνην· ἐδίδασκε γὰρ αὐτὸν ὁ

10 ἰηοοῦς τὸ μυστήριον τῆς βασιλείας τοῦ θεοῦ· ἐκεῖθεν δὲ ἀναστὰς·

ἐπέστρεψεν εἰς τὸ πέραν τοῦ ἰορδάνου· ἐπὶ μὲν τούτοις ἔπεται τὸ· καὶ

It seemed necessary at this stage to go a little further. Morton Smith himself (op. cit. pp. 357ff.) has drawn attention with painstaking detail to the way in which a great part of the pericope is paralleled in canonical Mark. We append an analysis, in part dependent on his work, but attempting to isolate phrases rather than individual words. We have underlined the relevant phrases in the appended text and refer to them by page and line number; within lines the first phrase discovered is identified as (i), the second as (ii), the third as (iii); where a phrase is continued from one line to the next we identify it by the earlier line. Where confusion might exist as to the end of one phrase and the beginning of the next a vertical line indicates the break. We have given each phrase a value; if it contains two significant words unvaried in comparison with some phrase in canonical Mark it is valued at 3; if there is some minor variation (e.g., change of person, number, tense, mood, gender or change of 'Jesus' to 'he'), then it is valued at 2; if there is more than one significant change then it is valued at 1; very common phrases

(e.g., 'he said to them') and vague parallels are valued at 1.
Longish phrases (consider III 3 (ii) and (iii)) have been broken
into sections otherwise the full value of their similarity would
not be made apparent; alternatively we might have given higher
values to them. Sample parallels are given, except in the case of
very common phrases. It is assumed that phrases will have at
least two significant words in common; the article, common
connecting particles, etc. are thus excluded.

II		Parallels	Value
23	(i)	8.22	2
	(ii)	3.1	2
24	(i)	5.6	2
	(ii)	frequent	1
24–25	(iii)	10.48	3
25	(i)	10.13	3
26	(i)	5.24	2
III			
1	(i)	1.26; 5.7; 15.34,37	2
1–2	(ii)	16.3	2
2	(i)	16.3	2
	(ii)	6.25	2
3	(i)	1.41; 3.5	2
	(ii)	1.31	2
3–4	(iii)	1.31	3
4	(i)	10.21	2
	(ii)	10.21	2
5	(i)	5.17	2
	(ii)	5.18	3
5–6	(iii)	1.29	2
6	(i)	1.16 + 10.22	1
6–7	(ii)	9.2	3
7	(i)	6.47	3
7–8	(ii)	1.40	2
8	(i)	14.51	3
10	(i)	4.11	3
	(ii)	7.24	3
11	(i)	10.1	3

The number of passages underlined shows that this passage is very similar to canonical Mark. There are 157 words in the passage; of these 91 words fall into passages with similarity rated 2 or 3. There are in fact two phrases of value 1, fifteen of value 2 and ten of value 3. Totalling these according to value we obtain a correlation figure of 62 (2 × 1 + 15 × 2 + 10 × 3).

It is now necessary to ask if we would find the same pattern of similarity if we were to take other pericopae from canonical Mark and compare them with the remainder of the Gospel. We have done this for three passages of content somewhat similar to the passage we have just discussed. We give detailed evaluation for 10.17-22 and the results for the two others. Our enumeration now follows verse numbers.

Mark 10.17-22

Καὶ ἐκπορευομένου αὐτοῦ εἰς ὁδὸν προσδραμὼν εἷς καὶ γονυπετήσας αὐτὸν ἐπηρώτα αὐτόν, Διδάσκαλε ἀγαθέ, τί ποιήσω ἵνα ζωὴν αἰώνιον κληρονομήσω; ὁ δὲ Ἰησοῦς εἶπεν αὐτῷ, Τί με λέγεις ἀγαθόν; οὐδεὶς ἀγαθὸς εἰ μὴ εἷς ὁ Θεός. τὰς ἐντολὰς οἶδας, Μὴ φονεύσῃς, Μὴ μοιχεύσῃς, Μὴ κλέψῃς, Μὴ ψευδομαρτυρήσῃς, Μὴ ἀποστερήσῃς, Τίμα τὸν πατέρα σου καὶ τὴν μητέρα. ὁ δὲ ἔφη αὐτῷ, Διδάσκαλε, ταῦτα πάντα ἐφυλαξάμην ἐκ νεότητός μου. ὁ δὲ Ἰησοῦς ἐμβλέψας αὐτῷ ἠγάπησεν αὐτὸν καὶ εἶπεν αὐτῷ, Ἕν σε ὑστερεῖ· ὕπαγε, ὅσα ἔχεις πώλησον καὶ δὸς τοῖς πτωχοῖς, καὶ ἕξεις θησαυρὸν ἐν οὐρανῷ, καὶ δεῦρο ἀκολούθει μοι. ὁ δὲ στυγνάσας ἐπὶ τῷ λογω ἀπῆλθεν λυπούμενος, ἦν γὰρ ἔχων κτήματα πολλά.

		Parallels	Value
17	(i)	10.46; 13.1	3
	(ii)	8.23; 13.3; 14.61	3
	(iii)	12.9; 15.12	1
18	(i)	frequent	1
	(ii)	2.7	3

		Parallels	Value
20	(i)	9.12	2
21	(i)	10.27	2
	(ii)	frequent	1
	(iii)	12.44	2
	(iv)	14.5	2
	(v)	2.14	3

It will be noted at once that the phrases for which similarity is suggested are shorter and contain fewer significant words than those in the non-canonical passage. The corresponding figures are 94 words of which 26 are accorded values of 2 or 3; there are three passages of value 1, four of value 2, four of value 3. The weighted correlation figure is 23.

The corresponding figures for 1.40–45 are: 97 words of which 23 are accorded values of 2 or 3; there are two passages of value 1, seven of value 2, one of value 3. The weighted correlation figure is 19.

The corresponding figures for 7.24–30 are: 129 words of which 17 are accorded values of 2 or 3; there are eight passages of value 1, six of value 2 and none of value 3. The weighted correlation figure is 20.

Summarising

	Number of words	Number values 2 and 3	% of Total	Weighted correlation figure	Fraction total number of words
non-canonical					
Mark	157	91	58.0	62	.395
1.40–45	97	23	23.7	19	.196
7.24–30	129	17	13.1	20	.155
10.17–22	94	26	27.7	23	.245

From these figures it can be seen that non-canonical Mark stands by itself. We noted earlier that it had Markan characteristics at unexpected places. We must now conclude that it is too much like Mark. All this implies it was not written by Mark but by someone who knew Mark well and picked up his phrases.

We might describe it as a·mosaic of Markan phrases. It looks as if its author thumbed through Mark until he found the phrase he wanted, if necessary modified it and then made it part of his text. Inadvertently he produced an 'overkill'. It is impossible to determine when or by whom this was done.

As Morton Smith's work shows many of the phrases not paralleled in canonical Mark can be paralleled from one of the other gospels. It is of course impossible to compare non-canonical Mark against other sections of canonical Mark in respect of use of Matthew and Luke since we know the latter used Mark. It is for the same reason impossible to decide whether Matthew and Luke knew non-canonical Mark or vice versa. It would not, of course, be surprising that by the time of Clement of Alexandria someone should know and use all three synoptic Gospels.

Chapter 12

The Markan Redaction of the Transfiguration

Since we are interested in the setting of this incident in Mark's gospel and his interpretation of it it is unnecessary to inquire after its origin, earlier *Sitz im Leben,* or meaning in the tradition before Mark; in particular we do not need to discuss Riesenfeld's[1] theory that it is closely related to the Feast of Tabernacles, for it is impossible that Mark could have expected his readers to pick up and understand this background. However there are other Old Testament motifs which may have helped to shape the account in its earlier stages and which could have been appreciated in Rome and we have to ask whether these were of importance in Mark's use of the pericope. The background has been found in the theophanies of Mount Sinai to which the idea of the new Moses would be related and in the apocalyptic scenery of Daniel which would bring in the idea of the Son of Man; it is not necessary that these should be regarded as alternatives; both may have affected the tradition.[2] Apart from this commentators have tended to divide in recent years between those who relate the Transfiguration to the resurrection and those who relate it to the Parousia.[3] There are obvious

[1] *Jésus transfiguré. L'arrière-plan du récit evangélique de la transfiguration de Nôtre-Seigneur.* Lund,1947.
[2] M. Sabbe, 'La rédaction du récit de la Transfiguration' in *La Venue du Messie* (Recherches Bibliques VI) Bruges, 1962,pp.65–100, traces both backgrounds in the account.
[3] The most recent survey is that of J.A. Ziesler, 'The Transfiguration Story in the Markan Soteriology', *Exp. Times* 81 (1969/70) 263–8, in which most of the literature is listed. It needs however to be supplemented by M. Horstmann. *Studien zur markinischen Christologie* (Münster, 1969), pp. 72–139. We should note also: M. Thrall, 'Elijah

connections in both cases. 8.38 and 9.1 immediately preceding the Transfiguration suggest the latter and are supported by the transformation of Jesus' body, which might be expected at the Parousia. The direct reference to the resurrection in 9.9f. linked to the prediction of it in Mark at 8.31 suggest the former.

Here it is necessary to distinguish carefully between the origin of the Transfiguration in a resurrection appearance which has subsequently been relocated in the earthly life of Jesus and Mark's alleged view that in the Transfiguration the risen Jesus and not the Jesus of the Second Coming is presented to the disciples. Despite Bultmann's endorsement of the former theory[4] it is not tenable; C. H. Dodd in a classic study[5] of the 'form' of the resurrection appearance narratives has clearly demonstrated that the Transfiguration lacks the characteristics of the resurrection 'form'. There is no initial sense of lonely abandonment on the part of the disciples, no introductory word of greeting, reproach, or command from Jesus to those to whom he appears, no recognition by them of the figure who appears as

and Moses in Mark's account of the Transfiguration', *NTS* 16 (1969/70) 305-17, W. Gerber 'Die Metamorphose Jesu, Mark 9.2f. par.' *TZ* 23 (1967) 385-95; A. Feuillet, 'Les perspectives propres à chaque évangéliste dans le récit de la Transfiguration', *Bib.* 39 (1958)281-302; R. Lafontaine et P.M. Beernaert, 'Essai sur la structure de Marc 8.27-9.13', *Recherches de Sc. Rel.* 57 (1969) 543-61; P.G. Bretscher, 'Exodus 4.22-23 and the Voice from Heaven', *JBL* 87 (1968) 301-311; F. Neirynck, 'Minor Agreements Matthew-Luke in the Transfiguration Story' in *Orientierung an Jesus* (Für Josef Schmid; edited P. Hoffmann) Freiburg, 1973, pp. 253-66; W. Schmithals, 'Der Markusschluß, die Verklärungsgeschichte und die Aussendung der Zwölf, *ZTK* 69 (1972) 379-411; T. A. Burkill, *Mysterious Revelation* (Cornell, 1963) pp. 145ff.; R.G. Hamerton-Kelly, *Pre-existence, Wisdom and the Son of Man* (S.N.T.S. Monograph Series 21; Cambridge, 1973), pp. 53ff.
[4] *History of the Synoptic Tradition* (Oxford, 1963), p.259. He was by no means the first to suggest a resurrection setting but his *imprimatur* has led to its wide acceptance without independent examination.
[5] 'The Appearances of the Risen Christ: an Essay in Form-Criticism of the Gospels' in *Studies in the Gospels* (Essays in Memory of R.H. Lightfoot), Oxford, 1955, pp. 9-35. Cf. also G.H. Boobyer, *St. Mark and the Transfiguration Story*, Edinburgh 1942; Sabbe, art. cit. Curiously C.E. Carlston, 'Transfiguration and Resurrection', *JBL* 80 (1961) 233-40, who advocates a misplaced resurrection account is unaware of Dodd's article; so also is Schmithals (see n. 3).

the earthly Jesus they have previously known, no commission or instruction from Jesus to the disciples. Instead we find, what we do not find in any of the resurrection accounts, that Jesus is silent, that there is a voice from heaven which identifies Jesus, not as the earthly one, but as the super-human (which seems unnecessary in a resurrection appearance), that he is accompanied by two heavenly figures, and that ὤφθη, the characteristic word of the appearances, is used of these figures and not of Jesus.

We possess at least two distinct traditions about the Transfiguration, for the account in 2 Pet. 1:16-18 does not depend on any of the synoptic accounts. Nearest to Matthew it differs from it considerably:[6] the mountain is described as 'holy' and not as 'high', the voice speaks 'from heaven' and not 'from the cloud', the words of the voice are in a different order from that found in Matthew, μοῦ is added to ἀγαπητός, ἐγώ inserted before εὐδόκησα and εἰς ὅν used instead of ἐν ᾧ. No mention is made of the cloud or of Moses and Elijah but this, it must be allowed, may only be because the account has been stripped of superfluous detail in order to confirm the authority of 'Peter'. The Ethiopian version of the Apocalypse of Peter (chs. 15-17)[7] may represent yet another tradition or be allied to that in 2 Peter since the mountain is again described as holy. The disciples are praying (in the Lukan account it is Jesus who prays) as they go with Jesus to the mountain, and their interest lies not in Jesus but in the heavenly figures; it is these, unnamed at first, who apparently are transfigured, and the point of the narrative seems to be that their transfigured form discloses the nature of heavenly existence. At its conclusion Jesus as well as Moses and Elijah is borne away by the cloud.

More interesting but much more difficult to evaluate is the assertion that Matthew and Luke had access either to another

[6] Cf. J. N. D. Kelly, *The Epistles of Peter and Jude* (London, 1969) ad loc. See also C. Bigg, *The Epistles of St. Peter and St. Jude* (Edinburgh, 1910); K. H. Schelkle, *Der Petrusbrief. Der Judasbrief* (Freiberg, 1964).
[7] See E. Hennecke and W. Schneemelcher, *New Testament Apocrypha* (ed. R.McL. Wilson, London, 1965) II, pp. 663ff. for this and for its relation to the Akhmim version.n

tradition in addition to that of Mark or to the tradition which
Mark used; as is well known there are a number of minor
agreements between them against Mark. The evidence has been
examined most recently by Schramm[8] and Neirynck[9] who reach
opposite conclusions. The discussion raises so many wider issues
in relation to synoptic source criticism that it is impossible to
discuss it here.

In order to determine Mark's understanding of the pericope
we begin with his redactional activity.[10]

In v. 2 κατ'ἰδίαν μόνους is clearly Markan for: (i) Mark loves
double expressions;[11] (ii) he uses κατ'ἰδίαν frequently in
redactional passages (4:34; 6:31,32; 7:33; 9:28; 13:3); (iii) he
regularly depicts Jesus as separating the disciples or a group of
them for special teaching (4:10,34; 7:17,24; 8:10 etc.); here we
have such a separation of three disciples from the remainder and
from the crowd (8:34) and they are given special instruction (9:7)
and revelation.[12] If these words are Markan how much of the
rest of the verse is his? The 'high mountain' could be (cf. 3:13;
6:46; 13:3) but is not distinctively so for it was in such general
use to describe a place of revelation (cf. in the N.T. Mt 5:1;

[8] T. Schramm, Der Markus-Stoff bei Lukas S.N.T.S. Monograph Series
14), Cambridge, 1971, pp.136-9.
[9] Art. cit.
[10] We do not need to examine the earlier course of the development of
the tradition; cf.F.Hahn, The Titles of Jesus in Christology, London 1969,
pp.334-7; Horstmann, op.cit., pp.74-80. H.P. Müller, 'Die Verklärung
Jesu', ZNW, 51 (1960) 56-64, divides the pericope into two distinct
earlier accounts, vv. 2ab, 7 (9) and vv. 2c-6,8, which he believes were
joined at the time when the Messiah Christology and the Son of Man
Christology were united. This will have been pre-Markan. Many of the
attempts to find two sources for the narrative derive from Lohmeyer's
view (which he later abandoned in his Markus) that the idea of
transfiguration in the story is a Hellenistic addition to an earlier Jewish
tradition; see his 'Die Verklärung Jesu nach dem Markus-Evangelium',
ZNW 21 (1922) 185-215. Some of the difficulties which have led to
division hypotheses can be accounted for more easily through the
hypothesis of Markan redaction.
[11] Cf. F. Neirynck, Duality in Mark: Contributions to the Study of the
Markan Redaction, Leuven, 1973.
[12] Sabbe, art. cit., thinks incorrectly that the secrecy derives from the
nature of apocalyptic revelation.

15:29; 28:16; Lk. 6:12)[13] that it was almost certainly part of the pre-Markan tradition; the scene must have had some geographical setting and it has the same setting in the independent tradition of 2 Pet. 1.16–18. None of the other words in the verse is characterisitcally Markan.[14] The association of Peter, James and John with Jesus is found also at 5.37; 14.33 (cf. 1.16–20; 13.3); it is difficult to determine whether Mark is responsible for their names in our pericope[15]; Peter is so much a part of the story that his name must have been present from the beginning; Mark could either have introduced the three in place of a general discipleship reference or in place of the sole name of Peter[16] (three disciples balances the three booths which Peter suggests building). The reference to 'six days' is surprising since Mark apart from the Passion narrative generally fails to supply temporal data; there is no clear six-symbolism in Mark (in its origin the number six may go back to Exod. 24.16); it is difficult to interpret within the Gospel. Mark tends to retain the irrelevant details that come to him in the tradition[17], cf. his retention here of the description of Jesus as Rabbi which both Matthew and Luke change. We conclude that the six days was found in the pre-Markan stage of the tradition.[18]

But if we ascribe the six days to the tradition this implies that

[13] W. Foerster, *TDNT* V pp. 475ff.; U. Mauser, *Christ in the Wilderness* (Stud. in Bib. Theol. 39), London, 1963; J. Schreiber, *Theologie des Vertrauens*, Hamburg, 1967, pp.164–7.

[14] Παραλαμβάνω does appear in Markan redactional passages (4.36; 5.40; 7.4; 10.32; 14.33) but it is a normal word on each occasion and it is used more regularly by Matthew (sixteen times to Mark's six).

[15] As a unit of three they are probably pre-Markan for they come at the head of his list of the Twelve in 3.16f. Andrew is pushed down the list from his natural position beside Peter, and the three are the only ones in it who have been given 'nicknames' by Jesus.

[16] Cf. Bultmann, op.cit., p. 260; Horstmann, pp.83–5; Müller, art. cit., παραλαμβάνω is also closely associated with these three names in 14.33.

[17] Cf. Best, 'Mark's Preservation of the Tradition', in: *L'Evangile selon Marc* (ed. M. Sabbe, Gembloux, 1974), pp.21–34, 'Markus als Bewahrer der Überlieferung' in: *Das Markus-Evangelium* (ed. R. Pesch, Darmstadt, 1979), 390–409; (info pp. 31–48).

[18] Luke has apparently failed to see what the reference was for he has changed the six days to eight.

in the tradition our pericope possessed a temporal connection
with some other event. Has then Mark broken or disturbed a
connection which previously existed? Schmithals (art. cit.) has
recently suggested a new theory which accounts for the six days.
He argues that it is inconceivable that Mark's source which
provided him with a connected and detailed account of the
arrest, trial and execution, death, burial of Jesus and included the
discovery of the empty tomb could have lacked resurrection
appearances. In fact the transfiguration followed in Mark's
source directly after the discovery of the empty tomb (after
16.8), and was dated as taking place six days after that event.[19] A
time dating here would correspond to the series of such data
throughout the passion narrative. Mark however decided that he
would not follow his source at this point. He inserted 14.28; 16.7
into it as a conscious replacement of 'appearances' and removed
the Transfiguration, leaving 16.8b which has caused so much
trouble to commentators. In the source the women kept silence
through fear but Jesus appeared to Peter. He assumes that only
Peter[20] was mentioned in the Transfiguration account in Mark's
source as vv.5f. would indicate, and thus the story corresponded
to the Petrine appearance of 1 Cor. 15.5. In the source also, as the
Matthean and Lukan accounts show for they had access to it,
Jesus' whole being was transfigured; Mark omits this and speaks
only of a transformation of his clothes because in the pericope's
new position it would be improper for the historical Jesus to
have had his existence transformed. Moses and Elijah, who
according to Jewish tradition could return as heavenly visitants,
indicate the eschatological nature of the event. Mark changed the
order 'Moses and Elijah' to 'Elijah with Moses' because he
wished to emphasise Elijah in view of vv.11-13; Matthew and
Luke restore the original order again indicating that they knew
Mark's source. The story ended in the source with the rapture of

---

[19] Bultmann, op.cit.,pp.259f., and others had already suggested dating
the Transfiguration six days after the crucifixion but had not suggested
that Mark himself moved the event. H.M. Teeple, *The Mosaic
Eschatological Prophet* (*J.B.L.* Monograph Series, X) Philadelphia, 1957,
p. 85, argues that the Transfiguration was originally an account of the
enthronement of Jesus as the Christ, a week after his resurrection.
[20] Cf. n. 16 supra.

Jesus along with Moses and Elijah; the cloud of course would be a suitable vehicle for such a rapture.[21]

The earliest tradition of the resurrection appearances not only recounted an appearance to Peter but one to the Twelve (1 Cor. 15.5) and Schmithals discovers this in 3.13–19, their call.[22] He also accepts the suggestion of E. Linnemann[23] that 16.15–20 is early but argues unlike her that it was the ending of Mark's source which he rejected but which survived and was later restored by someone who knew the source; thus the source gave the commissioning of the Twelve as well as their call. (It is difficult to see why Mark should discard such a clear commission and be content with 3.14, 15a, which according to Schmithals he provided, and with 6.7ff.)

Why did Mark carry out this extensive re-editing of his source? Had he not done so his Messianic secret theory would have been impossible; he needed to eliminate from his source those pericopae which set the disclosure of Jesus' secret after his resurrection, and he required pericopae which acknowledged it in secret before his death. By moving the story of the appearance to Peter, he was able to fulfill this purpose.

What are we to say to this? First of all the transference of the position of material which Schmithals suggests does not accord with what we know of Mark's editorial habits. H.W. Kuhn[24] has shown how Mark held together the larger complexes of material which he received, even though they sometimes contained units which he did not require; e.g. most of 10.1–45 came to him as a unit; he only wished to use the final section, 10.35–45, but because it was part of an existing complex he retained the whole – though of course adding to it and modifying it. As I myself have attempted to show in another paper he did the same with the smaller sections of the tradition, carefully preserving material though it was not necessary for his

[21] Cf. Acts 1.9.
[22] He omits vv. 14b, 15 as Markan from the account as it is alleged to have appeared in Mark's source.
[23] 'Der (wiedergefundene) Markusschluß', ZTK 66 (1969) 255–87.
[24] H.-W. Kuhn, Ältere Sammlungen im Markusevangelium, Göttingen, 1971.

wider puposes.[25] It was not then his habit to break up the sections of his sources. Turning now more directly to the Transfiguration account itself Schmithals several times assumes that Matthew and Luke knew not only Mark but the source which he used (in this way he accounts for their agreements against Mark). But Schmithals has also argued that the Transfiguration was not an isolated item in the pre-Markan tradition but part of a connected Passion narrative. Matthew and Luke can therefore only have known it as part of such a connected account. Why did they not restore it to its original position when at times they actually restored its original wording? They do not adhere to Mark's Messianic secret theory and were therefore under no compulsion to place it prior to Jesus' death. Matthew instead of restoring it substitutes another commission to the Twelve and dispenses with the appearance to Peter which ancient tradition required. Luke for his part shows his awareness of the tradition about Peter (24.34) yet omits the opportunity to narrate it; and he makes use of yet another commission. One of the points at which Matthew and Luke return to the source is in their agreement that Jesus' face shone, which Mark eliminated because it was unsuitable in a story about the earthly Jesus; would not Matthew and Luke also have been aware of its unsuitability? If Schmithals makes out Mark to be a clever editor he also makes both Luke and Matthew to be blunderers. In respect of the six day period and Mark's Passion source, so far as we can judge from Mark, the events of the source crowded in, one on top of another, without a long interval at any point; the six days would therefore be an unusually long interval. Neither Matthew nor Luke (in his Gospel), both of whom are alleged to have known Mark's source, have any interval after the resurrection before the Ascension.

We have already seen that the form of the Transfiguration narrative is very dissimilar to that of the resurrection appearance narratives and the structure of the Transfiguration which Schmithals supposes it to have possessed in Mark's source does nothing to increase the similarity. Schmithals also claims to find

[25] See note 17. Note the retention of the early title 'Rabbi' at v.5.

support for his view in the account in 2 Peter but the great majority of commentators on 2 Peter reject the resurrection suggestion and argue that the author has the Parousia in mind.[26] It is almost equally difficult as Boobyer has shown[27] to argue for the resurrection idea in the account in the Apocalypse of Peter.[28]

Returning once again to the account itself. If we reject the solution of Schmithals in respect of the 'six days' and all symbolic solutions[29] we have still to discover to what the six days referred in the tradition.

In 8.27-9.1 Mark combined with editorial additions three separate units of tradition, viz., 8.27-30, 8.31-33 and 8.34-9.1. The last of these is a set of sayings and 'after six days' would not follow it appropriately; the time reference implies a preceding incident. If 9.1, as is probable, was added by Mark to the tradition consisting of 8.34-38 then for the same reason the six

[26] This is worked out in great detail by J.N.D. Kelly, op.cit. ad loc. So far as I know the only recent commentator on 2 Peter to accept the resurrection view is C. Spicq, *Les Épitres de Saint Pierre* (Sources Bibliques), Paris, 1966.

[27] Op. cit., pp. 30ff.

[28] It is remarkable that Schmithals seems to be unaware of the literature which advocates the parousia connection – at least he lists none of it in his footnotes and writes as if no scholars adhered to it.

[29] Schreiber, op.cit., pp. 119f. and 'Die Christologie des Markusevangeliums', *ZTK* 58 (1962) 154-83 (at pp. 161 f.), takes the six days to be Markan and connects them to the length of the final stay of Jesus in Jerusalem and to his (i.e. Schreiber's) claim to find a gnostic Saviour myth in Mark. The latter we have already rejected; cf. Best, *The Temptation and the Passion*: The Markan Soteriology (S.N.T.S. Monograph Series 2) Cambridge, 1965, pp. 125ff. His particular view of the six days is too fanciful. This is true of all attempts to find theological meaning in the number. It is not clear why Horstmann, op. cit., pp. 100f., after allowing that the six days is non-Markan should then find deep meaning in Mark's use of it – six days is one day short of the fulfilled week, and so the Transfiguration is the complete fulfillment of 9.1. This could only be an accidental result of its insertion here; that is to say, Mark did not insert the Transfiguration at this point because it already possessed a 'six days' time datum. There may, of course, have been a 'six' symbolism at some stage in the tradition earlier than Mark. H. Baltensweiler, *Die Verklärung Jesu* (ATANT 33), Zürich, 1959, pp. 49ff., relates it in origin to the Day of Atonement and the length of the Feast of Tabernacles. 2 Pet. 1.17f. shows that the incident could exist without a time note at all.

THE TRANSFIGURATION 215

days will not have been attached to it. Unless then Mark has wholly detached it from its setting in the tradition, and there are no good grounds for conjecturing he did so, it will have been previously united either to 8.27-30 or 8.31-33. In both these passages Peter is isolated for special attention as in the Transfiguration itself. If it followed 8.31-3 then it provided confirmation that the one who had to suffer was God's chosen son, yet it is more probable that it originally followed 8.27-30 and spelt out Peter's confession of Jesus as the Christ; in that God declares him to be his son it was God's confirmation of that confession. Such a new description may have become necessary once Christianity moved into Hellenistic areas where Messiah was a term lacking real significance.[30] The 'six days', whatever symbolism or O.T. origin it may once have had, consequently tied the Transfiguration firmly to what preceded it. We shall later have to take account of the significance of Mark's insertion of intervening material. Rturning now to 9.2 we conclude that the tradition began 'After six days Jesus (taking Peter, James and John?) led the disciples (Peter?) up to a high mountain. And he was transfigured...'.

Within the pericope we find a Markan motif in the fear of the disciples (v. 6b).[31]. It does not fit appropriately with Peter's words in v. 5 καλόν ἐστιν. . . [32] ἔκφοβοι γὰρ ἐγένοντο is a typical short Markan explanatory clause utilising γάρ;[33] since he tends to insert these into existing material 6a may be from the tradition. On the other hand we find almost exactly the same

[30] 9.2-8 and 8.27-29 may not always have belonged together for Peter describes Jesus as Rabbi at 9.5 and not as Messiah as he ought to have done after 8.29. In the Markan context this use of 'Rabbi', if it is other than the preservation of pre-Markan tradition, would underline Peter's failure to understand what he had said in 8.29.
[31] Cf. 10.32; 9.32; 16.8b; 6.50; 4.41. On the 'fear' of the disciples in Mark see K. Tagawa, *Miracles et Evangile*, Paris. 1966, pp. 99ff. In Matthew the fear is a response to the Divine Voice, in Luke to the overshadowing cloud, i.e. in each case a definite psychological motive is offered for it.
[32] See C. Masson, 'La Transfiguration de Jésus', *RTP*, 14 (1964) 1-14.
[33] E.g. 2.15; 6.14; 7.3f.; 11.13. Cf. C.H. Turner, *JTS* 26 (1925) 145-56; M.Thrall, *Greek Particles in the New Testament*, Leiden, 1962, pp.41ff.; C.H. Bird, 'Some γάρ Clauses in St. Mark's Gospel', *JTS* 4 (1953) 171-87.

words used at 14.40; both there and here they are omitted by Matthew and Luke. Moreover the ignorance of the disciples is also a Markan theme.[34] It is probably better therefore to regard the whole of v.6 as Markan[35], though it is possible that Mark has re-written an earlier and vaguer allusion to the disciples as puzzled. The stupidity of Peter lay in the tradition and there was perhaps also always something which implied the difference between Jesus on the one hand and Moses and Elijah on the other.[36]

In v.7 the final clause ἀκούετε αὐτοῦ may be Markan. The independent tradition in 2 Pet. 1.17[37] lacks these words though it does have the first part of what the divine voice says. In 8.35 it is generally agreed that he added 'and of the gospel'[38] and in 8.38 'and my words'. Probably 'the word' (τὸν λόγον) in 9.10 is also his. The present phrase has similar import: the words of Jesus are to be obeyed.[39] Its appearance accords with the change from the second person to the third in the words of the Divine Voice as compared with the baptism. Mark lays considerable emphasis on 'hearing' (cf. 4.3a ἀκούετε, which is missing in Matthew and Luke; 4.9 is a detached logion which he inserts there and at 4.23; 7.16). The need for obedient hearing is closely linked to Mark's continual emphasis on the failure of the disciples to understand (e.g. 4.10–12; 7.14) and on the frequent references to Jesus as teaching, though Mark rarely gives his teaching. Yet at this

---

[34] E.g. 4.10–13; 6.52; 7.18; 8.17,21. See Tagawa, op.cit., pp. 174ff.; G.M. de Tillesse, *Le Secret Messianique dans L'Évangile de Marc*, Paris, 1968, pp. 174ff.

[35] So Horstmann, pp. 81–3.

[36] K.G. Reploh, *Markus – Lehrer der Gemeinde*, Stuttgart, 1969, pp. 112f., argues that the motif of fear is pre-Markan because it is essential to the story since v. 7 is an answer to it. But v. 7 might be an answer to the misunderstanding of Peter which was more probably in the tradition. Even if the 'fear' of the disciples was in the tradition Mark has re-written and intensified the motif as his characteristic wording shows.

[37] Vide supra and see n. 6.

[38] In Mark the Gospel is something to be proclaimed, i.e. it is conceived in verbal terms; cf. R. Schnackenburg, 'Das Evangelium im Verständnis des ältesten Evangelisten' in *Orientierung an Jesus* (see n. 3 supra), pp. 309–23; G. M. de Tillesse, *Le Secret Messianique dans L'Évangile de Marc*, Paris, 1968, pp.264ff.

[39] In Biblical language 'to hear' is almost the same as 'to obey'.

point he has supplied teaching. In 8.32f. Peter's failure to understand is brought out; the material in 8.34ff. which Mark has inserted breaking the earlier connection between Peter's confession and the Transfiguration is teaching of the highest importance to which the disciples must give heed. One of the two main strands of thought in 8.27–10.45 is the need for true discipleship. With all this the command to 'Hear Jesus' is most appropriate; even if Mark did not add it[40], it is central to his interpretation of the Transfiguration, as we shall finally see. Whether the clause is inspired by Deut. 18.15, αὐτοῦ ἀκούσεσθε must await decision until we have discussed whether Mark finds any Moses imagery in the event as a whole.

In v.4 we have the peculiar phrase 'Elijah with Moses'.[41] There are similar phrases in 4.10 ('those around him with the Twelve') and 8.34 ('the crowd with his disciples') both of which are redactional, though in each of those cases Mark may be uniting groups drawn from two different strands of tradition. It can be argued that each time the first name is the more important. Since in 9.11–13 Mark takes up the figure of Elijah but makes no further use of Moses it is probable that he has brought Elijah's name forward from an original 'Moses and Elijah' to give it the position of stress.[42] V.5, where the names

[40] Horstmann, op.cit. pp. 80–90, takes it as redactional. Hahn, op.cit., pp. 336ff., and others have held that the clause is original to the story and derives from Deut. 18.15; it therefore sets out Jesus as eschatological prophet. However it has by no means been proved that the idea of Jesus as the deuteronomic prophet was accepted everywhere in the primitive church. See the discussion of Moses infra.

[41] Matthew and Luke replace it with the simpler and chronologically more correct, 'Moses and Elijah'.

[42] So Horstmann, op.cit., pp. 85–8; Feuillet, art.cit., pp. 283f. We cannot accept the suggestion of Masson, art.cit., that Mark introduced the name Moses to an account which originally contained only Elijah's because Moses would have been a better known name in Rome than Elijah. Mark makes no use of Moses' name elsewhere. Masson's further theory that an original account of a transfiguration of Elijah was changed by Mark into one of Jesus lacks credibility; Masson fails to show the Markan editing which would have produced this result; all he can show is that a transfiguration of Elijah was a remote possibility at some stage in the transmission of the material. If the theory of H. Baltensweiler, *Die Verklärun Jesu*, op. cit., pp. 87–90, that the incident had its origin in a false Messianic temptation to Jesus is correct, then Elijah may well have been featured alone in the original form.

appear in the normal order, shows that both belonged to the tradition.

Two recent suggestions have been made about the significance for Mark of Moses and Elijah. (1) Ziesler[43] has developed U. Mauser's[44] suggestion that Jesus was for Mark the new Moses.[45] He discovers the imagery of Exod.24 in the transfiguration; Moses was transfigured (Exod.34.29ff.) as Jesus was; the tents are a reference to the wilderness and therefore introduce the exodus theme; the cloud and the voice are elements from the story of Mount Sinai. There are difficulties in this. The evidence for a Moses background is much clearer in Luke and Matthew than in Mark for it is in the former that Jesus' face is said to shine or be changed (cf. 2 Cor.3.7) whereas in Mark only his clothes are changed.[46] The cloud of 'light' in Mt. 17.5 recalls the shining cloud which guided the Israelites through the wilderness but is not mentioned in Mark. Even in Matthew and Luke the parallel with Moses is not complete for Moses is transfigured in conversation with God but Jesus with Moses and Elijah.[47] Elsewhere in Mark there is no clear Moses typology;[48] the new exodus theme is not present; as I have argued elsewhere[49], the wilderness theme is not prominent. If a connection is made with Exod. 24 and ἀκούετε αὐτοῦ is introduced as an extra argument then Jesus would be presented as the new Lawgiver; again this theme is much more fully present in Matthew; although Mark does stress Jesus as teacher he nowhere implies that he gives a new law. Finally this theory fails to account for the presence of Elijah on at least an equality with Moses. Methodologically Ziesler reached his result because he failed to consider the

[43] Art. cit.
[44] Op. cit. pp. 108–119.
[45] For the Moses symbolism in the N.T. as a whole see T.F. Glasson, Moses in the Fourth Gospel (Stud. in Bib. Theol. 40), London, 1963.
[46] If Matthew and Luke obtained their information from Mark's source then his omission of this feature would be very significant, for he would be destroying a reference to Moses.
[47] Cf. Gerber, art.cit. He finds closer parallels to the transfiguration in Jewish mysticism.
[48] Jeremias, TWNT, IV, in his reference to Moses in the N.T. has no section on Mark.
[49] The Temptation and the Passion, (see n.29), pp.25ff.

elements of Markan redaction and to set the Transfiguration
account in its total context.

(2) Thrall makes an interesting attempt[50] to account for the
presence of both Elijah and Moses. She argues correctly for a
contrast between Jesus on the one hand and Moses and Elijah on
the other. The suggestion of Peter that he and his fellow-
disciples should make booths for Jesus, Moses and Elijah put all
three on the same plane; this was Peter's misunderstanding (v.6
– the misunderstanding of the disciples is a common Markan
theme).[51] The divine voice corrects Peter in showing that Jesus is
unique. The situation within Mark's church was one of
hesitancy to accept the full apostolic kerygma and his church
was in danger of down-grading Jesus to the level of Moses or
Elijah. Against this we must argue: (i) Moses and Elijah were
already in the story and Mark does nothing by his redaction to
bring out the distinction between them and Jesus (though this
may have been important at an earlier stage in the tradition).[52]
(ii) Elijah, but not Moses, is singled out for special attention
perhaps in v.4, but certainly in vv. 11–13. (iii) Moses and Elijah
do not figure largely elsewhere in Mark's gospel and are not
therefore important for its Christology, as Thrall's suggestion
would necessitate. (iv) Thrall has not shown from the total
Markan picture that the rejection of the apostolic kerygma
which she supposes took the form she alleges; this one passage
cannot contain the whole key to the gospel. It is more likely that
the rejection of the apostolic kerygma took the form of a failure

---

[50] Art.cit.

[51] G.B. Caird, 'The Transfiguration', *Exp. Times* 67 (1955-56) 291-4,
goes further in suggesting that Peter's error was his failure to realise that
Jesus was the true 'tent'; John 1.14 may present Jesus in this way but
such a view reads far more into Mark than his narrative will bear.

[52] The attempt to make Moses and Elijah into representatives of the
Law and the Prophets so that 'Hear him' becomes God's call to turn
from the old dispensation to Jesus if it were true would support the
thesis of this paper but it has many weaknesses; it fails principally
because Moses and Elijah are not typical of the Law and the Prophets
(Moses is a type of a 'prophet', Deut. 18.15, 18). Mark's inversion of
the normal order of their names indicates he does not take them in this
way. Suhl, op.cit., pp. 107f., points out that in the Markan Transfiguration account there is no element of O.T. fulfilment.

to understand the necessity of the cross and of the place of suffering in Christian discipleship.

What then is the role of Moses and Elijah in Mark? They are heavenly inhabitants (cf. their role in the Apocalypse of Peter) setting the scene for the divine voice[53], though of course they may originally have had a different part to play.[54]

If we now look back along the path we have come we can see that the position Mark has given to the Transfiguration and the additions he has made to it cohere to emphasise the same theme. In the tradition as it lay before him the incident was connected to 8.27-30 and its purpose was christological – to confirm the confession made by Peter of Jesus' true identity.[55]But as is now becoming increasingly recognised Mark did not see Peter's confession of Jesus as Messiah as an adequate confession, at least for his community.[56] Peter may call Jesus the Messiah but he does not understand Jesus' mission; the title is therefore immediately changed to 'Son of man' and Peter is rebuked sternly for his failure. Now at the Transfiguration another title comes to the fore, son of God; this indeed is Mark's special title for confessional situations. If man, that is Peter, has confessed Jesus as Messiah, God confesses him as his son. Unlike the baptism the words are here addressed directly to the disciples – and the second clause used then 'in you I am well-pleased' no longer appears,[57] with the effect of concentrating attention on

[53] Boobyer, op.cit., pp. 73f., speaks of them almost as typical of the dead in Christ. Baltensweiler, op.cit., p. 68, points out that the 'whiteness' of Jesus' transfigured clothes is another indication of 'heaven' (Mk. 16.5; John 20.21; Rev. 2.17; 3.4f.; etc.). They may have been eschatological prophets at an earlier stage of the tradition (cf. Teeple, op. cit., for both Elijah and Moses as such).

[54] As fore-runners of the Messiah? (cf. Glasson, op.cit., p. 69).

[55] Boobyer, op.cit., p. 57, thinks that this is still the purpose in Mark though for Mark it is also a prediction of the parousia.

[56] Cf. Best, op.cit. (n.29) pp. 165f.; N. Perrin, *What is Redaction Criticism?* London, 1970, pp.53ff.; Schweizer, ad 8.27-33.

[57] Matthew and 2 Peter have it; it appears in some texts of Luke but is probably not original. Matthew wholly and Luke partially appear to have conformed what they found in Mark to their baptismal accounts.

the title[58] and the words that follow, 'Hear him'. Material has been inserted between 8.30 (or 8.33) and the Transfiguration which has to do with discipleship (8.34–9.1). Within the incident Mark has reinforced the attention given to the disciples, perhaps by adding the reference to Peter, James and John (9.2), certainly by introducing the fear on the part of the disciples and emphasising their lack of understanding (9.6), and either by adding the words 'Hear him' (9.7) or by stressing them through the omission of the second clause of the baptismal formula. These additions relate much more to discipleship than to Christology. Mark then has not neglected the original Christological setting of the pericope in the tradition[59]. but he has added to it another dimension – discipleship[60]– and this is in keeping with his whole train of thought in 8.27–10.45.[61] He acts as a good pastor, not just content to supply his congregation with a more adequate Christology but using this at the same time to exhort his readers to a truer discipleship. Scholarship today tends to have a Christological fixation; it is doubtful if the early Christians were as much concerned to express the nature of Christ as we are to understand their expression of it. Christianity was for living, not definition. To return to our passage. Christ, who was transfigured, has to be heard and obeyed; hearing and obedience do not lie in grandiose statements about his glory but in the claims to deny self, take up the cross and go on his way (8.34ff.). Thus the Transfiguration is given a new perspective. Fear and lack of understanding may be a reaction before the mighty deeds of God in Christ, and these mighty deeds were not

[58] In this form the words relate more directly to Gen. 22.2 and therefore point more clearly to the connection of the title to the death of Jesus, cf. Best, op.cit., (see n. 29) pp. 167ff.
[59] As in the tradition it still continues in Mark as divine confirmation of Peter's confession in which however the inadequacy of that confession of Jesus as the Christ is replaced by a confession appropriate to Mark's theology, the confession of his community, viz. Jesus as son of God.
[60] R.H. Lightfoot, *The Gospel Message of Mark* (Oxford, 1950, p. 44) points out that 'if we read St. Mark's version of the Transfiguration carefully without thought of the parallel versions in Matthew and Luke, we find that in Mark the whole event, from first to last, takes place solely for the sake of the three disciples.'
[61] Cf. Suhl, op.cit., pp. 108f.

confined to Palestine in Jesus' time but took place in Mark's own community as in all the early communities, but the true reaction is an obedience which is to be firmly governed by the cross. At the same time by the clause 'Hear him' Mark indicates that the sayings of the earthly Jesus[62] are also the sayings of the exalted Lord[63] having behind them all the authority of revelation. God tells men to obey his son. This can now be said in a way in which it could not be said at the baptism for the words of the son have been made known since then in his teaching.

It is appropriate at this point to return briefly to the question which has so agitated modern commentators: is it the risen Jesus or the Jesus of the Parousia who appears as the Transfigured? Is this a real question? Would Mark have been conscious of such a distinction? Since there are no resurrection appearances in his Gospel we do not know how he would have depicted the risen Jesus. The Jesus of the parousia was to come on clouds with his angels (8.38; 14.62), but presumably the risen Jesus was already in the sphere of the angels (16.5-7) and it is significant that δόξα is not applied in Mark to the Jesus of the Transfiguration[64] though it is regularly used in relation to the Parousia (8.38; 10.37; 13.26). Instead of being concerned with the distinction between the risen and returning Jesus Mark wishes to stress that the words of the earthly Jesus have behind them the authority of God.[65] And at all points the earthly Jesus of the cross and the exalted Lord are the same; for this reason Mark has at this point introduced 9.9-13 with its renewed stress on the suffering of Jesus. Our question can be put in a different way: is the transfiguration a prediction of the resurrection or the parousia? It is difficult to view it as either in Mark. Predictions of the resurrection are frequent in the Gospel (8.31: 9.31 etc.), and are made in such a way as to stress its predetermined nature but

[62] Whether 8.34ff. are actually ipsissima verba or not is irrelevant; Mark and his community believed they were.

[63] Horstmann, op.cit. p. 96.

[64] In Matthew Jesus himself and not his clothes only, is transfigured, and in Luke the word δόξα is used.

[65] If we wish to insist on the element of δόξα then it is seen in relation to the exalted Lord in Acts 7.55 and the idea is present in Paul's Damascus Road experience (Acts 9.3; 22.6,9,11; 26.13); see also Acts 3.13; Rom. 6.4; 1 Pet. 1.21; cf. Carlston, art. cit.

the pericope hardly functions in this way in its present position.[66] As a prediction of the parousia the transfiguration might have had some relevance to Mark's readers in their time of persecution, assuring them of the victorious outcome of the Christian faith. But what then is the point of ἀκούετε αὐτοῦ? [67] The returned Christ will be obeyed by men without question; no other option will be open to them!

In so far as Jesus is set out as the one whose words are to be obeyed he is given a unique position vis-à-vis the disciples, one which cannot be exhausted by the category 'imitation', but one which explicates further what 'following' means. Obedience to Jesus is part of discipleship, perhaps the main part (cf.3.35) in so far as he commands his disciples to go in his way, the way of the cross. Thus at this point a new facet of the meaning of discipleship is brought out. Previously interpreted as 'following' now it is explained as 'obedience'.

If Mark has thus set 9:2-8 in relation to the whole of the preceding section 8:27-9:1, has he given it any special relation to 9:1?[68] 9:1 was added by Mark[69] to the sequence of sayings in 8:34-38 which probably came to him as a unit. Did he add it to complete the sequence or to prepare for the Transfiguration account, or indeed to fulfil both purposes? From patristic times it has been argued that the Transfiguration represents the fulfilment of 9:1; Peter, James and John, from among those standing with Jesus when he spoke the logion, are those who before their death see the Kingdom of God in power and do so in the Transfiguration. Thus interpreted the Transfiguration draws the sting of the very difficult logion, 9:1, which might imply to Mark's readers that the Parousia must come before all the original Twelve are dead. We have however already seen that Mark does nothing to bring out the Parousia significance of the Transfiguration. Moreover Mark's readers would not necessari-

[66] This could have been its meaning if it was ever an incident in the life of the historical Jesus.
[67] Interestingly Boobyer who strongly advocates this view nowhere comments on 'Hear him' in his detailed exposition of the passage!
[68] I assume that for Mark at any rate 9.1 refers to the Parousia.
[69] Note the introductory καὶ ἔλεγεν αὐτοῖς, a Markan phrase; cf. Kuhn, op.cit., pp 130f.

ly take the logion as referring to the historical disciples but perhaps as referring to themselves, i.e. some of them would still be alive when the Parousia would come. There is a certain ambivalence about Mark's attitude to the Parousia, so much so that some writers think he expected it to come very shortly (14:27f.; 16:7; in Galilee?) while others conclude that Mark did not know when (13:32), perhaps soon, perhaps after an indefinitely long period. No one can deny that Mark has a strong interest in the coming of the End: his inclusion of chapter 13 proves that and from it we know that he drew his material from different strands of the tradition. He does what any pastor who believes in the parousia might do – at one moment he stresses its imminence, at another he guards against the abandonment of daily life which this might produce. Thus there is no reason to doubt that Mark and his readers could have referred 9.1 to themselves and not therefore think of the Transfiguration as its fulfilment – they were probably not interested in solutions to historical problems in the way we are. In addition to this there is a strong connection between 9.1 and 8:38; as we have said Mark added 9:1, and his introductory phrase καὶ ἔλεγεν αὐτοῖς is used to link material to what *preceded*. The sequence of sayings in 8:34–38 which starts with the challenge to deny oneself and take up the cross ends on a menacing note in 8:38; those who fail will suffer at the parousia. In the Q tradition the parallel to 8:38 is balanced with another logion which says that those who confess Jesus will be confessed by him to his Father (Luke 12:8f.; Matt. 10:32f.). 9:1 has the same function here in balancing 8:38. Mark thus added it to 8:38 to remove the threatening note on which otherwise the sequence of sayings would end. Thus 9:1 is not really the introduction to the Transfiguration but the conclusion to 8:34–38 and the Transfiguration is not to be explained through 9:1.[70]

[70] We cannot agree with Hamerton-Kelly, op.cit., p.54, who considers 'that the Transfiguration in its present position, is intended to reveal who this humble, suffering Son of Man is, for the sake of those who might be tempted to be ashamed of him because of his suffering' (op.cit., p. 54). Bultmann, op.cit., p. 121, Horstmann, op.cit., pp. 57f., Loisy, *Marc.*, p. 262, have all argued that 9.1 was connected in the pre-Markan tradition to 9.11-13. The grounds for their assertion are slight. If we require to attach 9.11-13 to anything in the pre-Markan

To summarise: Mark has begun with Peter's confession (8.27-30); out of it he has shown the centrality of the death of Jesus and implied the difficulty of understanding this (8.31-33); he has then taught the necessity of self-denial and suffering in the life of the disciple (8.34-7), a failure to appreciate which leads to the disciple's ultimate exclusion (8.38), yet he does not leave his readers here with a threat but encourages them (9.1). He now returns to the tradition where he had left it at 8.27 and commences again with the Transfiguration in which he supplements and corrects the Christology of Peter's confession and at the same time affirms the necessity of accepting the teaching he has just given on the meaning of Jesus' death and the place of suffering in discipleship, and by 'Hear him' sets God's authority behind that teaching. The same authority is given to the 'word' of 9:9 on the necessity of suffering. Finally he brings in John the Baptiser, who is Elijah, and who has already witnessed his confession in death: Jesus must do the same; the way to glory lies through suffering. This is equally true for Mark's community. Thus the Transfiguration is fully integrated into Mark's major emphases and interests.[71]

---

tradition then a better case could be made for 8.38 since in both there is the use of ἔρχομαι, the title 'Son of Man', and the πρῶτον in v. 11, on which the argument of Bultmann etc. hinges, is still as relevant as in the case of 9.1. In addition the parallel of the coming of Elijah to the coming of the Son of Man (8.38) is better than that to the coming of the Kingdom (9.1);. But there is probably not even sufficient reason to see 9.11-13 as attached earlier to 8.38.

[71] Some of the material relating to the Transfiguration in Mark which has appeared since the delivery of this lecture is discussed in my *'Following Jesus: Discipleship in the Gospel of Mark'* (JSNTS 4; Sheffield 1981), pp.55ff.

AUTHOR INDEX

Abrahams, I. 25.
Achtemeier, P.J. 125, 156, 178, 179, 185, 193.
Aland, K. 93.
Ambrozic, A.M. 90, 95f., 138.
Baltensweiler, H. 87, 214, 217, 220.
Bammel, E. 25.
Barbour, R.S. 166.
Barclay, W. 96.
Barr, J. 33.
Bauer, J.B. 38.
Bauer, W. 52, 54.
Beasley-Murray, G.R. 93, 94.
Behm, J. 168.
Benoit, P. 162, 165.
Dillerbeck, P. 90, 92, 147.
Black, M. 26, 27, 41.
Betz, H.D. 81.
Bird, C.H. 52, 91, 215.
Blass, F. and Debrunner, A. 66, 91.
Bigg, C. 208.
Boobyer, G.H. 138, 207, 220, 223.
Bretscher, P.G. 207.
Brown, R.E. 83, 93, 164, 175.
Bultmann, R. 29, 43, 57, 71, 72, 89, 90, 102, 131, 162, 165, 169, 207, 210, 211, 224.
Bundy, E.W. 40.
Burgers, W. 135, 157.
Burkill, T.A. 33, 155, 168, 186, 188, 207.
Caird, G.B. 219.
Cangh, J.M. van 192.
Carlston, C.E. 207, 222.
Clarke, W.K.L. 94.
Citron, B. 116.
Court, J.M. 179.

Coutts, J. 61, 159.
Cranfield, C.E.B. 138.
Crossan, J.D. 50, 51, 55, 56, 57, 59, 60, 107, 172.
Cullmann, O. 92, 164.
Daube, D. 87, 93, 122.
Davies, W.D. 106, 156.
Delling, G. 38.
Delorme, J. 128, 140, 156, 172.
Dewey, K.E. 167.
Dideriksen, B.K. 87.
Dibelius, M. 22, 57, 68.
Dinkler, E. 164.
Dodd, C.H. 56, 90, 93, 125, 155, 167, 207f.
Donahue, J.R. 122.
Dupont, J. 38.
Evans, C.F. 14, 106, 158, 172.
Feuillet, A. 207, 217.
Foerster, W. 210.
Freyne, S. 102, 116, 119, 140.
Fridrichsen, A. 185, 188.
Fuller, R.H. 27, 106, 164, 172, 177.
Funk, R.W. 91.
Gerber, W. 207, 218.
Glasson, T.F. 218, 220.
Glasswell, M.E. 191, 195.
Gnilka, J. 138, 140.
Grässer, E. 59, 187.
Grundmann, W. 37, 87.
Haenchen, E. 3, 19, 24, 39, 43, 144.
Hahn, F. 33, 164, 209.
Hamerton-Kelly, B.G. 207, 224.
Hartmann, G. 419.
Hauck, F. 25.
Hawkin, D.J. 119.
Hawkins, J.C. 50.

Reumann, J. 164, 175.
Riesenfeld, H. 206.
Rigaux, B. 134.
Robinson, J.M. 190.
Roloff, J. 159.
Sabbe, M. 206, 209.
Schelkle, K.H. 208.
Schelling, F.A. 94.
Schenk, W. 122, 151, 152, 167, 169, 170, 172, 173.
Schenke, L. 106, 122, 151, 153, 154, 166, 169, 172, 178, 181, 182, 183, 187, 188, 189, 192.
Schlatter, A. 37.
Schille, G. 158.
Schmahl, G. 102, 132, 134, 137, 142, 147, 148, 152, 156, 160, 174.
Schmid, J. 87.
Schmithals, W. 135, 136, 137, 207, 211-4.
Schnackenburg, R. 41, 93, 132, 188, 216.
Schneider, G. 122, 151, 168, 170.
Schramm, T. 73, 151, 209.
Schreiber, J. 39, 50, 99, 101, 162, 172, 210, 214.
Schroeder, H.-H. 49, 53, 54, 58, 60.
Schulz, A. 81, 137, 138.
Schürmann, H. 73, 150.
Schweizer, E. 19, 21, 33, 35, 39, 43, 44, 62, 87, 145, 183, 187.
Senior, D.P. 152.
Smith, M. 83-6, 92, 199-205.
Smith, J.Z. 124.
Snoy, T. 181, 182, 193.
Soden, H. von 62.
Spicq, C. 214.
Stein, R.H. 106.
Stemberger, G. 106, 156.
Stock, K. 102, 139, 143, 147, 148, 149, 154, 155, 156, 173, 174.

Strack, H.L. see Billerbeck
Strecker, G. 132.
Streeter, B.H. 79, 87.
Suhl, A. 169, 219, 221.
Sundwall, J. 144.
Swete, H.B. 44.
Tagawa, K. 116, 145, 182, 183, 184, 188, 189, 190, 195, 215, 216.
Taylor, V. 18, 19, 21, 33, 37, 39, 42, 43, 44, 46, 50, 68, 72, 73, 135, 144, 145, 150, 151, 152, 167.
Teeple, H.M. 211, 220.
Theissen, G. 179, 184, 189, 190, 193.
Thrall, M. 41, 52, 91, 144, 147, 206, 215, 219f.
Thompson, W.G. 75, 90, 142.
Tiede, D.L. 183.
Tilberg, S. van 132.
Tödt, H.E. 73.
Trocmé, E. 35, 59, 116, 120, 121, 129, 138, 162, 174, 184.
Turner, C.H. 36, 52, 88, 91, 103, 117, 118, 131, 144, 215.
Turner, N. 66, 91.
Tyson, J.B. 38, 99.
Walker, N. 38.
Walsh, P.G. 123.
Walter, N. 17, 18, 19, 21, 22, 36.
Wansbrough, H. 49, 53, 54.
Weeden, T.J. 46, 99, 101, 106, 107, 115, 120, 121, 123, 131, 140, 172, 184.
Wellhausen, J. 22.
Weiser, A. 126.
Weiss, J. 120.
Weiss, K. 94.
Wenham, D. 52, 54.
Wichelhaus, M. 163.
Wilcox, M. 170.
Wink, W. 83.
Wohlenberg, G. 37, 88, 92.
Zeisler, J.A. 206, 218f.

INDEX OF SCRIPTURE ETC